"Are Those Kids Yours?"

"Are Those Kids Yours?"
American Families with Children
Adopted from Other Countries

CHERI REGISTER

FP

THE FREE PRESS

NEW YORK   LONDON   TORONTO   SYDNEY   TOKYO   SINGAPORE

THE FREE PRESS
A Division of Simon & Schuster Inc.
1230 Avenue of the Americas
New York, N.Y. 10020

THE FREE PRESS and colophon are trademarks
of Simon & Schuster Inc.

Manufactured in the United States of America

10 9 8 7 6 5 4 3 2 1

Library of Congress Cataloging-in-Publication Data

Register, Cheri
    "Are those kids yours?" : American families with children adopted
from other countries / Cheri Register.
        p.   cm.
    Includes bibliographical references and index.
    ISBN 0-02-925750-6
    1. Intercountry adoption—United States—Case studies.
2. Interracial adoption—United States—Case studies.   2. Adoption
—United States—Psychological aspects—Case studies.   I. Title.
HV875.5.R44   1990
362.7'34'0973—dc20
                                                        90-37734
                                                        CIP

To my kids,
Grace 근영 *and Maria* 은숙

Contents

Preface

The day my new ten-month-old daughter was due to arrive from South Korea, I woke up in such agitation I knew there would be no point in attempting a normal workday. To keep myself occupied while the time passed, I pulled out the sweaters that had accumulated on the closet floor and began washing them. As I lifted a machine-knit acrylic out of the water by its shoulders, the label caught my eye—"Made in Korea." Never again would I read that phrase without loading it with associations: Did my daughter's birthmother run the knitting machine? Did she paint the round blue eyes on the plastic baby dolls lined up at the discount store? She had chosen to reveal nothing about her situation when she entered the maternity hospital and asked that her newborn baby be placed for adoption. I had only the typical case to go by in fleshing out her story: a young woman from the countryside, away from her family, putting in long workdays at a factory that produces goods for Western consumption. What would it mean for me to raise the child she relinquished, whether out of economic necessity, social injustice, family obligation, or personal choice? What set of historical circumstances, economic patterns, geopolitical dynamics, and cultural transformations had made it possible for me—a white, middle-class American—to adopt a child who was also, one might say, "made in Korea"? And what responsibilities came with this privilege?

The sweater label was a timely, graphic reminder of questions I had been asking myself and others all along in the sixteen months since my husband and I began the adoption process. We came to the agency knowing that there were extremely few American-born Caucasian infants to be adopted, and that our likely options would be older children in foster care, handicapped children, or infants born in other parts of the world. The latter fit most realistically with our habits and capacities as career-minded, first-time parents. Adoption from Korea best suited my ethical requirements: There was no doubt the mother made the decision to have the baby adopted; the legal separation was firm and final; there was no attempt to hide the fact the child was being sent abroad; there were no better possibilities for the child in the country of her birth. Taking a child out of her original culture and moving her to a very different setting where she would be in a racial minority seemed a rather drastic measure. I did not want to think of myself as a greedy, imperialist consumer of imported children. On the other hand, I wanted a baby, and a chronic illness prevented me from bearing one myself; moreover, the baby we were to adopt needed a family.

Two years later, as we anticipated the arrival of a second child, I was consumed by different questions entirely: Can there possibly be another child as wonderful as the one we have already? Am I capable of loving two children at the same time? How will we manage, with the emotional and physical demands upon us doubled? These were the very same questions that plagued my friends through their second pregnancies. The documents that came with my daughter's referral identified her birthmother as an unmarried university student, bringing to mind the years of my adolescence when girls not unlike myself "got in trouble" and had to give up their babies to spare the children and themselves a life of shame. This time, my sense of justice was provoked less by global economic inequality than by patriarchal sexual morality, to which I, too, was subject. A divorce has since given our family's situation an ironic twist. Born to single mothers in a society where fatherless children are stigmatized and disadvantaged, my daughters are now being raised by a single mother in a society where one-parent families are becoming ever more common. Sometimes I wish their birthmothers and I could work at this together.

Over the years, the hyperrational edge on my political conscience has been worn smooth by the daily reality-testing of motherhood. The ethical questions are still valid, but global concerns give way to more immediate responsibilities: packing school lunches, luring weary children from the television to the bathtub, explaining why friends sometimes hurt you. We have become a family in the most ordinary sense—living together, loving each other, fighting it out at times. Sometimes I even forget that my daughters don't look like me. Yet, we are not an ordinary family. As natural and normal as it feels to us to be together, we are still anomalous. How many other parents are regularly approached by strangers demanding to know, "Are those kids yours?"

The question is more puzzling than those who ask intend it to be. It is ambiguous, reflecting the paradoxical nature of adoption itself. No, I did not give birth to them. They are not "my own" or my "biological" children, depending on whose jargon you use. Yes, I am the one raising them, and I am doing it in the same fashion as any "real" or "natural" mother would. The firmest answer might be a declaration of ownership: Yes, they are mine *now*. I have the papers to prove it. Social science literature takes adoption out of the realm of the material and speaks instead of "entitlement": Yes, I am entitled to these children. I have been duly approved to exercise the rights of parenthood. None of these answers really suits me, however. My relationship with the children is solid enough that strangers who pose the question get an unqualified "yes." But in my mind, I prefer to live with the paradox: They are mine, yet not mine. Rather than claim ownership, I hope to fulfill the obligations of stewardship as the one to whose care these human lives have been entrusted.

Adoption agencies, of course, have long appreciated the potency of "entitlement." In the past, they kept the issue muted by sealing records to ensure that the birthparents' ties to the child would remain severed. Now, open adoption and modified variations of it affirm the right of birthparents in the United States to know about the child's life or even to have some influence over its course, while also protecting the adoptive parents' legally established right to raise the child to adulthood. The literature about adoption reflects this ongoing negotiation of rights and interests. Jerome Smith and Franklin Miroff called their 1981 sociological and psychological study of adoption *You're Our Child,* a deliberate response to the title of Robert Silman's book, *Somebody Else's Child,* published in 1976.

I have just as deliberately chosen *"Are Those Kids Yours?"* as the title of this book to suggest that international adoption complicates the issue of entitlement. To begin with the obvious, most international adoptions are also interracial. No matter how firmly our children are bonded to us, to our extended families, to our religious communities, or to any other groups we might belong to, their race remains unchanged. A Korean-born girl named Bridget O'Leary is still Asian to the world-at-large, and that facet of her identity needs to be affirmed and nurtured. White parents cannot draw on personal experience to help with that. Instead, we have to recognize that our child belongs to a group from which we ourselves are excluded. Further, many children adopted internationally were born in poverty, which may even be the reason for their needing a home. They have been relinquished by parents who cannot provide for them and adopted by people who have the resources to pay agency costs, legal documentation fees, and travel expenses. Adoption brings the children out of destitution and into the middle or upper class of one of the most affluent countries in the world. No matter how benign the motives involved, this great disparity between adoptive parents and birthparents makes it look as though one is benefiting from the other's misfortune.

The competing claims of entitlement in international adoption are not simply between birthparents and adoptive parents. There is a third party involved: the child's birth community, whether that be ethnic group, race, or nation. The National Association of Black Social Workers raised the issue of community entitlement to children in their 1972 statement opposing the adoption of black children into white families. Transracial adoption, they said, was a form of "cultural genocide." It deprived the black community of its children and deprived the children of the heritage the black community had to offer them, including skills needed to survive in a racist society. Similar fears of loss and suspicions of ill will are heard in the opposition to international adoption voiced in the countries from which children are being sent for adoption abroad. *"They* are taking *our* children" is the simplest way it gets expressed. Citizens of countries whose natural resources have been mined and tapped to meet North American and European needs, and whose labor is bought cheaply to make export goods might, understandably, feel that sending children abroad for adoption is a severe form of exploitation. Occasional baby-selling scandals and rumors of child abuse feed the fear.

Responsible advocates of international adoption in the children's birth countries do recognize the community's entitlement to children as a worthy ideal in the abstract. In practice, however, they see it challenged by the community's inability to provide for children who are homeless and destitute. Most agencies that place children internationally rank the *child's* entitlement to a loving family first among the principles that govern their work. If there are no families in the home country ready to take the children, the agencies will send them abroad, knowing and regretting that this means forfeiting their cultural heritage, just as separation from birthparents means losing one's ancestral history.

Adoptive parents have had little voice in this controversy. Unless we visit our children's birth countries or read publications with an international orientation, we may not even know that what we have done is controversial. Yet, our daily lives keep us aware of the ambiguities and require us to work at resolving them. This happens when a child asks, "Why don't I live in Colombia?" It happens when a child is assigned to do a family tree for school. When a child is taunted with racial epithets. When adoptive parents and members of an immigrant community get together to set priorities for an ethnic culture camp. When a teenager longs for a peer group that will be totally understanding. When a young adult goes off on a search for both genetic and cultural roots.

My intention in writing this book is to identify some of the ethical issues raised by international adoption and to show how they are played out in the actual, day-to-day experience of adoptive families. I have interviewed thirty-one adoptive parents and fifteen people, from ages six to thirty, who have been adopted, asking them not for answers to controversial questions but simply for their stories. I wanted to see how they would portray their families and their shared lives and what experiences they would highlight as critical to understanding how international adoption works over the long run. I had originally intended to interview entire families, but changed my mind along the way, to avoid the particularities of internal family dynamics and collect more evidence of experiences common to all or many adoptive families. It was more enlightening to hear the mother from one family describe a mother-daughter conflict and have it echoed by the daughter in another family. Everyone I interviewed has been given a pseudonym to ensure privacy. Except for a few quotations from published sources, the voices heard here are only those of adoptive parents and children. I have not attempted to speak for birthparents, for citizens of the children's birth countries, or for professionals working in adoption.

My task, as author of this book, is to interpret the stories I have been told in light of the paradoxical nature of adoption and the ethical questions inherent in international adoption. Some excellent books have already been written on the more general nature of the adoption experience, especially its psychological implications, so I have tried to keep my focus on the cross-cultural aspects. In raising and clarifying the ethical questions, I make no pretense of answering them conclusively. My hope has been that the complexity of the issues will be apparent and that readers will be moved to discuss them, to test their feelings about them, and to work alongside others involved in international adoption toward a common resolution.

Adoption is not the only area where entitlement to children is at issue these days. The question "Are those kids yours?" has a renewed and expanded practical urgency. Courts and legislatures are trying to set appropriate legal boundaries on surrogate childbearing, while the general public discusses the ethics of such arrangements. The new reproductive technology calls for new definitions of parenthood: What, for example, is the relation between a baby conceived through artificial insemination and the donor of the sperm? Who would be considered the "real" parents of a baby born of a donated egg fertilized in a Petri dish and implanted in an infertile woman's womb? With the high rate of divorce, many parents have found themselves explaining to lawyers and judges why they feel entitled to raise their children. Public child protection agencies are challenging parents' claims to children whom they abuse or neglect, while advocacy groups make sure that parents' rights are not jeopardized simply by poverty and differing cultural norms. The ethical debates prompted by these developments may have some bearing on international adoption, as well.

"Are those kids yours?" is a question of much greater depth and scope than even these recent developments suggest. What does it mean to own a child, anyway, and who can ultimately make that claim? I was dragging my reluctant younger daughter through a clothing store one afternoon, just past naptime. She was dressed, according to her usual habit, in costume—this time an oversized Hallowe'en chicken suit. Each time I stopped to feel another item of clothing, she whined, "I want my real mom." This in no way threatened my sense of entitlement. I don't think it even had to do with adoption or with our racial difference. Our temporary difference in species was more to the point. How well I remember those moments when I too yearned for a real mom, not the one with the nose just like mine who was feeling everything in the store, but the one in my imagination who would meet every one of my needs instantly. This daughter is particularly smitten with fairy tales, and Cinderella's fairy godmother still has more reality for her than the young woman in Korea who bore her. All these lovely fantasy mothers who die from a fatal prick of the needle and are replaced by wicked stepmothers must have some grounding in human psychology, as does the myth of the changeling, the troll child placed in the kidnapped human baby's cradle. The emotional bond between parent and child is always subject to strain. How those bonds are sealed, maintained, and tested in families formed across racial and cultural boundaries is a central subject of this book.

This book is not intended as a practical guide on how to adopt internationally, but it will certainly help new and would-be parents prepare for family life. I have described the experience in ways that need not rely on concrete, statistical data. The factual information cited has had to be continually updated in the course of writing. As the book went to press, the government of Vietnam began allowing orphaned children to be placed abroad, and American and European parents were making inquiries about the many children reported to be living in orphanages in Rumania. Adoption policies and procedures vary from country to country and can change very abruptly. Readers contemplating adoption who want to know what the process is like currently are advised to consult an adoption agency.

Anyone who writes about adoption is immediately caught up in disputes about appropriate language. Because adoption is often perceived negatively, as second-best to parenthood by birth, the vocabulary used to talk about it quickly becomes tainted. Thus "give up" and "put up for adoption" were replaced by "abandon" and "relinquish," which were replaced in turn by "place for adoption" and then "make an adoption plan for." The trend is usually from the judgmental to the descriptive to the euphemistic. I believe strongly that euphemisms only help perpetuate the aura of negativity by making certain aspects of the adoption experience taboo. To say that a birthmother "made an adoption plan" for a child she left behind in a bus station leaves the child's true history enshrouded in shame and misleads us into thinking that the mother made a free and thoughtful choice. To say the child was "abandoned" compels us to recognize the hurt the child experienced and to ask what awful circumstances can drive a mother to leave her child to an uncertain future. I prefer the term "relinquish" to describe the act of turning children over to child welfare workers or adoption agencies. According to my dictionary, it "connotes giving up something desirable or prized unwillingly and regretfully." Throughout the book, I choose terms that best preserve the paradox—the simultaneous gains and losses—at the heart of adoption.

Selecting terms to describe race and ethnicity is also a challenge. "Black," which came into being during the civil rights movement as an emblem of pride, is being replaced in some quarters by "African-American," which, like "Italian-American," specifies geographical origin rather than race. "White" has a more colloquial ring than "Caucasian," which sounds pretentious at times. "White people," however, often suggests racial polarization rather than mere difference. "Oriental" has been the standard term for people of the Far East, but is giving way to

"Asian," which includes India, Pakistan, and other South Asian countries, as well. Yet, "Asian" used to denote physical appearance usually
means East Asian. Since all of these usages are in flux and there is not
yet consensus about them even in the ethnic communities they represent,
I have used them alternately, trying to be sensitive to the particular
meaning in each instance.

Many people have kindly provided me with information, resources,
comments on segments of the manuscript, and/or alternate interpretations: Linda De Beau-Melting, Richard De Beau-Melting, Gail Dekker,
Jean Erichsen, Susan Freivalds, Carolyn Hoolahan, Kashmira Irani, Virginia Jacobson, Carol Rae Jasperson, Peggy Meyer, Myrna Otte, Marietta
Spencer, Ana Trejo, Jean Wakely, Karla Williams, and many others
who suggested people to interview. One who deserves a special thank
you is Hyun Sook Han, who, in addition to doing all of the above,
served as travel agent, door-opener, interpreter, and shopping companion
on my trip to Korea. There I received the gracious hospitality and
assistance of Dr. Kim Duk Whang, Dr. Kim Do Young, Mr. Kim Hak
Joo, Mr. Kim Young Bok, Mrs. Wee In Sook, Miss Paik Soon Young,
Miss Che, and other staff members of Eastern Child Welfare Society,
Mrs. Kim Young Sook and Miss Hong Choon of the Ae Ran Won
Home, Dr. Park Kyung Sook, and Mrs. Cha Jeom Ye.

Once again, I am grateful for the ever-ready encouragement and finely
honed critical skills of my Friday morning work group, which has guided
this book from proposal to publication: Sara M. Evans (a.k.a. Rachel's
mom), Amy Kaminsky, Elaine Tyler May, and Riv-Ellen Prell. My
editor, Gioia Stevens, contributed not only her professional expertise
but also her personal observations as the sister in an internationally
adoptive family. Of course, I owe thanks to the adults, children, and
"grown-up kids" who shared their stories with me. The latter, especially,
made it very hard for me to stop doing interviews and get the writing
done. Their voices need to be heard much more, and I feel privileged
to have been the conduit this time. Finally, I want to pay my respects
to the source of inspiration: my daughters, who weathered this process
very well. Maria never balked at watching a little more television while
I finished a train of thought. Grace survived the last frantic weeks
before the manuscript deadline by running to the piano whenever things
got too tense and playing "Blest Be the Tie That Binds" as fast as
humanly possible. And blest it is!

1

Children in Need of Families

In 1967, Kyung Chun was living with his mother in Korea in a village near a military installation. His father, an American serviceman, had finished his tour of duty and gone back to the United States, abandoning responsibility for the son he had engendered. Kyung Chun's curly hair and wide eyes identified him as an Amerasian child. As long as he was tiny and cute, he received the fond attention that Korean adults bestow on toddlers. He learned very early how to win acceptance with his good humor and charm. Yet, as he approached school age, he began to be set apart and mistreated. His mother realized that a mixed-race child without a father would face many obstacles in a homogeneous culture where social status depends on one's patrilineage. Having no resources herself to help him overcome those obstacles, she put him in the care of the Holt Agency, a rescue mission begun by Harry and Bertha Holt of Eugene, Oregon, in 1956 to aid children orphaned by the Korean War. A description of Kyung Chun and his background was sent to adoption agencies in the United States, and Dan and Marlene Duval made a request to adopt him. Marlene, a homemaker with two children in elementary school, had attended a lecture about homeless children given by the mother of a large, interracial family. She and Dan decided that they, too, had "room for one more," the slogan the speaker had used. Kyung Chun, renamed Steven, arrived in time to celebrate his sixth birthday with his new family. The next year, the Duvals adopted a second Amerasian child.

The plight of Korean war orphans had been well publicized in the American popular press in the 1950s. The homeless Korean child became an object of both compassion and sentiment. Elementary school students like myself packed cigar boxes full of pencils and toothbrushes and small toys to send to those less fortunate children "across the ocean." Mine was not the first generation that learned to practice charity that way. Both world wars of this century left children orphaned and homeless,

1

and both wars elicited a response among people of conscience in countries that escaped devastation. During World War I, women from Britain and the Scandinavian countries united in an organization called Save the Children to find homes for Belgian orphans. Within a year after the Allied victory that ended World War II in Europe, the officially authorized U.S. Committee for the Care of European Children brought in just over 300 unaccompanied minors, the majority of them Polish. For several years after the war, children from Germany, Greece, Italy, and other countries were admitted to the United States as "displaced orphans." (Unless otherwise noted, the statistics on international adoption come from the United States Immigration and Naturalization Service, which publishes them in an annual report.)

The Korean War, however, raised new issues of international responsibility. The children left homeless in its aftermath were not only orphans whose parents had been killed in the fighting. For many, "orphan" was a misnomer. They were, rather, the offspring of sexual relationships between American and United Nations soldiers and Korean women— wives, lovers, prostitutes, rape victims. Certainly, this is an age-old wartime phenomenon. But in this case, because the fathers were white or black and the mothers Asian, the children's heritage was evident in their physical appearance, making it much harder for them to be integrated into the postwar society. Social ostracism and poverty impelled their mothers to put them into orphanages, and compassion moved families like the Duvals to adopt them.

A debate arose about whose responsibility these children were and to which culture they properly belonged. According to Korean practice, their ancestry and identity would be derived from their fathers, so emigration to the United States was a preferred solution, even though it meant separating children from their mothers and from a familiar environment. The question of responsibility was debated even more intensely toward the end of the war in Vietnam in 1975. As it became clear that the Saigon government was going to fall, the United States began evacuating children from orphanages in what came to be called "the Vietnam baby-lift." Some Americans who had spoken out against the war itself saw this move as a last-ditch exercise in anti-Communist fervor, based on the presumption that Vietnamese children were better off displaced in the United States than reunited with their families or villages under North Vietnamese rule. The crash of a U.S. Air Force plane carrying children out of the country aroused wider public controversy about the wisdom of rounding up children in the chaos of war. Behind these headline events, however, a more systematic process of adoption was taking place. The Holt Agency, for example, had been working in Vietnam since 1972 and was already placing legally designated orphans in families in the United States. Holt speeded up its efforts when the end of the war became imminent but kept a distance from the babylift by refusing an offer to use military transport planes. For some American citizens, mention of international adoption still evokes memories of the Vietnam babylift.

Steven Duval was one of 1,905 children counted by the Immigration and Naturalization Service in 1967 as "orphans adopted abroad or to be adopted by U.S. citizens." Twenty years later, in 1987, 10,097 children were brought into the United States for the purpose of adoption. Nearly 59 percent, or 5,910 of these children were from South Korea, only a few of them Amerasian. 1987 was a peak year for international adoption. The following year, 9,120 orphans were admitted, 4,942 of them from Korea. International adoption is no longer a wartime rescue effort and is not limited to countries that have suffered a violent upheaval. Many of the countries involved are, however, going through the disruptive social transformation that typically accompanies industrialization and urban development. Adoption from Latin America is on the increase, with new links established each year between adoption agencies in the United States and orphanages and agencies in most countries of Central and South America. Colombia has been the primary country of origin for Latin adoptions, with 699 children arriving in the United States in 1988. Six hundred and ninety-eight children from India and 476 from the Philippines joined American families that same year. For these three countries, too, the figures were down somewhat from the previous year. The United States is not the only destination. Western Europeans, particularly the Scandinavians and the Dutch, also adopt internationally, as do Canadian and Australian families.

Each of the nearly 200,000 children who have found new families in the United States since the end of World War II has come with a life history marked by misfortune. The reasons for separation from birth-parents and the manner in which they have been separated vary, but there are common themes in the case histories that are truly universal. The following examples are specific, real life illustrations, drawn from the adoptive families I interviewed, yet each could as well be a fictional composite representing hundreds or thousands of others whose circumstances are the same:

- Soon Young's parents brought her to an orphanage when she was six years old because they could no longer manage her care. Her leg muscles were atrophied as a result of polio and she had severe curvature of the spine. The orphanage outfitted her with braces and crutches so that she could walk a little. She spent the next six years there, until she was adopted by an American family who had requested a handicapped child and had the resources to pay for surgery and physical therapy.

- David was the fifth child born to a poor woman living in Tegucigalpa, the capital of Honduras. Her husband had left her during the pregnancy and she knew it would be difficult to raise the four children she already had, let alone a new baby. After he was born, she turned him over to a lawyer who handled adoptions and David was put into a foster home until his adoption at five months by an American couple with one other Latin American child.

- Anita was found on the street in Guatemala City after a beating by a group of older boys. She did not know her birthdate but seemed about seven years old and had been living on her own for a year or so. She spent the next two years in an orphanage until her adoption by a divorced woman with one child. Only when she had been in the United States for several months and had grown accustomed to her new family did she feel secure enough to reveal that she had run away from an abusive father.

- Asha weighed less than four pounds and was malnourished when her mother, a young, unmarried woman in northern India, left her at a clinic a week or so after her birth. She was placed in the care of a Sikh couple who run a small orphanage, and spent a year there until she had been legally cleared for adoption and emigration. Her new mother is a single woman who had been waiting several years for a child.

What would have become of these children had they not been adopted? Steven Duval would have grown up in an orphanage among other Amerasian children, orphaned children of full Korean heritage, and handicapped children like Soon Young, relinquished by parents unequipped to care for them. There, his basic needs for food, clothing, and shelter would have been met and he would have received a minimal elementary school education. After that, he would have been on his own to earn a living at unskilled labor. For Soon Young, even that option was limited. With no public welfare system to aid her, she would face a life of deprivation. David's family, having to stretch their meager resources six ways, would face a daily, arduous struggle for subsistence. Unless they could find suitable ways to help supplement the family income, the children might be pressed to beg or scavenge. They would certainly not have the means to go to school. David or any of his siblings might end up among the streetchildren who live by their wits in cities and towns throughout much of Latin America. The police who found Anita beaten saved her from that fate. The orphanage where she was housed prepares teenage girls for work as domestic servants and warns against prostitution, which may be more rewarding financially. Asha would very likely have died in infancy.

All around the world—and the United States is certainly no exception—there are children who live in jeopardy because of poverty, malnutrition, physical or mental disability, inadequate health care, abuse and neglect, or true orphanhood—the death of one or both parents. In addition to the children living in foster care and orphanages, an estimated thirty to one hundred million children worldwide live on the streets with no adult support or supervision. Adoption improves, or even spares, the lives of a relative few. Nor is a massive, global relocation of children an ultimate solution to this heart-rending problem. It would be better and more just to move the resources around and thus secure these children's lives in their own countries. On the other hand, the "one life at a time" approach puts human faces on statistics so astonishing as to be incomprehensible otherwise.

In many countries, international adoption remains the best or only hope for a particular category of children, known officially as "illegitimate," a term that puts the onus on the child by declaring its very existence null and void. We might instead call them the "fatherless." Birth out of wedlock is the most common peril in the early lives of children adopted by American families. The simple fact of being born to an unmarried mother, often in defiance of cultural taboos, is enough to place a child at risk of ostracism and lifelong poverty. In countries where patrilineage determines identity and social status, children born outside marriage are anomalies with no legal existence. Even where the stigma of sexual immorality has been eased, as it has in the United States, children raised by young, single mothers face a distinct material disadvantage. In much of the world, desertion by the father leaves children of a formal or common-law marriage in similarly dire circumstances. Women deserted by husbands fare very poorly in countries that have no laws obligating fathers to support their children and no public welfare systems. Abandoning children so they will be free for adoption is often a painful sacrifice made on the children's behalf. Despite the fact that it puts millions of children at risk, "fatherlessness" is regarded neither as a historical cataclysm, like war, nor as a natural disaster worthy of global attention. It is perceived, rather, as an individual stroke of misfortune, a parental error—usually the mother's in the case of illegitimacy—for which the child itself pays recompense. The immediate solution for each of these children is adoption into another family—a solution that the child's birth culture may not offer.

Thus, the typical child adopted from abroad by an American family in the 1980s is, like the typical native-born child adopted by American families in the 1950s and 1960s, an infant—or by the time of arrival, a toddler—born out of wedlock. Viewed from the American perspective, international adoption is, for the most part, an extension of domestic adoption across national boundaries that has been brought about by changing social mores in the United States. When I was entering puberty in the late 1950s, the greatest horror imaginable was getting pregnant before marriage. It happened frequently in my hometown, and the girl— as she still was—was whisked away to an undisclosed place where her abdomen could grow in anonymity. When the baby was born, it was "put up" for adoption, and the mother returned home to live among whispers until public memory of her transgression had faded. By the time I was ready to become a mother myself and had learned that pregnancy would endanger my health, the situation had changed dramatically. New methods of contraception and legal abortion had reduced the risk of unintended pregnancy, and a change in sexual mores had made it less socially hazardous for an unmarried mother to raise her child. The book Chosen Children by William Feigelman and Arnold Silverman (New York: Praeger, 1983) reports that 65 percent of Caucasian babies born out of wedlock in the United States in 1966 were placed for adoption. Twenty years later, that figure had fallen to five percent. At the same time, the incidence of infertility, the primary reason for domestic adoption, seemed to be on the rise, attributed in part to a voluntary delay in childbearing among college-educated women, and in part to damage caused by intrauterine contraceptive devices and environmental health hazards. Resolve, Inc., a national infertility education and advocacy network, estimates that one in six American couples of childbearing age is experiencing infertility. According to the Bureau of National Affairs, two million couples and one million single people sought to adopt children in 1987.

White prospective parents learn at their initial inquiry that there are extremely few healthy Caucasian infants waiting to be adopted. Transracial adoption in the United States is limited, as well. Following a statement by the National Association of Black Social Workers in 1972 objecting to the adoption of black children by white families, many agencies stopped making such placements, and one-fifth of the states passed statutes requiring that only black families be considered. In part because of insufficient efforts to recruit African-American families, that rule has left many children waiting in foster care. The current trend is toward a three-tiered policy that would place a child, first, with another relative, then with a family of the same race, and then with a family of another race sensitive to racism and African-American culture. The federal Indian Child Welfare Act of 1978 reserved the right of determining a child's custody to the tribe in which the child is registered in order to end the forcible removal of Indian children from their parents' homes on the grounds of poverty or "incompetence," a judgment open to racist attitudes. The tribal governments prefer to place children, first, with parents who are members of the tribe, second, with other Indian families, and as a last resort, with non-Indian parents who can demonstrate genuine interest in Native American culture. As a consequence of all these changes, white Americans who want to adopt infants are advised to look abroad.

International adoption is not, however, an easy and problem-free solution to infertility. Adopting across racial lines, national and cultural boundaries, and economic classes raises complex ethical questions and provokes political controversy. Opponents of international adoption tend to view it in the aggregate and see it as a simple matter of supply and demand, an international trade in human lives, parallel to the trade in natural resources. The Western industrialized nations, with a growing "demand" for adoptable infants and a short "supply," turn to poorer countries where children born out of wedlock are still likely to be abandoned at birth. It is troubling to speak of children in terms usually associated with inanimate commodities and to see the family's acquisition of a child as an expenditure of money, and this arouses suspicions that those engaged in international adoption are profiting by it.

Moreover, adoption itself is not a universal phenomenon and is not accorded the same meaning or value in the cultures where it is practiced. The twentieth-century American practice of absorbing a child born to someone else into one's family on an equal status with the family's birth children may have no counterpart in the child's original culture. In countries where children enter the labor force as young as six and poor children may work for wealthy employers for subsistence only, it takes no leap of the imagination to assume that foreigners adopting children intend to exploit them in some way. In countries where long-raging civil strife has exposed much of the population to violent atrocities, nothing is beyond belief. Thus, similar apocryphal stories about babies killed and hollowed out for drug smuggling, their organs sold for transplants, crop up in very distant parts of the world.

More reasoned opposition comes from advocates of social change who see international adoption as an impediment to needed political and economic reforms. Elizabeth Bartholet, a professor at the Harvard Law School and mother of two children from Peru, summarizes this argument in an article in the book *Adoption Law and Practice* (New York: Matthew Bender, 1988):

> For the poorer classes in these countries, international adoption is said to represent exploitation by their own government; the argument is that by exporting the children of the poor, the government avoids coming to terms with the economic and social needs of its most powerless members.

To its proponents, who are more likely to focus on case-by-case examples, international adoption proceeds from the same benign motives and fills the same mutual needs as a domestic matching of would-be parents and children whose birthparents are not in a position to raise them. The benefits to the children—family security, sufficient food, health care, education—are more tangible measures of good than abstract arguments about national integrity. Rosemary Taylor says this forcefully in a comment piece in the 1988 *Report on Foreign Adoption* published by the International Concerns Committee for Children (ICCC): "The nationality or citizenship of a child is a meaningless concept to a child who is dead, or subnormal from the deprivation of institutionalization."

Proponents emphasize that adoption has always involved dislocation of some sort: from one family to another, from the tuberculosis-ridden slums of the city to the invigorating countryside, from England to the British Commonwealth, The "orphan train," which brought more than 100,000 East Coast children—some of them European immigrants—to the Midwest between 1854 and 1929, has been replaced by the jumbojet, and the children encounter not only new landscapes and social mores but new languages, new physiognomies, new food, new rituals. This greater displacement raises new issues, as well, that are best clarified by keeping both the aggregate and the individual in mind.

While the cross-cultural transitions are major ones, the stories sketched out on the social history forms of adoption agencies are not always culturally specific, especially in cases of infant adoption:

> Father unknown, mother age 22. Bio-mother was hospitalized alone without her relatives and left asking that her baby be adopted to a happy home because she was not able to bring up this baby by herself. There was nothing to be known because bio-mother avoided answering. No one has come to see or ask about the baby.

The hint of secrecy and shame in this birthmother's silence are certainly not lost in the translation from Korean to English. It would come through as well in Portuguese, Spanish, or Bengali.

Sometimes the social histories tell a compelling story of false hope and heartbreak that reiterates what seems to be a universal theme:

> Birthparents had been living together for some time, but separated during pregnancy. Birthfather left the area without promising marriage. Birthmother has tried to raise child alone for four months, but has no support from parents and can no longer continue.

Occasionally there is enough detail reported to give the outlines of a cultural context that makes the situation different from that of the typical teenage pregnancy in mid-century America, as in this account relayed by the adoptive mother:

> My son had been born with rickets. The mother was an orphan, post-polio, walked on crutches. The father walked with a limp. He was also post-polio, but his family was well-to-do. They were "of class" and didn't approve of her and refused to allow them to get married. And so they together made the decision that he should be

adopted to the United States. They broke up ten days before he was born. She worked in a factory. She went to work in the morning before the sun came up and she worked until after the sun went down, so she was never in the sunlight. And she couldn't afford to eat properly.

The country in question here is South Korea. It is important to understand the circumstances that put so many children in need of adoption in developing societies like South Korea, certain Latin American countries, or India.

In its emergence as a modern industrial nation with leadership in technology, South Korea has only recently begun to find ways to deal with the many adverse effects of industrialization, such as urban crowding and the disruption of family ties and traditional social structures. The young women who migrate to the cities to work in factories seem to have borne the brunt of the change, and an increased rate of unintended pregnancies in the 1970s and 1980s is symptomatic of that. The social disruption brought on by the war, which left Korea divided into two hostile nations, and then by South Korea's rapid industrial development cast many rural young people into an urban environment with new and unfamiliar values and weakened the family's control over the younger generation. Although out-of-wedlock birth is now in a rapid decline, the typical unmarried mother can still be characterized as a woman in her early twenties living apart from her parents, who has an elementary or middle school education and works in a factory for a wage barely sufficient to support herself that she nevertheless shares with her family back home. She knows very little about sex and reproduction and becomes pregnant in a short-lived relationship with a man she has met at work or perhaps in her leisure time at a teahouse.

Usually, the decision to relinquish the child is made before the birth. Being the mother of an illegitimate child would make it impossible for a woman to keep her job or marry anyone other than the child's father, who has no legal or moral obligation of support and, even if he loves her, may encounter family opposition. There has been no public aid for single-parent families, even in cases of death or divorce. After divorce, legal custody of children is automatically granted to the father, because they are considered members of his family lineage. If he chooses not to take them, however, the mother has no formal recourse to financial support. Even widows often have to relinquish their children because they have no means of supporting them. If a divorced or widowed mother remarries, her new husband may refuse to accept her children because they belong to another man's family. Many of the older children who have come to the United States from Korea were placed for adoption by loving mothers who saw no other way to ensure the children's well-being.

Korean people trace their cultural origins to Confucius and are infused with the Confucian values of male supremacy, filial obedience, and reverence for ancestral memory. The multigenerational, patriarchal family is the cornerstone of Korean society, and a birth outside the bounds of the family is intolerable. Not only the mother, but the child, too, is marked by shame. Every Korean baby born within a legal marriage has its name entered in the father's family registry, a document of lineage that is all-important in Korean economic and social life. A prospective employer or the parents of a potential spouse may check the family registry to make certain it reveals nothing improper. A baby not legally acknowledged by its father cannot be entered into the public record except as the founder of a new family, which is culturally unacceptable. The child may as well not exist.

The care of these large numbers of children born out of wedlock fell first to the orphanages established after the Korean War, some run by the government and others privately administered. Postwar child welfare has been in large part a Christian endeavor, involving both Korean citizens and Western missionaries of several different denominations, from the Maryknoll Fathers, a Catholic order that follows the social gospel, to more evangelical organizations such as Holt International. They are similar in that they meld the Christian admonition to love thy neighbor and care for widows and orphans with the Confucian emphasis on family stability. Most child welfare advocates do not see institutional life as a favorable mode of upbringing and have promoted adoption instead. The justification for international adoption has been that a loving family is more important to the child's welfare than preserving national identity for its own sake. The four agencies licensed by the Korean government to place children abroad operate as social service agencies and are motivated by their commitment to the well-being of the children in their charge. Eastern Child Welfare Society, for example, which had cared for my children, was founded by Dr. Kim Duk Whang, a retired public official and Methodist layman, as a personal ministry to needy children. Eastern has actively sought adoptive homes in Korea

and has been prepared to cease international adoption altogether whenever domestic adoption meets the need.

Adoption has been practiced in Korea all along, but it has been
rare, extralegal, and highly secret. In preindustrial society, a family
might hide away its pregnant daughter, register the baby as the child
of the oldest brother, and then bring the child up within the household.
There were many women who had no such protection, however. Their
recourse was to abandon the child by the gate to a wealthy family's
home or in front of a police station, where it would not go unnoticed
long enough to endanger its life. A family without a son might take in
an infant found abandoned and enter him as a birthchild in the father's
registry. Since 1976, there has been a legal process for relinquishment
that has almost completely replaced physical abandonment. The same
law also allows adoption of nonrelatives and is meant to encourage
Korean families to take responsibility for the many homeless children.
Through the 1980s, in-country adoption saw a slow but steady increase,
but there have been many cultural barriers to overcome. In Confucianism,
to count as heir someone of a different bloodline violates the sanctity
of patrilineage. Those couples who do adopt may use several subterfuges
to avoid offending their own or their families' propriety. They almost
always plan to keep the adoption secret from the child and look for an
infant with similar physical traits and a compatible blood type. Sometimes
they go so far as to feign pregnancy so that even family and neighbors
do not know. And, wary of the stigma attached to fatherlessness and
adoption, they will register the child as a birthchild if they can.

Attention of the media, both domestic and foreign, to the "export"
of Korean children has kept the practice of international adoption under
very close and demanding government scrutiny. During the Seoul Olympics in 1988, a feature story on the adoption of Korean children was
broadcast to an international television audience. The South Korean
public was ashamed and outraged by the numbers of children involved—
the Health and Welfare Ministry counted 109,579 from 1954 to 1988,
compared to 24,317 adopted within Korea—but also moved to find
internal solutions for the needs of homeless children. More families
are seeking to adopt, and the government is giving financial support
to in-country adoption. This has abruptly diminished the number of
children coming from Korea to the United States. Other factors are
also at work. The number of out-of-wedlock births is declining, as contraception and abortion are more readily available and more widely prac-

ticed, and vigorous family planning efforts have slowed the country's population growth. There is also a slight change in public acceptance of single mothers who are of age. A 1988 survey found that seven percent of the unmarried women giving birth planned to raise their children themselves, and the percentage is expected to increase. The Ae Ran Won Home in Seoul, which has offered housing and vocational training to pregnant women intending to place their children for adoption, now operates a day-care center and a transitional home for unmarried mothers who need assistance as they begin their new lives. Finally, with economic stability, Korea is now in a position to finance social programs that will benefit children and families.

While Korean adoption has served as precedent for the placement of children outside their home countries, adoption from Latin America does not follow the Korean model. The differences relate both to the socioeconomic conditions in the countries involved and the structure of the adoption process. There are significant national and regional variations among the Latin American countries, as well, and generalizations do not apply across the board. Colombia, which accounts for the greatest number of adoptions to the United States (699 children in 1988), also has the most coherent policy and procedures. Paraguay was second, with 300 children, but a new government temporarily suspended adoptions in 1989 in order to review the policy. Chile was next with 252 American placements, followed by Guatemala, Brazil, Honduras, Peru, Mexico, El Salvador, and Costa Rica. Several other countries each placed fewer than 50 children in the United States in 1988.

Adoption from Latin America began on a random, case-by-case basis, on the initiative of foreign citizens seeking to adopt. Bob and Rita Garman's story offers one example of how it came about. When the Garmans went to Ecuador as missionaries in 1972, they were newly married and intended to remain childless in order to devote themselves fully to their work. As Rita began orienting herself to the community and looking for places to be of service, a Peace Corps volunteer invited her along to visit a state-financed orphanage. Rita recounts what conditions were like there:

> The babies were left swaddled, and they were basically left in cribs to lie all day and all night. Their bottles were propped. They were changed, my guess is, once a day. And chronic diarrhea. It just reeked.

And the diaper rash! They had sections partitioned off for babies who were left because they were dying. You would pick up a seven-month-old and it was just limp—no pick-up reflex. Children terribly, terribly ill. It was a real bad situation. We went to try and give the children stimulation—play with them, hold them, wash them.

Rita began making weekly visits to the orphanage and found herself drawn again and again to a particular infant girl. The nuns who staffed the orphanage explained that the mother had brought her there and said she would be back, but they did not know her name or how to locate her. While Rita saw more children come into the orphanage, she rarely saw one leave again. Those who survived the many health hazards would spend their entire childhoods warehoused in that way. Rita began the long and complicated legal proceedings to take her one favorite baby into her home and talked to other people about the children's need. The legal process included putting out public notices calling on relatives to claim the child if they wished. At the same time, Rita was put in touch with a maternity hospital at which many newborn infants were being relinquished and was asked to help find alternatives to the orphanage for these babies. When the Garmans' missionary assignment ended after two years, they returned home as a family with two small children and had found adoptive parents in the United States for several others.

The Garmans' experience is not unique. Other North American and European missionaries, volunteer workers, business people, exchange teachers, and foreign service employees returned home from Latin America in the 1970s with newly adopted children. The omnipresence of streetchildren makes the severity of homelessness very obvious and difficult for a comfortable North American with a sensitive social conscience to bear. These few families made themselves available as advocates for international adoption and offered assistance to others seeking to adopt. Heino Erichsen and Jean Nelson Erichsen, who adopted twin daughters from Colombia in 1972, published a guidebook, *Gamines: How to Adopt from Latin America,* in 1981, and opened a consulting service, Los Niños International Aid and Adoption Center, to assist with private, parent-initiated adoptions. Los Niños gradually evolved into a full-fledged placement agency operating in eleven Latin American countries, and other U.S. agencies sought their own Latin American contacts. As rumors spread that South Korea might soon be closed to international adoption, Latin America was promoted as a new "source" of adoptable children.

The number of homeless children in Latin America seems limitless, but this is due less to sexual mores than to poverty, particularly the poverty that afflicts women who have sole responsibility for their children. In deference to the Catholic Church's stance against premarital sex, and the extra force with which it is applied to women, wealthy families will go to great expense to protect their pregnant daughters' privacy. Among the poor, however, long-term cohabitation without the formality of a wedding ceremony or a civil marriage license is very common. Some governments have made cohabitation quasi-legal by passing laws granting equal status and rights of inheritance to children born to unmarried parents. Yet, if the parents have no possessions, or if the father leaves and paternity has not been established, this makes little difference. Indeed, these relationships are quite unstable, and it is not unusual for a woman to bear children with two or three partners in succession. In a common adoption story, a young woman bears a child in an ongoing relationship but has no firm promise of support from the baby's father. He leaves, and she turns to her family for assistance. The family consists of her mother, who is also unmarried, and several sisters who have small children. Sometimes, there is no man contributing to the support of any of these children, and the financial need is greater than the family can manage. The young mother may see no recourse but to relinquish her child and might leave the child at the hospital right after birth or take it to an orphanage. Or, to guard her privacy, she may abandon the child in a public place, where it is likely to be found and provided for. In some countries, voluntary relinquishment of parental rights is against the law, making physical abandonment the only option. With increasing knowledge of international adoption, more women are contacting agencies, lawyers, and professional "childfinders" and requesting that their children be placed in wealthier countries, where they will have an opportunity for education and other advantages the mothers could never afford.

The out-of-wedlock children who are adopted abroad are most often the offspring of the poor, since wealthy families can afford illegal abortions or arrange private, in-country adoptions. With the exception of Chile, the children are more likely to be Indian or mestizo than of full European ancestry, and some are of African heritage. Many of the children have been born to domestic servants whose employers will not allow them to raise children on the premises. In some cases, the father is the employer himself or a member of his family.

The single mother is certainly not a new phenomenon in Latin America, but her numbers are increasing. The ideology of machismo, with its emphasis on virility, sexual prowess, and masculine dominance, has traditionally offered some leeway for men to avoid paternal responsibility. It is not considered shameful for men to leave their spouse or partner and form new relationships, or to have two families—one with a wife and one with a mistress. The growing impoverishment of the rural areas has strained and broken family bonds and increased the risk of abandon-ment. First, the men go off to the cities to look for work, which is hard to come by. Many men never earn enough money to bring their families along, or they find new partners and lose interest in returning to the old way of life. More recently, women and children have joined the urban migration. Poor women left alone with several children have extreme difficulty providing for them, especially in an unfamiliar and intimidating environment. They may feel compelled to house one or more of them in an orphanage, at best, or, at worst, to "lose" them in the marketplace or at a bus depot. Having three children to feed rather than four may make the difference between constant hunger and outright starvation. In addition to the children of poverty, there are thousands more who have been orphaned by war and political violence in Central America.

The three Frazee children, adopted from Colombia at 5, 4, and 3, were placed for adoption by their mother. What John, the oldest, recalls from their early life is living in a house about the size of the Frazees' dining room, watching rats crawl on the floor at night, and helping their mother wash clothes in a central square. He remembers a father who disappeared without explanation. One day a car came to pick up the children and drove them off as their mother waved goodbye. Three months later they were in the United States.

The staggering figures on homeless children and impoverished fatherless families in Latin America raise the question, What about birth control? The poor use it infrequently, for many reasons. First of all, the Catholic Church's prohibition against the use of artificial contraception has limited its availability. Supplies tend to be expensive and beyond the means of women who might otherwise use them. Narrative accounts of poor women's lives tell, for example, of two women sharing birth control pills and taking them on alternate days, which is, of course, ineffective. Even birth control campaigns that offer free or inexpensive contraceptives often meet with skepticism. Those run by foreign aid programs or by dictatorial governments arouse fears of genocide. In addition, many women worry about the health risks. They have heard about women left sterile or unhealthy as a result of the testing by North American pharmaceutical companies of pills and IUDs not yet approved for use in the United States. Added to this is a cultural attitude that children are gifts to be treasured and the promise of a better future. In countries that have no social security system, parents depend on their children for support in old age. Where incomes are low, it takes many children to earn a surplus large enough to support a parent.

With so many homeless children, the challenge for adoptive parents has been to select a child and to negotiate the often ambiguous legal procedures necessary to adopt the child and bring it to the United States. With Colombia excepted, about half the children available for adoption have been physically abandoned. Usually, a child can only be designated an orphan after an attempt has been made to find relatives and the case has been reviewed by the courts. The task of finding adoptable children and providing legal counsel has been taken on largely by attorneys based in the various countries who pursue each case as a private adoption. The system is rife with opportunity for abuse, and there have, indeed, been instances of fraud, of exorbitant fees for deficient services, and of outright baby selling. The 1982 arrest of a Colombian attorney on kidnapping charges received wide publicity and generated new opposition to international adoption. Subsequently, Colombia instituted a uniform national adoption policy with licensing procedures centralized in the Bogotá office of the government family welfare agency. As a result, Colombian-born children arrive in healthier condition and within a more predictable period of time, and Colombia is the major country for infant adoption.

International adoption is a sensitive political issue for Latin American governments. Without denying the need for solutions to poverty and homelessness, many people object to sending children abroad as a violation of national pride and a sacrifice of cultural values. In this view, the United States, particularly, is seen as a materialistic, self-indulgent culture lacking in religious values—a detrimental setting in which to raise children. To counter the trend, both public and private efforts have been undertaken to keep families intact through sponsorship programs, women's craft cooperatives, housing subsidies, free meals, and other supportive measures. Without a public welfare system, and short of significant and unencumbered economic development, these programs will continue to meet only a small portion of the need.

In response to public opinion, some countries have, from time to time, limited international adoption to children identified as having "special needs," such as handicapped children, older children, and sibling groups. Lengthy residency requirements in Uruguay, Venezuela, and Argentina make international adoption from those countries impractical for most North American families. In Argentina, adoption is clouded by the memory of the serious violations that occurred with children born to women held in political detention, many of whom "were disappeared" in the "dirty war" of the 1960s and 1970s. Throughout Latin America, regulations and procedures on adoption are in constant flux. A change in government can, in fact, change the country's entire stance on international adoption.

Although it is the visibility of streetchildren, known as "gamines" in Colombia, that makes it seem as though Latin American countries would be receptive to international adoption, the true streetchildren are the least likely to end up in the adoption process. Those who have learned the ways of the street are not necessarily amenable to being confined in an orphanage while a family is found. Not all of them have been abandoned by their families. Some maintain contact with parents or other relatives who would not think of severing the legal bonds, even if they cannot or do not provide for the child's care. While the children who are adopted abroad might become streetchildren if adoption were not available, those who are already living on the streets are usually doomed to stay there.

In India, international adoption is a relatively new form of relief for poverty, a problem of long duration, and for a more recent increase in the number of births out of wedlock. By global economic measures, nearly 40 percent of the Indian population lives below a subsistence level. This figure includes 108 million children. A 1987 article by Kamal Krishna reprinted in the International Mission of Hope newsletter claimed that there were five million abandoned, destitute children in India, only one-tenth of whom could be accommodated by existing institutions. An article published in the journal Child Welfare in 1989 estimated that by 1991 there would be 30 million orphans in India, 12 million of them without access to the resources necessary to maintain life. Homelessness among children is thus an overwhelming problem. There are children living on the streets, toddlers living in the "nursing homes" or maternity hospitals where they were born, children crowding the state-run orphanages. Private orphanages help meet the need for housing but vary greatly in quality of care. Children who live in these institutions may be malnourished.

Physical abandonment of children is still more common than legal relinquishment, so there is not always certainty about the child's origins. Abandoned infants are presumed to be born out of wedlock. Unwed motherhood is both stigmatized and financially difficult, unless someone in the mother's "joint family," as the extended family is known, has the means to raise the child or maintain the child as household help. This was the solution in the past, but increasing urbanization has broken the joint family into smaller units with fewer resources to manage extra children. Older children become homeless when parents die—and early mortality is high among the poor—or when their families can no longer afford to care for them. Children born to beggars, or to handicapped parents without resources, are destitute from the start. Widowhood often leads to impoverishment and, sometimes, loss of children. Remarriage does not necessarily keep the family intact, since the new husband may refuse to accept the children.

The first Indian children to be placed abroad were sent to Northern Europe and to Italy in the 1960s to families designated as their guardians. International adoption was not legally recognized in India at that time, and each child's case was handled individually through the court system, in keeping with the Guardians and Wards Act of 1890. According to an article in the July 1976 issue of *The Indian Journal of Social Work*, there were 99 such placements between 1963 and 1970. By 1975, the major countries involved in Indian adoption were Sweden, Belgium, West Germany, France, and the Netherlands, accounting for 978 of the 1220 children placed in the previous three years. Only thirty-one were sent to the United States in that period. The fact that infants could be adopted from India caught public attention in the United States in 1978, with the founding of the International Mission of Hope (IMH) in Calcutta. Cherie Clark-Prakash, an American woman who had worked with children in Vietnam during the war, began touring nursing homes in Calcutta in search of abandoned newborns and took custody of children who had been housed in the jails for lack of better shelter. Many of the babies were premature, and nearly all were malnourished. IMH's urgent appeal for families to adopt these children was addressed to single people as well as married couples, thus opening a new avenue for single would-be parents to pursue adoption. The IMH babies were sent to the United States as soon as they could survive the flight. My sister tells a story of waiting for a plane at the Boston airport and hearing a mewing sound from a basket across the aisle. She peeked in, expecting kittens, and saw five tiny babies lined up in a row—babies so fragile she would hardly dare pick one up.

Indian babies do not arrive so tiny anymore. In 1982, India's Supreme Court decreed that adoption agencies must be registered with the government, that all adoptions must be cleared by the Council of Child Welfare, and that there be a waiting period while efforts are made to find the birthparents. Birthparents who sign relinquishment papers are allowed a further time in which to reconsider their decision. The legal process varies by state and can be long and intricate. Although the government does operate orphanages, most social welfare is conducted on private initiative. Children adopted internationally are generally found and cared for by private placement agencies. Typical for India is the small, family-operated orphanage and adoption agency. As of 1988, approximately ninety different agencies were licensed by the government to refer children for adoption abroad.

The Supreme Court ruling also required that preference be given to Indian families seeking to adopt. In some states, adoption agencies must document their efforts to recruit Indian families. This is a slow process, since adoption across family lines is largely a foreign concept. Hindus, who constitute 80 per cent of the population, do have a long-standing practice of adoption, mostly to clarify lineage and inheritance, to provide security in old age, and to assure that there is a son who can perform last rites at the father's death. Hindu adoption preferably operates within extended families, and almost always within caste boundaries. The Muslim community, 11 percent of the population, has not been amenable to interfamily adoption because it is not compatible with Islamic religious law. Indian families that do adopt tend to be quite selective, preferring boys and specifying religion, caste, and skin color.

Because adoption across ethnic boundaries is alien to most Indian people's conception of the family, there is widespread suspicion about the motives of people from other countries seeking children in India. Rumors abound that the children are being sold into prostitution or servitude or used in medical experiments—some of the very same apocryphal stories that circulate in Latin America. To assuage these fears, many adoption agencies and state governments require the parents with whom they have placed children to submit periodic reports, including photographs of the children in their new homes. In response to negative public opinion, some state governments have been tightening the restrictions on international placements. The courts themselves can be even more restrictive than the legal code specifies. Rulings in individual adoption cases are very much subject to the particular judge's attitude toward placing Indian children abroad. Adoption workers in the United States have begun to caution their clients that India, despite continuing poverty and homelessness, is not to be regarded as an unlimited source of adoptable children.

In describing the factors underlying international adoption, there is a risk of portraying the children's birth countries as primitive or barbaric in their treatment of children. No country willingly deprives its children of the conditions needed for a good life, nor eagerly sends its homeless children abroad to be done with them. In all countries, there is great sorrow for the children who are thus cut off from their cultural roots. Lourdes G. Balanon, assistant director of the Bureau of Child and Youth Welfare in the Philippines, believes, "It is a sign of political maturity for a country to accept that it cannot provide for the needs of its children" (*Child Welfare*, March/April 1989, p. 253). David H. Kim, the Executive Director of Holt International Children's Services, urges parents to see a country's placement of children abroad in a positive light:

> I think that the decline of Korean adoption is a reminder to all of us that it is a very special privilege to be entrusted with a child from another nation. Children are a nation's most valuable resource. When that nation allows one of its children to become a part of a family in another country, they deserve to know that their nation will be respected and that its culture will be honored in the home that adopts the child. (*HI Families*, March/April 1989)

The same cultures that are perceived as offering insufficient help to needy children may, in fact, hold children in high esteem. Korean parents, for example, will make very significant economic sacrifices to provide for their children's educations. Children are omnipresent in Latin America and are loved for their vitality and the joy they bring.

American society is hardly more hospitable to children. We segregate children from adult life much of the time, and we have, until recently, tolerated child abuse as a private family concern. One-quarter of American children live in single-parent families, and only one-quarter of these receive child support payments from the absent parent. Despite an ever greater need for facilities, child care gets grudging and inadequate government support. Homelessness in the United States is a growing social problem afflicting not only the alcoholic and drug dependent and the "deinstitutionalized" mentally ill but more and more poor families with young children. The difference between these homeless children and the streetchildren of other countries is that they are less likely to be abandoned, though lack of shelter is, in some jurisdictions, reason for removing children from their families' care. The children are homeless together with their parents—most often their mothers. There are also thousands of children in the United States who have no permanent families and are in foster care awaiting adoption. I do not mean to romanticize the other countries, either. No matter how much love and affection are bestowed on children in any culture, there is an underside. Older children come from Korea, India, and Colombia, too, with histories of physical or sexual abuse.

Rather than passing judgment, we in the industrial nations need to look at our own history and understand how recent a phenomenon adoption is. It was a late nineteenth-century response to economic conditions that caused mass migration from Europe to the United States and from countryside to city, that impoverished families and separated children from parents, that put children to work at manual labor. Adoption, in its early phase, was not a heaven-made match between infertile parents and cherished babies. Child welfare agencies recruited families to take in "poor orphans" out of kindness, or in exchange for the children's labor on the farm or in the household. There was no expectation that the child would become a full member of the family. That idea emerged later in a more prosperous and urban America, where children were no longer valued for the work they contributed but as embodiments of the family's love.

Even the countries now rating lowest in infant mortality and highest in public benefits to children once experienced the social upset that comes with industrialization and leaves the most vulnerable in need. Years ago, doing research on women's history and literature in Sweden, I read through Swedish women's magazines from the decade of the 1910s. I was surprised to come upon photographs of children in need of adoption. They had been found in the street or turned over to charitable institutions by their impoverished mothers. Some were products of "Stockholm marriages"—short-lived relationships between young women who had come from the country to work in factories or sweatshops and men they met at work, in overcrowded rooming houses, or at dance halls. In rural Sweden, orphaned or abandoned children were auctioned off to the lowest bidder—the adult who would accept the lowest subsidy from the local parish for the child's care. In effect, they became indentured farm laborers or domestic servants. This method did not suffice for children left homeless in the city. They sold their labor on their own as best they could. Some of these children found their way to America as part of the "Great Migration" of 1880–1920. The families they engendered, whether in Sweden or in the United States, may well include Asian or mestizo great-grandchildren.

We do best, in the long run, to look at the common conditions that put children in peril: poverty, malnutrition, lack of medical resources, and, across seemingly impenetrable cultural boundaries, failure of paternal responsibility. These conditions afflict some segments of the population even in wealthy countries. Such massive problems are best addressed in a global perspective, with conscientious attention to the larger factors that cause and maintain them. Yet, the need for long-range solutions does not preclude short-range ones. Focusing on the particular—a single child's life—can sharpen our vision of the whole, if we stay attentive. Seen in its broader context, international adoption may increase our sense of urgency about the millions of lives still at risk.

2

Families in Search of Children

Even though adoption into an American family profoundly improves a child's material well-being, social status, health, and access to education, parents who adopt from other countries seldom do so primarily for altruistic reasons. Earlier in the history of adoption, families took in homeless children out of charity, and virtue's reward was the additional labor the children could provide. The ethos of adoption has changed since then, and prospective parents usually sense that wanting to do a good deed is, if not the wrong motive, at least insufficient in itself. Charity moves people to send UNICEF cards at holidays or make monthly payments to sponsor a child in a Third World country, but charity alone cannot sustain a relationship as emotionally demanding as that between parent and child.

Most parents recoil when others try to credit them with selfless generosity. Bill MacNamara, the father of two Korean-born children, speaks for many when he says,

> The most offending thing that I get is, "Oh, aren't you nice for doing that?" I tell everybody—and I tell them rather quickly, "No, I'm lucky. I'm the lucky one, not them." I have a pretty short fuse on that one.

Left unanswered, such unwarranted praise can make you feel a little deceptive. Linda Truman, whose Korean-born daughters are now grown, confesses,

> People say, "Oh, what a wonderful thing!" and I think, Oh, if they only knew, because it was completely selfish. I wanted the kids and was filling my own need. It just happened that it helped both of us as far as I could see.

What Linda calls selfish—wanting the children—is, indeed, the most trustworthy impulse behind adoption. Adopting children without first wanting them would be foolish. The parents' objection to the "wonderful" accolades is not simply that they are unwarranted. They are, at worst, uncomprehending. Those who bestow them presumably see our families as aberrant, linked by benevolence rather than bonded by "real" or "natural" family ties.

We who have adopted from other countries have had a series of opportunities to examine our motives, so by the time the children arrive, our reasons for pursuing this unusual mode of family formation should be evident, at least to ourselves. First, you must decide whether or not to have a child—or an additional child, as the case may be. Second comes the decision to adopt rather than to bear a child, which, for some, might require medical intervention. Third is the decision to adopt internationally; fourth, the choice of a country to adopt from. Finally, you must agree to the adoption of a particular child whose other attributes—age, sex, state of health, temperament, developmental progress, previous history—may be more decisive than nationality. For a relatively small number of families, like the Garmans who found themselves drawn to a certain child while living temporarily in Ecuador, this process is foreshortened. Wanting a child is simultaneous with wanting *this* child. By the time these steps are completed, whatever pride we might take in doing a good deed for a homeless child ought to be balanced by an honest reckoning of our own needs, especially those we hope the child will fill.

The majority of children are, of course, born into the world without a great deal of parental forethought. In moments of existential crisis, contemplating the prospect of nuclear war, for example, young people may well ask themselves, Is it worth it to have children? but, if they go ahead and do so, they are hardly ever asked to explain themselves. Friends and relatives may ask, Why *now*? but the desire for children is itself a given. Indeed, it is the married couples who remain childless who are pressed to justify their unusual condition. Adoptive parents, however, *must* be able to articulate their reasons for wanting children to the satisfaction of domestic adoption agencies and agencies and courts in the child's birthplace. What explanations might people offer for giving birth to children, if obligated to do so? Apart from societal expectations, a desire for genetic continuity, sexual irresponsibility, and contraceptive failure, the motives for giving birth are probably not much different from the motives for adopting.

Looking back through my journal, I found an entry in which I was either rehearsing the answers I would list on the agency's application form or convincing myself of the wisdom of giving up what I had been calling my "childfree" lifestyle. Why did I want children?

> I want to develop the sensitivity and the capacity for caring that I observe in my friends who have children. I want to end my isolation from all that has to do with children and break out of this confining adult insularity. I want to reexperience—from a new vantage point— the aspects of childhood that I remember so vividly. I want to have a major project for [my husband] and me to work together on. I want some part in setting a future course. I want to learn responsibility for someone other than my independent self.

And on and on and on. In my effort to make the case irrefutable, I left out the obvious, primary—or, rather, primal—reason. How much more succinctly Judy Pollard said it in explaining why she stuck it out through a four-year ordeal of false hopes and broken agreements that finally brought her a daughter, a toddler from Honduras: "I wanted to love a child, to share my life with a child, and hopefully enrich and broaden her life—love her and have her love me." The fundamental human need to love and be loved—that is the first "why" of international adoption. Subject to failure and misuse it may be, but it is still the firmest foundation on which to build a family, whether by nature or by law.

Then, why *adoption?* For Judy, who is single, the choice was clear. There are, of course, other alternatives—artificial insemination, or getting pregnant in a courtship of convenience—but adoption seems the least morally ambiguous. Judy herself was adopted in infancy and had a happy childhood in a loving family, so she had no qualms about adoption itself. Her only hesitation was whether she, as a single woman, could provide a child with the kind of nurturance she got from two parents. The majority of adoptive families become so because adoption is the best hope for meeting the need to love and be loved. Often, the choice comes quite naturally, as it did for me. Long before I really wanted children, I knew that pregnancy would exacerbate my chronic illness and possibly endanger my life and the child's, too. So, even in my fantasies, my children were usually adopted.

For very many families, however, the decision to adopt marks the end of a long, stressful effort to conceive and bear children. It is made with mixed emotions: sorrow for the impossible, joy in the possible, and apprehension that this, too, may come to naught. Patti and Jim Cronin come close to being the typical internationally adoptive parents, as do Mary and Bill MacNamara. According to *American Demographics* magazine of March 1988,

> A 1986 survey of adoption agencies found that parents who adopt foreign-born children are generally college-educated, suburban couples earning an average of $36,000 a year. Although most have no children of their own, the couples—who are likely to be in their mid-30's— have been married an average of seven years. (p. 38)

In addition to matching this sketch, the Cronins and the MacNamaras are white, live in the state with the highest per capita rate of international adoptions, Minnesota, and adopted from the country which accounts for the greatest number of adopted children, South Korea. Another common denominator implied, but not explicitly stated, in the sketch is infertility. Patti Cronin describes her experience:

> We never considered that we would not be able to have children until we started trying. After about a year, it was evident to us that something was wrong, so we went to an infertility specialist and began infertility testing. It took about a year to discover that there was nothing wrong with Jim, but it was probably me, so I went through about four years of infertility testing and surgeries. It was discovered that I did have endometriosis, and so I had a major surgery, two so-called minor surgeries, and a major infertility surgery. Being an infertility person, I think you have to go through that to understand the emotional strain that has on you. When you want children so badly and you can't have them, you're on an emotional yo-yo. You go to these doctors and you're told, "We can treat this possibly. There's no guarantee, but keep your hopes up." So every month you're thinking, Oh, I'm pregnant, or I'm going to be, and then you're not. It's up and down and up and down.

All through the infertility testing and treatment, Patti and Jim held on to adoption as a worthy solution to childlessness, but that did not eliminate the sorrow. Mary MacNamara tells about the emotional adjustment she and Bill had to make in order to go ahead with adoption. She uses an image familiar to many in such circumstances:

> When we started thinking about adoption, first we had to go through a thought process that was sort of like a funeral. We had to emotionally

bury that fantasy child. I had thought about a little boy who would have hair the color of my husband's and would be like him, because he's a real nice man. I thought, Oh, he'll inherit that. It will be so nice. And so I had to let go of that, and it surprised me that that was difficult to do. Once we started getting involved in the adoption process, it was OK. The funeral was over, so to speak.

In the past, when there were many newborn white babies in need of adoption in the United States, agencies did their best to replace that fantasy child with a reasonable facsimile. Adoptive parents and birthparents were "matched" for hair and eye color, physical build, even talents and hobbies. If they chose, the adoptive parents could keep up the pretense that the child had been born to them, even withholding the fact of adoption from the child. International adoption rarely offers that possibility; the child's "difference" will probably be apparent to just about everyone the family encounters. This is an insurmountable barrier for some infertile couples seeking to adopt, and the process stops there; or else they turn to private sources or place themselves on a waiting list several years long in the hope of eventually adopting a white infant. Others react positively to the prospect of widening their horizons and welcome the clarity that interracial adoption brings. I remember feeling relieved that there could be no pretense that this was anything but an adoption. The evidence would be open, for all to see, and my family would not be tainted by the shame-ridden secrecy with which we human beings often mask our deviations from the norm.

Before deciding to adopt a child of another race, or even one darker in hair color or smaller in stature, white parents typically go through a kind of self-examination, considering the meaning of difference and thinking through how it might affect their parental relationship with the child. They may ask themselves, How will it feel to have a child who doesn't look at all like me? Will I really love this child like my own? Am I capable of handling any problems the child might run into as a minority person at school or elsewhere? Jack Gaartner grew up in a white, working-class, urban neighborhood that bordered on a poor black neighborhood. As the black neighborhood expanded, racial hostility grew more intense:

I never would have heard the words "Negro" or "black" in my growing up years. It was always "niggers," whether it was my father or my grandfather or the next-door neighbor. It was just the way it was done, so I grew up with the same orientation. It wasn't until I got lots of education and out of that kind of environment and had other experiences that I really challenged it. That's really powerful stuff for a long, long time—so much so that when we got to the point of deciding to adopt, I can remember kind of questioning myself, saying, I don't think I'm that way anymore, but what if I am? What if we adopt this Asian kid and I'm prejudiced against her? That was a real struggle, even though I felt like I had left all that crap behind a long time ago. But the issue still surfaced.

Bill MacNamara, on the other hand, took his recovery from that kind of overt racism to mean that race would not be a significant issue:

We were pretty much determined to have children. As far as the foreign adoption goes, I just never even thought about it. There was nothing in my mind at the time we decided to have children whether he was black, white, pink, purple. It didn't matter. It just never even dawned on me that there would be a difference. And even through the process, right from the day of orientation—although the agency made a big deal about it—it never really hit me. We met with other families who were doing the same thing, and they had some questions. I can remember, because of my size, one of the people looked at me and asked me what kind of sports I played—I played basketball. One of his questions was, "What if your son is a little, short Korean?" I said, "Well, I'll make him a shooting guard."

Bill talks with some amazement about his naivete and has become one of the most vociferous advocates of emphasizing and affirming difference and of preparing adoptive parents for racism, whether it be their own or that of the world around them.

One clue to how comfortable people are with difference at the outset is to see whom they include in the decision-making process. It is not at all unusual for prospective parents to worry about how their child will be received by relatives and to be silent about their interest in adopting until they have actually applied for a child or even received a referral for a specific child. Getting past a presumed point-of-no-return seems to be a safeguard against family opposition. Mary and Bill MacNamara had intended to wait until just before the baby's arrival to announce the news, but they found that "we were so thrilled with the possibility that we might get a child that we couldn't keep it in." Their families' reactions were very unexpected:

> We were concerned about telling Bill's family about adoption, because he comes from a real blue-collar family that is kind of racist. We thought, No problem with my mother. It was the exact opposite. Bill's family was so open and immediately accepting, and my mother acted like Archie Bunker. I called my mother up and told her, and there was a long silence on the phone, and then the only thing she said was, "Oh, Mary." I wanted to slam the phone down, I was so mad. And then she didn't want to talk about it anymore. I talked to my sister afterwards, and my mother was real opposed to it. She said to my sister, "What if when he grows up he wants to go back to his own kind?" And my sister said, "Well, Mom, Mary and Bill will be his own kind." I never expected that from my mother. I remember talking to her about it years afterwards and saying something about her negative reaction, and she said, "Well, Mary, I just didn't want anything bad to happen to you." "Mom, something bad had already happened to me. I had been married eleven years and no baby."

Where the adoptive parents suspect racism, the prospective grandparents often explain their initial reservations as an impulse to protect their children from possible ostracism or heartbreak. My parents looked stunned when I first told them, and I read their expression to mean, Here she goes again, doing something real different. What will people think this time? When they heard the situation described and, especially, when they saw my daughter's referral pictures, all hesitation melted away. Convincing my 88-year-old Danish grandmother took about five minutes: "Why do they have to come from so far away? What do Koreans look like? Well, how is *that* going to work?" When she heard that there were lots of other families in the Twin Cities with Korean children, she breathed a very audible sigh of relief and said, "Well, then, that's good."

Convincing the hesitant to go ahead and adopt is not the best way to serve children, of course. Fully accepting a child of another race or culture as one's own child requires more than good intentions, and not all families are suited for raising internationally adopted children.

Betty Ringstad makes that observation after twenty years of childraising and of working with other adoptive families in her community:

> In the early years, when people would say, "Oh, I could never do that, never adopt a child of another race," we always said, "Yes, you could. It's no different." But in the last years, my husband and I both said, "Yeah, we're different." There are some people who could not do it and should not do it, and there are some people who have anyway. We have really come to the conclusion that the people who adopt cross-culturally are unique persons generally in their thinking and beliefs and feelings.

Adoption agencies with long experience in placing children from other countries generally do see a need to discuss the impact of racial and cultural difference in the preadoptive counseling they require. Seasoned social workers will even read indifference to difference as a warning sign and will probe into the sentiments underlying statements like "Color doesn't matter to me. She will just be my child." Colorblindness is a luxury enjoyed only by members of a dominant group with its power unthreatened. A child who grows up not only as a minority in society at large but as a minority in its own family is not likely to feel indifferent about the fact. Parents who set out denying difference may end up negating or trivializing their child's experience. Bill MacNamara broached this issue with another parent who insisted, "She's not Korean. She's an American and that's the way she's going to be brought up." Bill's response was quick and vivid, "All she's got to do is wake up and look in the mirror and *she* knows she's Korean."

It is vitally important for parents to realize that adopting a child whose appearance is obviously different from theirs turns the family itself into a minority family. Everyone in it becomes different from the norm. The family will be interracial not just through childhood, but for generations. People who make the decision to adopt internationally ought always to come to terms with difference before proceeding. A popular rule of thumb is, if you would not marry interracially, you should not adopt interracially. In the beginning, we may not know precisely how difference will affect our family's daily life, but we need to be alert to it and learn some ways to respond that will affirm our children's dignity and our family's unusual make-up.

Despite the best efforts of adoption agencies to raise these issues ahead of time, there are some parents who slip through the process believing, for instance, that a Korean infant is just an updated version of the healthy white baby of yesterday, or that finding a light-skinned Latin American child will make issues of ethnicity irrelevant. Moreover, some agencies require only a single home visit and do not offer the kind of preadoptive counseling that would elicit consideration of difference. These parents are underrepresented in this book because they are harder to find than the others. They do not join organizations or read newsletters for adoptive parents. Their children do not attend ethnic festivals and summer culture camps. They do not make use of agencies' postadoption services. "They don't check back in with us," one social worker told me. "I know they're out there, and I worry about them."

So far, I have focused on the typical internationally adoptive family, but there is a large category of parents who have followed an alternate route to the decision. Not all adoptive parents are infertile. Many choose adoption in preference to birth, either the first time, or, more commonly, after bearing children. Sometimes this is an ideological choice, based, for example, on concern about overpopulation or, more specifically, about bringing new children into a world where others remain homeless. Or adoption might be a more certain means to a desired end, such as adding a girl to an all-boy family, or vice versa. For Sally Anderson, who is very fond of children and has happy memories of growing up in a large family, adoption was a sensible, appealing way to have such a family, and it had the advantage of not overtaxing her somewhat frail body:

> I started thinking about adoption back in grade school. It was
> international adoption, too, that I was thinking about. I guess I've
> always felt that it was my calling or mission in life or that God has
> put it in me because it goes back so far. I read a lot of books and
> stories about families that maybe started with biological kids and
> then filled in with international kids. I had a good home life, and I
> enjoyed being a kid, and I wanted other kids to enjoy being kids.
> Even before we got married, I told Gordon that I wanted a big family.
> He knew that, and it meant having a couple of biological kids and
> then adopting.

As it turned out, Sally and Gordon adopted two children from India first and then had one by birth. Having had the experience of caring for infants, they now look forward to adopting an older child, very possibly a so-called "hard to place" or "special needs" child with a physical handicap.

While the frequency of international adoption is attributed to the shortage of healthy white infants in the United States, many parents choose international adoption for its own sake and fervently challenge the implication that it is second best. Not all parents who adopt from other countries are white. A few are immigrants themselves, or second or third generation Americans, who adopt from the country of their own heritage. Several of the people I interviewed entered marriage with a definition of "family" that was bound neither to reproduction nor to homogeneity. As Fred Truman puts it, "I didn't feel an overriding desire to procreate myself. There were enough children in the world that needed help. If my biological son hadn't been born, I wouldn't be any sadder today that I hadn't created something." Well before Fred married Linda, they found that they shared a vision of their future children as Asian. Linda sees her dream as highly idiosyncratic but rooted in a childhood experience:

> I always wanted Oriental children. My mother says that when I was about eight and it was the end of the Korean War, there were lots of pictures of Korean kids in the newspaper. I told her, "Let's get one of those kids." There must have been something about kids being adopted. I didn't come up with this idea. So, I asked my mother if we could have one of these children and she said, "No, your father would never stand for it. You'll have to wait until you grow up." I was a very obedient child. I did.

By the time Linda put the plan into action, it was more than a childish whim. She imagined her potential children as adults, to convince herself that she was not just "fixed on them being cute little kids." She attended preadoptive counseling sessions that outlined the problems that older, interracially adopted children might encounter. And she asked herself whether she "might be doing them a worse service" by removing them from the culture of their birth. To explain the persistence of her desire to adopt Asian children, Linda examines her psychological makeup, wondering whether it had to do with being lonely as an only child, or with getting enjoyment out of doing things against the grain, or with an aesthetic fascination with Oriental facial features.

Other parents who looked forward to having multicultural families explain their preference as consistent with their values and perspective on the world. Elsbeth Saunders traces the impetus to adopt a child from India to her husband's habit of "looking at the world as an international citizen." Since she herself is a Swiss immigrant who grew up bilingual and spent part of her childhood in Africa, the idea seemed very compatible with her own worldview. The Saunders family now includes a child from India, a child of mixed black and white heritage born in the United States, and two birthchildren. Tina Molinari talks of "wanting to set up a sort of world community in my house. I always felt that you set up within your own walls what you want on the outside. The personal and the political should be the same." Tina's family, too, lived outside the United States during her adolescence, and she attended school with students of many nationalities.

There is an idealism in this that may make the statement "How wonderful of you to do this" seem justified. Tina is aware of the idealism, and also of how quickly it is tempered by reality:

> That was the goal, and then I found out you couldn't just deal with ideals. There were real people involved here. Slowly but surely they teach you how to not deal with ideals, and how to be realistically nurturing and caring. Quickly you find out that they're doing you a favor. They're teaching you to be a better human being. Kids in general. Not just adopted ones, but kids in general.

What is important here is that in setting up a "world community" at home, or in behaving like "international citizens," the Saunders and Molinaris were primarily intent on having a *family* and bonding it together with parental and filial love, not just moral responsibility.

Linda and Fred Truman knew all along that they wanted children from Asia, most likely Korea. Edward Saunders had a prior interest in India, having been there several times. Donna Frazee, who has a truly multicultural family, including a birthchild and children adopted from the United States, Colombia, and India, was acquainted with the work of the International Mission of Hope in Calcutta and had sent donations to help support it. Like many parents who adopt from India, she saw the need there as exceedingly great and was aware of health problems that some parents might be reluctant to risk. As an experienced mother, she felt she was ready to take a chance on a malnourished baby. Most other parents approach international adoption only vaguely informed about where their children might come from. What knowledge we have usually depends on acquaintance with other families that have adopted.

There is some security in adopting a child of the same ethnicity as friends' or neighbors' children, even if that isn't the primary factor in selecting a country.

The only parents I talked with who expressed as a major concern finding a child whose appearance was not strikingly unlike theirs were Reba and Michael Perlitz. It was not denial of difference but rather an acute awareness of its real social impact that led them to choose Latin American adoption. Michael explains,

> We decided that, inasmuch as we are Jewish and it's hard enough to bring up children Jewishly, to have the added difficulty of being cross-cultural within that religion was just too much for ourselves and for our kids. So we decided we would adopt from Central or South America because the children would look most like us. We had some friends over who had adopted a child from Korea, and she said there just weren't any Korean kids in the after-school Hebrew school. Being Jewish is hard enough in this society. It would be hard to raise kids Jewish who would be the only Korean kids in school. It was a harder lesson than we wanted to saddle our kids with.

Anticipating the child's experience of difference also affected my choice of country. I grew up in a Minnesota town with an economically disadvantaged population of Mexican migrant workers subject to a good deal of racial prejudice. In the spirit of the civil rights movement, the Hispanic population in Minnesota has bolstered its ethnic pride and solidarity, while still encountering discrimination. Even though the first fantasy children I envisioned for myself had mestizo features, I decided against pursuing a Latin American adoption. Following some of the reasoning in the National Association of Black Social Workers' recommendation that black children not be adopted by white parents, I worried that Hispanic children growing up in my Anglo, middle-class home would feel a divided allegiance and perhaps some bitterness about not fitting into the local Hispanic culture and not sharing fully in its pride and solidarity. The Korean immigrant community in the Twin Cities, on the other hand, was not struggling with a long history of hostility from the white majority, so there would not be the same tension. I might have made a different choice if I lived in a West Coast community with a large, cohesive, and economically segregated Asian population.

A reason frequently cited in favor of Korean adoption is the generally good health and easy emotional adjustment of children arriving from Korea. These can be attributed to the regularity and efficiency of the Korean adoption system, which has been gradually refined over the thirty-five years since Korean children were first placed abroad. The child welfare agencies that engage in international adoption are well managed and subject to licensing procedures that hold them legally accountable. They employ trained social workers and health care professionals and house children in private foster homes as much as possible. Their orphanages and health care facilities benefit from voluntary fund-raising efforts by parents with whom they have placed children. Some Americans who do not know this long history conclude from observation that Asian children are of a better quality somehow. As adoption from Korea has declined, some people who had hoped to find children there have begun making inquiries about other possible sources in Asia. Rumors come and go that children are available in Japan, for example. Japan, however, has a low rate of unintended pregnancy and little of the poverty that leads to abandonment of children. There are enough Japanese families ready to adopt children who do need homes. North American families should not expect to request children from any country in the world. Simply wanting children does not entitle us to adopt them without regard for the children's best interest, the birthparents' circumstances, and the birth country's efforts to find healthy solutions to homelessness.

The diminishing need to send children abroad for adoption has given the Korean government more leeway to impose restrictions on the sort of parents with whom children will be placed. Single people have not been eligible for healthy infants, for example, and no parent is allowed to be more than forty years older than the child. Some Korean agencies disqualify parents who have certain chronic illnesses or who are overweight. Colombia has a similar age limit. Single people wishing to adopt have a more limited choice not only of country but of programs within each country. Individual agencies and orphanages may pose other restrictions having to do with age, number of marriages, number of children, religion, and so on.

By far the most decisive factors in choosing a country to adopt from are very practical ones: parents' eligibility, costs, numbers of children legally free for adoption, length of wait for placement, and so on. Some of the parents I talked with who had adopted from Korea cited its predictable cost, about $5000 in 1988, which is considerably lower than the $10,000 to $30,000 people adopting from some Latin American countries end up spending on attorney's fees, foster care, documentation, travel, and hotel accommodations. Even though some agencies operate on a sliding fee scale based on family income, defer payments, or ask for ongoing donations rather than a set fee, international adoption is still out of reach for many families who might otherwise adopt. When Chuck Stensrud talked with excitement to an old high school friend about his son's arrival from Korea, the friend commented, "Well, that's clearly a yuppie activity." The average adoptive family may be comfortably suburban, but the elite stereotype does not describe all such families. In my search for parents to interview, I found quite a few who had made serious financial sacrifices to adopt their children and others who had chosen children ahead of the proliferation of consumer goods and leisure-time activities that characterize the "yuppie" class.

Whether or not parents must travel to pick up their children, rather than having them escorted, can be the decisive factor in choosing a country. Because they have made no special provisions to distinguish international adoption from domestic adoption, most Latin American countries require that the parents stay on for days or weeks while the legal adoption itself is completed. In many cases, the trip is made on a few days' notice and the length of stay is indefinite. This is prohibitive for those who do not have easy access to cash and the leeway to take time off from work. Korean, Filipino, and Indian adoption are preferred, then, for their greater convenience. On the other hand, parents who do have the means to travel appreciate the opportunity to see their child's birthplace and meet the people involved in the child's early care.

Parents who have been through the trials of infertility testing and have reached the midthirties in the process tend to feel some urgency about getting the child into the family quickly. First-time parents are usually eager to experience as much of their child's infancy as possible. The anticipated length of wait between application and referral or between referral and arrival may thus be of prime importance in selecting a country. Which country this is varies with legal changes and the popularity of the adoption program. Sally Anderson applied for a child from India precisely because they were the youngest children arriving in the United States. Her son's arrival was delayed a bit, but he was still only two months old. Since then, changes in the legal process have considerably increased the wait for an Indian child. There are, in summary, many factors that determine a family's choice of a country to adopt from, but one that figures very often is chance. The parents inquire at an adoption agency that is nearby or has been recommended to them, and that agency may be bringing children from only one or two countries.

Before my husband and I made the decision to adopt from Korea, I wanted to be satisfied of the ethical soundness of what we were about to do. I felt certain that I was adopting out of my own desire for children and not to do a good deed, but I wanted assurance that I was not harming the child or anyone else in the process. I especially did not want my good fortune to depend on another woman's oppression. As one who sympathized with anticolonialism in the Third World and international movements for economic justice, I was concerned that what I was doing might in effect perpetuate injustice. Above all, I wanted to be sure that I was not depriving the child of some better alternative. To assuage these reservations, I needed to know *why* these children were available for adoption. Why, for instance, were there so many orphaned Korean babies? Who were the children coming from Latin America and how did they end up in the custody of lawyers specializing in adoption to North Americans and Europeans? Were there grounds for suspicion of baby-selling or kidnapping in any of the countries we could adopt from? Were there opportunities for children to stay in their birth countries that would serve their needs better than adoption in the United States?

Going through the orientation and preadoptive counseling, I was surprised that other parents seemed to take the fact of unwed pregnancy or abandonment as answer enough, without probing into the cultural meaning of out-of-wedlock birth and the conditions that impelled parents to abandon children. The answers I received from the agency at that time were rather sketchy, though not inaccurate or misleading, and I felt that I at least knew enough to go ahead with a Korean adoption. Since then, that sort of information has become somewhat more available. In its first edition, a book called *Understanding My Child's Korean Origins* by Hyun Sook Han of Children's Home Society of Minnesota described the sleeping and eating habits and childcare practices that Korean children would be accustomed to prior to adoption. A revised version of the book, co-authored with Marietta Spencer, contains material on cultural mores and social conditions in Korea and several examples of situations that are likely to result in the relinquishment of parental rights.

In the decision-making stage, prospective parents tend to see the children as simply "available for adoption" and not to question how and why separation from the birthparents came about. Birthparents become a flesh-and-blood reality when the referral papers for a particular child arrive, bearing what is known of that child's personal history. Patti Cronin's experience with infertility helped her to identify with the birthmother's loss:

> Lisa's mother did try to keep her there and raise her there for two months before she brought her to the agency and released her. It was because of the abuse she was given for being an illegitimate child. And they don't have any welfare system to help support the mother and child over there. An illegitimate child and mother are really looked down upon there, so I'm sure it was a terrible struggle for her alone. But she was so determined to try it. I think of how these Korean mothers must feel, giving up these children and knowing they're coming to America and they'll probably never see them again. But especially in Lisa's case, I think of that mother so often. Here I am, having these two wonderful children and she must live with that daily. She wanted so desperately to keep that child and tried to raise her over there and was unable to because of the economic situation and the culture. How she must feel, oh, torn.

Perhaps because parents are encouraged to think and talk honestly about their personal motives for adopting and the needs that adoption will fill for them, these broader social questions do not arise as readily as they would if the parents saw their motive as serving the cause of child welfare. People looking forward to adoption thus focus more on their future as a family than on the child's origins, whether it be the birthparents' situation or the conditions in the child's birth country that made international adoption necessary. The parents I interviewed had anticipated early in the process that the child might experience some *confusion* about identity in adolescence, but they did not necessarily see international adoption as a displacement entailing *loss* for both the child and the birth country. Margo Speiser was one who did raise questions about loss, which she attributes to being an anthropology major in college:

> I was attracted to foreign adoption. It wasn't that it was second choice. I was real excited and proud to look forward to the privilege of having

children from a different culture than my own. But I wasn't without conflict about bringing someone away from their culture. How much of a person is determined by their culture and how much is determined by the fact that they are genetically from this pool? We don't really know that yet. Can you really take someone out of their culture? Is that a moral thing to do? Even with the children here, I still think I struggle with it.

The parents most likely to speak of cultural loss are those who have had some cross-cultural experience already, such as Roy Brower, who works with an international human rights organization:

I remember when we were leaving Bogotá the first time with our son. He was on my lap, and I looked at my wife, and I said, "You know, this is really a heavy thing we're doing." We were taking him out of his culture, taking him out of his cultural roots, and raising him in a culture that, frankly, has a lot of values that are not the kind I want to instill in my child. In fact, the culture out of which he comes has a number of values that I think are very positive, that he's going to be separated from.

In the pendulum swing from promoting adoption as a righteous act of charity to acknowledging our private longings for family, we risk losing sight of its firmest justification—Is it truly in the child's best interest? During the preadoptive counseling process, agencies can help parents first ask and then answer that question to their own satisfaction by including accurate, culturally sensitive information about the general child welfare picture in the countries from which children are being adopted: why children are homeless; by what legal process they become eligible for adoption; whether other means exist to support them and their parents; who in the birth country makes decisions about placing children abroad, and so on. It does occasionally happen that adoptive parents are left with doubt about the ethics of their child's adoption. This is not easy to live with. In fairness to the children and to both sets of parents, information about improprieties—illegal activities or simply shady ones—that have occurred in a particular country in the recent past should be shared with people intending to adopt from that country.

There is another very appropriate forum for discussion of these issues: the many organizations for adoptive families that have sprung up across the United States. Some of these unite parents who have adopted from one country or region of the world, while others build on the commonality of adoption itself, whether domestic or international. The largest and most influential of these groups is Adoptive Families of America (AFA), based in Minneapolis, which began as an informal support group of ten families whose children arrived from Korea in December of 1967. Known for its first two decades as OURS, it has now grown to a nationwide membership of 15,000 families and has more than 200 affiliated support groups, most of which welcome prospective and waiting parents to their meetings.

The May/June 1986 issue of OURS magazine includes an item from one of the support groups in the AFA network that is striking in its rarity but promising as a model for other groups to follow. The KIN Adoptive Family Group of Seattle-Everett, Washington, announced a meeting on "Children of Latin America," which was described as follows:

> The program will include a discussion of why many children in Latin
> America are in need of adoptive families; information about local
> agencies with Latin American adoption programs; as well as groups
> involved with child welfare projects in that region; and an overview
> of cultural identity issues for adopted Latino children growing up in
> the United States. In addition, parents who have adopted children
> from various countries of South America will share their experiences.

Ideally, prospective parents should have access to a comprehensive presentation of this sort before making decisions about where to look for a child. An adoptive parent organization is a very appropriate clearinghouse for such information.

Many prospective parents turn to OURS magazine for guidance in adopting and for support during the process. In fact, many adoption agencies recommend it as a resource for learning what the adoption experience is really like. Until quite recently, the magazine depended almost exclusively on reader submissions and was thus dominated by the "happy ending" adoption stories that virtually all of us long to tell and gladly hear. Ethical issues have surfaced mainly in cases where the parents themselves have encountered some hardship—not receiving a promised child, or having a child arrive in poorer health than anticipated. Parents reporting on a trip to the child's birth country have been more likely to offer travel advice or specific procedural tips than to relate what they learned about social conditions there, the country's approach to child welfare, or its overall adoption policy. Recent issues of *OURS* have shown more thematic focus and more deliberate intent to solicit certain kinds of submissions, including some that address controversial topics. An issue that focuses on a certain country or region would be a very suitable place for discussing child welfare problems and practices, including the social factors that have led the country to international adoption.

Another parent-organized group, the International Concerns Committee for Children (ICCC) based in Boulder, Colorado, defines itself as filling a need for a "nationwide resource in the United States to which interested citizens, prospective adoptive parents, and adoption agencies can turn; a resource that has as its concern the welfare of children in foreign countries as well as those in the United States." Its founders include parents affiliated with the Open Door Society, a group that promoted transracial adoption in the 1960s and has thus had experience dealing with difficult cross-cultural issues. In its 1988 *Report on Foreign Adoption,* the ICCC urges people considering international adoption to think through its complexities ahead of time. Those who feel entitled to a child simply because it has no home, or those who see immigration to the United States as an absolute good for any Third World child are reminded, "It is important to keep in mind that children are removed from their own country ONLY because they essentially have no future in that country, and no possibility of being cared for by permanent, nurturing parents, either by adoption within that country, or strong long-term foster care." There are, unfortunately, exceptions to this rule, but it is a policy to which the most established adoption agencies subscribe. Holt International Children's Services, for example, holds to the following priorities:

1. Enable the child to remain with his biological parents if that is best for the child.
2. Place the child in an adoptive family within his own country.
3. Place the child in an adoptive family of another country.

The ICCC asks prospective parents to try a mental exercise that is really quite provocative: "Imagine a child you know and love being sent to a foreign country to be adopted." In other words, what concerns arise if the direction of international adoption is reversed? I had an opportunity to try that out in real life about four years before I made the decision to adopt, and it was quite startling. While staying with friends in Sweden, I was invited to attend parents' day at their daughter's day-care center. A woman with a black girl about three years old on her lap asked me, "And whose Mama are you?" Since I wasn't responsible for any of the children, I sat down to hear her story. She told me all about the wonderful new life she was offering to this poor child of the ghetto who would have been a casualty of racism had she not brought her to Sweden where everyone is equal. A relative had found the child and arranged the adoption privately, and it had taken some maneuvering to get her out of the United States. As she went on about how fortunate the child was—with the girl sitting in her lap listening the entire time— it became apparent that this mother knew very little about African-American culture and had no respect for what she did know. I worried about that little girl growing up as a minority child in a country that was at that time much more homogeneous than the United States. Would she feel the gratitude that her mother expected?

When I brought my ethical concerns into preadoptive counseling, it was with the specter of this woman looming large in my conscience. She is still there as a constant reminder that there is no cause for self-righteousness in international adoption. The best gift a parent has to offer a child is the promise of love and support that comes with full and genuine membership in a family. That promise is not fulfilled by the adoption alone but is tested over a lifetime. Our children offer us the very same gift in return, plus the opportunity—if we take it—to push back our horizons to encompass a little more of the world.

3

Making the Match

Getting a referral is the bland bureaucratic name for an event that internationally adoptive parents invest with drama as a truly fateful moment in their families' histories. Here is how Mary MacNamara recalls it:

> I realize now that this was wrong, but we were so scared all the time that they weren't going to give us a baby. It seemed too good to be true. We had been married for so long—eleven years and no children—that it was hard for me to believe that I really was going to have a baby finally. The day our social worker called to tell us he had this referral, it was like forty minutes before their office was going to close. I drove over there as fast as I could, because I wanted that picture before he changed his mind. I thought that once I had it in my hand, he wouldn't be able to take it back.
>
> And then when I picked it up, I remember thinking, I'm not going to look at it until my husband gets home and we can look at it together. And so I drove home with this envelope on the seat blinking like a flashing light. I got off the freeway here and pulled over. I couldn't go on. I couldn't make it all the way home. And I thought, Oh, this is the most beautiful child that was ever born.

When the referral does include a picture, no matter how tiny or grainy, that first glimpse of your child-to-be produces a bodily sensation that is accurately described as "tugging at the heart strings." Over and over again, parents talk of being "instantly bonded" or "falling in love." "The most beautiful child that was ever born" may look rather unremarkable or even homely to a casual observer, but long expectant parents easily imbue the child with a beauty that can fulfill dreams, just as biological parents do with the squished up faces of their newborn babies. Tina Molinari talks about what it means to bond to a photograph:

The day I got that little picture, I put it in a little picture frame
and it hasn't changed since. That is immediate, having the picture.
You have this capacity to love, regardless of what your love object
is. It's your own capacity to nurture. You initiate that process. It
starts with that picture, and then the child comes and makes it grow.
But you've got it going for you with the picture.

Putting the picture in a frame, having enlargements made, running
multiple photocopies, pulling out the wallet at opportune moments in
conversation—all these gestures help make the parents' hope for the
future indelible. Looking at the picture again and again is also useful
preparation for integrating a child of another race into the family. Very
quickly, the first impression of almond eyes or dark skin gives way to
familiarity with the features that distinguish this individual child from
others of similar origins. This is not quite the same as colorblindness,
which usually means overlooking race altogether. In my mind, the image
evoked by the word "baby" is clearly Asian. And the real-life babies
that are sure to elicit my maternal sighs are not the bald, pale newborns
that my relatives and Caucasian friends bring home from the hospital.
Getting the referral, like our other most consequential life experiences,
leaves us with conditioned reflexes.

There is no magic in photography, however. As Tina Molinari reminds
us, "It's your own capacity to nurture. You initiate that process." Our
nurturing capacity might remain dormant a bit longer if we did not
already entertain visions of children and family life that can be easily
projected onto the photograph. The child is, after all, still only two-
dimensional, immobile, and silent. We may read personality into a
facial expression, as if that expression were constant, and forget that
the camera has simply frozen a single instant in the child's day. But
we are primed for instantaneous bonding, as long as the child in the
photograph bears a close enough resemblance to the child dwelling in
our imaginations.

Occasionally, prospective parents do turn down referrals—if the child
selected does not fit their health or age requirements, for example, or
if it carries the memory of a troubled past that the parent does not
feel equipped to handle. Refusing to take a child is not an easy matter,
as Marlene Duval remembers. Just before her fourth child was due to
arrive, she was informed that the girl's two-year-old brother had also

been relinquished for adoption. Suddenly the single six-year-old she was prepared for had become a pair of siblings.

> We were afraid that if we said no, we might ruin our chances for Anne, too, and at that point, she was our kid. We went round and round and Dan finally said to me, "Well, if you think you can handle a little one plus the others, that's OK with me." So then it was in my lap, and it was very hard. I just can't tell you how hard it was, but I honestly didn't feel like I could do it. And so I told the social worker that. She said, "I want you to tell me what's real. Don't tell me what you think I want to hear, but tell me what's real to you." So I did, and she said, "OK." The hardest thing I had to do was just let go of that and be true to myself and ask God to work through everything. Well, it turned out that a couple that lived just a few blocks from us and had come over to visit us because they were interested in adoption ended up adopting him, so the kids grew up together and went to the same grade school, and they're still very close. But it was scary, very scary, because talk about rejecting somebody! It was like, Well, if I don't do it, who will?

The parents I talked with who had turned down referrals were fortunate to have social workers who understood the power of the referral picture. They made tentative inquiries to avoid moral pressure: Would a couple who had requested an infant accept a two-year-old? Could first-time parents manage a child with a hernia and possible vision problems? Would the family have room for twins? Jack and Peggy Gaartner answered a few such queries, not without difficulty, but when their social worker finally brought them a complete referral, they felt that their decisions had led to the right conclusion. Peggy says, "As soon as we saw the picture and read her history, it was immediate that that was our child. That's when bonding, for me, took place. If something had gone wrong, I would have grieved as if that had been a child that I had carried and had lost shortly before delivery."

Adopting a child is an entirely voluntary act and, as such, it affords the privilege of selection. Parents may specify the characteristics they desire in a child, although some parents are more privileged than others. For example, national or agency policies often reserve healthy infants for couples rather than single parents, or sometimes even for parents who can produce medical documents attesting to their infertility. To those who adopt healthy infants, there is comfort in knowing that, whatever uncertainties international adoption might entail over the long run, you can at least start with fewer physical risks than ordinary childbirth poses. The privilege of being selective does, however, have an obverse side: For every characteristic you specify, you may be excluding a large population of waiting children. My husband and I left one agency's orientation meeting stunned by guilt. The social worker opened the group session by saying, "I suppose you're all here because you want cute little babies like the one down the street." Then she told us some sample stories about older children in foster care in the United States. This was her introduction to "truth time," which we did not choose to endure under her skeptical eye. But we certainly faced it on our own: Did wanting a healthy child mean we could not love a child with medical problems? Did wanting a baby mean we were leaving an older child homeless? Did pursuing a Korean adoption mean we were rejecting a particular child close at hand? These are troubling questions that push you up against the limits of your humanity. Fortunately, the next agency we consulted asked us first to examine the practical reality of our own lives. It may be a noble gesture to adopt three older siblings, one with a serious handicap, but could I, in my situation, do them justice? Guilt is a poor substitute for genuine love and nurturance and the practical resources that raising "special needs" children requires.

Of the legally designated orphans admitted to the United States in 1986, 64 percent were under one year of age, and another 21 percent were ages one through four. Some in the latter category were referred as infants from countries where the bureaucratic and legal procedures leading to emigration take quite a long time. The majority of parents do, indeed, want cute little babies, though not exactly like the one down the street. The remaining 15 percent of the children who arrived in 1986 were already of school age, presumably adopted by parents who had expressed a preference for older children. Among the people I interviewed, the reasons for adopting older children were quite individually distinctive. Jessica Martinson, for example, was not content to let divorce keep her from having more children or deprive the one child born to her of a sibling. As a single mother, she could not afford to take time off work to care for an infant, and the expense and inconvenience of day-care were prohibitive. Her daughter Anita was almost nine years old when she arrived from Guatemala. Linda Truman's intentions were very clear from the start:

It was real important to me that the children have some memory of
their own of Korea. It was part of the concern about taking them
out of their culture. I felt that they should have something that was
theirs, that I couldn't give them and I couldn't take away from them.
I also wasn't all that thrilled with babies, and I had had one. I thought
they got to be a lot more fun the older they got. They were also
more available.

One might ask why parents who want older children do not adopt
from among the many children currently waiting in foster care in the
United States. Linda and Fred had determined early on that they wanted
a multicultural family, specifically with Asian children. Jessica, on the
other hand, had intended to do a domestic adoption but was told that
as a single woman she was unlikely to get a referral for a healthy child.
Her job did not provide the income or allow the flexibility needed to
meet the needs of a handicapped child, so she looked to Latin America.
The Frazees, in adopting from Colombia, acted out of a sense that the
need was greater abroad, that children in the United States at least
had the option of foster care.

The public image of children in the foster care system may be a
disincentive for some families intending to adopt school-age children.
There is a common belief that children from other countries are a safer
bet than American children who have been shuffled from one foster
home to another, or who may have been forcibly removed from their
birthparents because of abuse or neglect severe enough to leave emotional
scars. Concern about parental drug use and fetal alcohol syndrome also
figures here. The 1988 *Report on Foreign Adoption* of the International
Concerns Committee for Children contains an item-by-item comparison,
prepared by Norma Lucas of PLAN (Plan Loving Adoptions Now), of
the typical features of older children adopted within the United States
and from other countries. The last item on the list for domestic adoptions
is "often emotionally troubled" and for intercountry adoptions, "relative
emotional stability." Ms. Lucas cautions that "this list is not meant to
stereotype any child, for there are always exceptions." Nevertheless, it
does mirror and perhaps reinforce a common perception that older American children present more behavioral problems. I, for one, entertained
that notion when I first began considering my options for parenthood,
and I found that it was shared by other prospective parents. I have
since heard stories about the emotional consequences of sexual abuse
from Korean and Latin American children and have a better understand-

ing of the psychological impact of abject poverty and the daily fight
for survival that it requires.

Silvia Kowalski, who was adopted from Colombia at age 12 along
with her 9-year-old sister, would caution parents to expect some difficulty
with older children. "I'd be willing to say that 99 percent of the kids
have been traumatized emotionally," she says, speaking with the force
of conviction and experience, rather than from objectively measurable
evidence. It was certainly true in her own case. At age three, she
watched her father die:

> He gets on his horse, leaves the house. Within minutes he was back
> and he had two or three gun wounds in his stomach and he was
> bleeding. My mother was about eight months pregnant with my sister.
> I was like my Daddy's little girl. Anything that has happened to me
> since I watched my father die, I will never forget. I remember every
> single experience, good or bad, but mostly bad, that I had for quite
> a while. Some people block out experiences like that. Immediately I
> felt like I was taking responsibility for all the pain in the world.

Four years later, Silvia's mother disappeared without a trace. Silvia, at
seven, spent two weeks caring for her four-year-old sister and a new
baby in their apartment until a neighbor alerted the police and they
were taken to an orphanage. The two older girls were sent to a group
home, despite Silvia's pleas to keep them all together, and the baby
was placed for adoption in Colombia, without Silvia's knowledge. While
they lived in group homes, they attended school, but Silvia also went
out to work, cleaning houses and taking care of younger children. Thinking herself capable of independence and adult life, she did not want to
be adopted, especially not if it meant leaving Colombia. "I had gone
through a lot and I considered myself pretty mature," she says. "I couldn't
accept that I was just a kid. Physically I was, but inside of me I wasn't."
She finally agreed to be placed abroad because it would offer her the
only chance she had for education beyond age 15.

Any parent would be proud to claim the adult Silvia as a daughter,
but few parents would eagerly choose the trouble that she says she
caused her adoptive family. They knew that she and her sister had lost
their parents, but she doesn't think they were prepared for the degree
of emotional trauma. Her story, and others I heard, help support the
argument that parents who are apprehensive about adopting older children in the United States should not expect international adoption to

be easier. In all adoptions of older children, parents must be prepared for a mutual relationship with a human being who comes with habits, feelings, and, often, a complex history.

While specifying the age of the child you wish to adopt is usually considered a legitimate request, there are some other limits to how selective applicants for international adoption are allowed to be. Designating skin color is rarely an option, unless the parents are prepared to undertake an independent search through private channels. Holding out for a white child is not only frowned upon as evidence of racism but is discouraged for practical reasons, as well. Most children coming from Latin America have Indian features and are recognizably Hispanic. The children from India are Caucasian by race but may have skin the same shade as their African-American classmates. It is very important for parents to know that and try to anticipate both how their children will look and how their extended families and communities are likely to receive them. Dark-skinned children may encounter prejudice, and parents must be prepared to respond. But requesting a child who can pass for white in order to circumvent the issues that international adoption raises is unwise and could be detrimental to the child's comfort in the family. Jessica Martinson was troubled by the motives of a few of the parents she met as she was beginning the adoption process:

> The reason, I think, some people were in the Latin American program is that they had some issues about Asian kids. I was really taken aback by that. I thought, My God, are you naive. How can you raise a minority child? I thought they were doing their Latin American kids a real disservice then. What? They're more acceptable? Kids are smart. They see through that. How can you pick one minority as better than another? In becoming an international family, you have to deal with all your prejudices.

The validity of specifying a boy or a girl is still open to question, though answers are being suggested by the very demographics of international adoption. There has been, all along, an overwhelming preference for girls. Initially, there were more girls in need of adoption from countries like Korea, where family continuity depends on a male heir, or India, where turning daughters into desirable marriage partners can drain a poor family's resources. Yet, the preference for girls has tipped the balance so that boys, though less numerous, are often more readily available. Agencies will sometimes tell applicants that the adoption will proceed faster if they are open to a boy. At the time of my first daughter's adoption, in 1980, we were told that 85 percent of the Korean children coming through the agency we worked with were girls. By 1986, the overall figure for Korean adoption was 59 percent female. For India, it was 62 percent. The figures for Latin American adoption are fairly balanced, except for Brazil, which sent 116 boys and 77 girls. Many agencies have stopped asking parents to state a preference, and may refuse to grant one to first-time parents or people adopting infants.

There is much speculation about why adoptive parents prefer girls, while studies of biological parents show a preference for boys, especially the first time around. The topic is discussed in adoption literature and among parents themselves when they speak about their own choices. Yet there are more questions than sound answers: Is it, indeed, true that most adoptions are initiated by the potential mother? Do most women really have a stronger desire for daughters than for sons? Are some families really reluctant to pass on their name and the heritage that goes with it to a son who is not truly of their blood? Are they, then, even more reluctant to pass it on to a boy who is of a different race, as well? Are parents indeed more fearful of the kinds of behavioral problems that boys might exhibit if the adoption does not work smoothly? Do boys, in fact, act out the negative feelings they might have about adoption in more destructive ways than girls do?

Some of the parents I interviewed wondered if the preference for girls has its origins in racism. As Bill MacNamara sees it, his daughter is "a cute little—I hate the saying—'china doll.' " His son, on the other hand, "is one of these days going to be that young man who might want to date their daughter. So he's a threat." American popular culture does purvey a stereotype of Asian women as exotic beauties, while the beauty of Asian men is obscured by unflattering caricatures: the World War II cartoon portrayals of Japanese men with buck teeth, or the evil warlord of science fiction fantasy literature. White people may also confuse the smaller stature and smoother skin of Asian men with effeminacy. With these stereotypes in mind, potential parents may well assume that girls will have an easier time bearing the turmoil of adolescent social life, or that their families and friends will more readily accept a lovely "china doll." Bill MacNamara takes pride in challenging those stereotypes: "We changed that by adopting Billy. Everybody saw Billy and said, Aaaaahhh, I'll have a boy."

The MacNamaras did not set out to raise consciousness in this way.

Bill had a very mundane—and stereotypical—reason for wanting a boy: "There was no question about it. I wanted a son I could play ball with and go fishing with and all the rest of that stuff." Two years later, they filled out the family with a girl. The Gaartners, too, were thinking ahead to parent–child activities, but they chose a girl. As Peggy explains it, "I think in our culture girls are now a little more flexible. They can do basketball, and they can wear dresses. So, thinking it would probably be our only child, from which sex would we be able to get the most shared experiences?" No one I talked with offered any more elaborate reason than that for their own choice, and most had not expressed a preference at all. Even those who did were quick to add that it didn't really matter. Had the agency not given them the option, they would have taken the next available child, regardless of sex.

Of course, I also had to ask myself why I did in fact choose daughters. The first time, we wrote "either" on the line that asked our preference, but I fully expected it to be a girl, given the sex ratio of children arriving from Korea just then. The social worker sensed that in our conversations—probably from the pronouns I used—and called to check on my intentions when eleven referrals for boys turned up on her desk. "I can give you a referral for a boy this week if you want one," she said. To my honest surprise, this news hit like a thud in the pit of the stomach. What about that girl I had been conjuring up in all my daydreaming about the future? The social worker waited a week and assigned us a girl. Our plan had been one of each, but as we moved closer to the second adoption, my imagination wrought a little sister.

I guess I would attribute this unexpected preference for female children to familiarity; I grew up in an all-girl family. As a nervous parent-to-be, I couldn't imagine myself straying too far afield from what I knew. Also, the women's movement fired my enthusiasm for introducing daughters to an expanded realm of possibility. The thought of preparing sons to stretch the limits of the American ideal of masculinity was more sobering. I was reminded of that one day years later when my principles gave way and I bought some Barbie paraphernalia to go with the doll a classmate had given my daughter for her birthday. I was standing in the check-out line at the toy store, feeling powerless against social pressure, when I noticed that the woman in front of me had an armload of machine guns and grenades. At least it's not that, I thought. I realize that my children help to throw the statistics off balance, but I don't know how to generalize from my choice or that of other parents whom

I talked to. It may be that racial stereotypes or strict notions of kinship underlie the preference for girls, but these are not the explanations that the parents themselves offer.

One preference that is generally regarded as legitimate is the desire that most parents express for healthy children. Illness and disability are seen not just as matters of "difference" but as conditions that require an extra measure of very practical, ongoing health care and intervention. Like birthparents who pursue genetic counseling or undergo amniocentesis, adoptive parents measure risks, assess their readiness to handle difficulty, and make their choices accordingly. Relatively few parents, however, pose their preference as an either/or choice: Give me a healthy child or I won't adopt at all.

Neither is "healthy" itself an absolute. International adoption illustrates the degree to which health is subject to cultural definition. Children often arrive from Third World countries with intestinal parasites that can usually be eliminated by medication over a period of weeks or months. There is a slight chance that Asian children may be carriers of the hepatitis B virus but be free of symptoms themselves. Are these children healthy or not? In countries afflicted by broad-scale hunger and malnutrition, a child who is still too weak in the legs to walk by eighteen months is not seriously ill. Americans may hesitate to adopt this child, who is developmentally delayed by Western standards, while poor parents in India would be happy that the child had survived infancy. In countries where even basic medical care is beyond the means of most families, a child born with a disfiguring feature such as a cleft palate or a clubfoot is considered handicapped and may even be relinquished for that reason alone. Parents who adopt children with disfiguring conditions expect that they will be healthy and normal after routine corrective surgery.

Health, in adoption parlance, does not mean perfection. To clarify the parents' expectations, adoption agencies often ask what medical conditions they will accept and which they would exclude. Some agencies even provide a checklist of illnesses and disabilities, which may read, depending on your frame of mind, like a catalog order form or like a multiple choice test to evaluate your sense of compassion. From the agencies' perspective, this checklist is a means of placing handicapped children with the particular parents who can best meet their special needs. The agencies' foremost task is placing the children in their charge with families who are truly ready to love them fully and to care for them sufficiently. They do not simply fill orders for special needs children.

When Ron Josephson and Gwen Ryan first inquired about adoption, they were "thinking in terms of a special needs child, just because it seemed the right thing to do. It was a little bit altruistic." They had a meeting with a social worker whose experience was mainly with children born with spina bifida. She knew that it would take more than altruism to meet the needs of such a child.

> It was real clear to her after ten minutes that unless we radically changed our lifestyles, we were not the people to take this on. She gave us a little idea of what a routine day would be like. She did it very gently—how would you arrange such-and-such day to day? I don't think we'd even considered how we would arrange for it with a normal functioning child.

They ended up with a healthy Korean baby. The second time around, however, the agency entrusted them with a referral for a six-month-old baby whose condition was still uncertain:

> They gave us all the outs we wanted. There was no pressure. They kept saying things like, "Now don't feel like this is God's will just because we've offered this child to you. It doesn't necessarily mean that you have to take the child. It certainly doesn't mean that nobody else will. You make your decision." On the other hand, how can you?

He turned out to be what is called a "failure to thrive" child, one who had had too little care and stimulation to develop at a normal pace. After one year with Ron and Gwen, he was declared healthy.

Of course, no child arrives with a warranty. Some develop problems after arrival or come with undiagnosed or unreported conditions. This can be heartbreaking, as it would be for biological parents. In the case of unreported problems, adoptive parents may also be angry and feel deceived by the adoption agency. Some stories have happy endings, however, and even ironic twists. A mother who spoke at a workshop on special needs adoption reminisced about going through the agency checklist and feeling generous when she agreed to accept a child born prematurely with some developmental delays. She got a referral for just such a baby who showed no signs of permanent disability. The child arrived looking healthy, but was not yet as responsive to her environment as a full-term baby of her age would be. As the months passed, there was no improvement, and tests determined that the child was deaf.

The mother reported both on the very real struggle to find resources to help the child live with her handicap and also on the positive benefits for the family. Their daughter, now of school age, has initiated them into a new culture—not only Korean culture, but a culture of people who speak with their hands and can help them see how the world looks without sound. The child herself is bright, cheerful, well-behaved. The mother recalls that deafness was one condition she and her husband had said they could not accept, and she is thankful now that their daughter sneaked through with no diagnosis. Families that have such an experience often end up very open to children with special needs. As Cynthia Peck, the editor of the adoptive family magazine *Roots and Wings*, explains,

> I never started out to adopt an "at risk" child, but once a problem surfaces and you've discovered that you *can* cope, then why deny another child a home because of the same disability? I didn't "choose" special needs adoption. *All* kids have special needs . . . so do parents. We just happen to go together!

The Means and Solberg families came into the adoption process wanting children who would benefit from the extra health care that they were, indeed, ready to provide. Special needs was clearly a first choice, made freely. They ended up adopting internationally only by chance. Laurie Means wanted an older daughter to fill the six-year gap between her two sons. As a pediatric nurse, she thought she could take on the challenge of a medical condition that would give other parents pause. She and her husband did draw some limits, though, excluding profound handicaps and mental retardation, which she was afraid would be emotionally draining for the family. The U. S.-born girls known to their agency at the time were older than the age range that Laurie and Jim had requested. They received a referral, instead, for a five-year-old Korean girl with tuberculosis. Her illness is now controlled by medication, and she is otherwise healthy. The Solbergs added two daughters disabled by polio to their nearly grown-up family after Arnie had a dream about adopting a handicapped girl. A devout Lutheran, Marjorie explains their decision this way: "I really felt that the Lord was leading us in this direction. We wanted to do something for someone else, but really didn't know what it would be, and the Lord led us to the adoption." They requested children whom they could help to become independent and self-supporting, which limited the range of handicaps they would consider. There were not very many American children who fit their description so they, too, ended up adopting from Korea, where orphaned handicapped children are numerous.

There are many children in orphanages and hospitals around the world who would be regarded as disadvantaged and in need of special care in any culture: retarded children, blind and deaf children, children with cerebral palsy, children immobilized by birth defects or paralyzing illness. Some of these children are victims of diseases, like tuberculosis and polio, that have been virtually eradicated in Western industrial countries. They are without families either because their handicaps are stigmatizing and culturally unacceptable or, more likely, because their parents do not have the means to provide for their care. Government funds and charity campaigns are seldom sufficient to fill so many children's need for food and shelter, let alone education, medical care, or the special aids that would enhance their lives and allow them some degree of self-determination. Lori Wedeking, who edits a section on single parenting in OURS, has written about her daughter's situation prior to adoption. When the Colombian orphanage where the girl was living suddenly closed, she was to be transferred along with some other handicapped children to an asylum for mentally ill adults, where they would be housed indefinitely. The woman who was to deliver them there refused to do it and instead took personal responsibility for the children until they could be placed for adoption. Five years later, Lori and her daughter went back to Colombia to adopt another child and visited this woman, whose assessment of the situation is worth repeating:

> She looked me in the eye, and said, "I saved this child's life," and there was no doubt in my heart that she was right. At the same time, she looked at Elena and the progress she had made, and said, "When you do work like this [running an orphanage and placing children for adoption], it takes your heart and soul, and you think you can't do this anymore; then you see a child like Elena and think you can do it two more years." (January/February 1987, p. 31)

International adoption is an alternative for some but not all handicapped children. Sometimes it is the only apparent hope for the child's survival, because the medical technology required to save the child's life is available only in the world's wealthy countries. Would providing surgery or medical treatment in the child's birth country allow the child to be restored to its original family? This option seems especially appropriate for children with correctable defects that are not life-threatening, such as a cleft palate. There are many children, some with multiple and profound handicaps, for whom there is no medical remedy even in the United States or Western Europe. Whether to place these children for adoption abroad depends on whether membership in a family and consistent care by one or two parents would significantly enhance the child's life.

Pictures and short biographies of physically and/or mentally handicapped children appear in albums of "waiting children" and in the magazines of adoptive parent organizations. Jack Gaartner's response is a common one: "I quickly learned that I couldn't read those things. You'd read them and you'd be crying so much you couldn't finish the last half of the story. It's like either we can't read it or we're going to have a family of twenty kids here." Those of us who are moved by these stories but feel unequipped to adopt handicapped children can find other means to act on their behalf, perhaps by contributing financially to their care, by supporting international efforts to prevent disabling illness—including immunization and basic hunger programs, or by joining an advocacy group for handicapped children worldwide.

There are a number of parents who are indeed ready to adopt waiting children on the basis of these portrayals, even if it means having an unusually large family. Such families are often the subject of newspaper feature stories that emphasize their uniqueness and ascribe special virtues to parents who would deliberately open themselves to such challenges. Marjorie Solberg cites a television program about the De Bolts, a large adoptive family with handicapped children, as a source of inspiration. We who have requested healthy children often puzzle over the possible differences between these parents and the rest of us: Are they more virtuous, do they possess extraordinary gifts, or are they just more experienced and thus less mystified by handicaps? One such parent who is widely known in adoption circles, in part because of the books she has written, is Grace Sandness, one of the founders of Crossroads, an agency that welcomes single and handicapped parents. She herself is quadriplegic, which makes her extraordinarily qualified to offer her twelve adopted children and additional foster children the love, understanding, esteem, and inspiration that she knows do not come easily to handicapped children. While I cannot begin to imagine the daily logistics in the Sandness household, I can certainly understand how fulfilling it must be to have the opportunity to affirm the human worth of each of her children.

She offers an answer to the natural *Why on earth have you done this?* in her book, *Commitment: The Reality of Adoption* (Maple Grove, MN: Mini-World Publications, 1984):

> For the children first of all, and out of our need to make some small difference somewhere in the world. Imperfect as they are, the children wait. Imperfect as we are, we are here. Together we can, with the addition of a small bit of insanity, find something to give to a union—which for them may be the only chance.

It is important to realize that parents who adopt four, five, or more special needs children are also choosing to devote a significant portion of their time and resources to medical care and advocacy work in the schools and community. What starts as an act of love becomes a mission with consequences for other handicapped children, as well. Like any other life mission, it may dawn gradually on people who perceive themselves as quite ordinary.

Children selected from photos of waiting children are among the relatively few for whom the aging euphemism for adopted children— "chosen"—really fits. Most of us rely on agency personnel to make the match for us. However it is that parent and child end up with common destinies, the bonds begin to seal as soon as the "choice" has been made. Anticipation is vital preparation for parenthood, and it is much easier to anticipate when you can attach your vision of the future to a specific child. How difficult it must be then when the process of finding a child goes awry, as it kept doing for Judy Pollard. As a 39-year-old single woman, Judy had fewer options to begin with than the more typical adoptive parent. She signed up on a waiting list for a child from India and also filed an application with a placement program in Brazil. After two years of submitting paperwork and waiting for a referral, she was told that the Brazilian program had closed down. In the meantime, she had barely moved up on the Indian waiting list.

A friend who knew of her disappointment and frustration told her about an unmarried, 19-year-old local woman who was pregnant and planning to give the baby for adoption. The young woman was very willing to entrust her baby to Judy, and a lawyer advised them that it could be done, in spite of stringent state restrictions on private adoption. Two months before the baby's due date, the legal process broke down and the birthmother turned to a licensed agency with a long waiting list of married couples. Again, the possibility of a Brazilian adoption arose—this, too, a private arrangement with a young, unmarried woman. Shortly before Judy was to fly to Brazil to pick up the baby, she got a call informing her that the birthmother refused to sign the papers relinquishing the child for fear of having her out-of-wedlock pregnancy made public. She was presumably going to abandon the child anonymously instead. Without the legal release form, Judy could make no claim to this particular child.

After several more months had passed, Judy learned about a new program in Honduras that was open to single parents. She applied and was given a referral for a one-year-old girl. There was no picture and the information about her was very sketchy. After her previous failures, Judy was a little apprehensive. "It was strange," she recalls, "but I wasn't all thrilled and excited the way I thought I would be." Through the summer and fall, she kept calling the agency to inquire about the child. By Thanksgiving, she was told that the child was severely malnourished and was no longer eligible for adoption. "I truly don't know if the child ever existed," Judy says.

A month after that adoption fell through, just as she was ready to give up, she got another referral, this time for a newborn baby. This adoption looked like a sure thing, so she flew to Honduras to start proceedings. Judy was given custody of the baby on her arrival and kept the infant with her in the hotel where she was staying. It turned out, however, that Judy's baby was the twin of another baby staying in the same hotel who had been assigned to a couple from another region of the United States. When Judy asked the lawyer if this was appropriate, he assured her that it was but then apparently grew worried that the court would object. He told the other parents that they would have to accept both children or surrender their new son, and it was left to them to inform Judy about this decision.

To say it was hellish is an understatement. I've heard people here say how they bond with a picture, and I'm sure they do, and I understand that, but I had that baby five and a half days. And the other parents were just beside themselves, because they were not ready to cope with another baby financially. But they realized they couldn't say no and take their son, so they had to say yes. There were times when I thought, This must be a nightmare. This can't be reality. This couldn't be happening.

The night I had to give her up, the woman from the adoption

agency here and my lawyer went out and when they came back, they said, "We have another little girl." This was at 10 o'clock at night. They brought her to me at 10:30 in her little nightgown. She had been asleep. And here I am still holding this seven-week-old baby girl in my arms. I was just senseless. And the woman from the agency said to me, when they walked in with her, "What do you think?" as though we were looking at furniture. "What do you think?" I could hardly talk. I choke up now. When I talk about it, it just brings it all back. It was just overwhelming to deal with the separation and the coming together of the two of us. All I could say was, "She will be fine." Then they said to me, "Do you want to take her with you?" I still had the baby in my arms. I had to give the baby to them in the back seat of the lawyer's Mercedes. I said, "No, not tonight. Would you keep her? I won't be in any state to take her."

The next day, Judy went to claim the new child, still in grief at the loss of the baby she had expected would be hers. She had planned to go home, but stayed on another week in Honduras to allow herself time to adjust to the change. "Of course you don't let go in a week, but I could gradually begin to think, Yes, I *do* have my little girl." A woman who worked in the hotel and had learned of Judy's traumatic experience offered to keep Mimi as a foster child until she was free to emigrate. Judy found this very reassuring, and she had many phone conversations with this family in the three months before she could return to Honduras and bring her daughter home with her.

Four years after beginning the adoption process, Judy could finally settle in with a child whom she truly loves as her own. But there is a gap in Mimi's history that was left unfilled because of the trying circumstances in which the two of them were brought together. Questions remain, such as, where was this little girl before she was brought to Judy? Why was she available for adoption? Why was the lawyer so unclear about her age? In a calmer situation, with more certainty of having the matter resolved, Judy would have insisted on verifiable answers. As emotionally wrought as she was by this time, she was not about to risk another loss.

One might wonder how and why Judy persisted after so many false starts. She herself was adopted, and she describes her desire to adopt a child and have a family as something of an obsession, "something I wore on my back: I *had* to do it." As for getting through the ordeal, she says, "When you're in it, you just *go* through it. You don't choose to do it this way, but you get yourself through it. You do question yourself," Judy acknowledges. "You think, Is this all worth it? Is this experience what I wanted to put myself through? After you get through the horrendous part, you look back and say, Of course it was all worth it. She's just filled my life."

Judy's quest for a child is by far the most grueling, as well as the most unyielding, that I heard about in the interviews I did, and it offers strong arguments for establishing firm policies, with government supervision, and enforcing them evenly. Yet, even those parents who receive their referrals neatly tucked into an envelope to carry home on the front seat of the car find the waiting period that follows more trying than they expected. Seldom do parents feel that it all happens too fast, unless, perhaps, their second adoption, which requires fewer steps, follows too quickly on the first. Linda and Fred Truman completed two adoptions and one foster placement in a single year. "Now I know why people have to wait nine months to have a baby," Linda jokes.

Once the referral is in hand, the geographical separation between parent and child can get very worrisome. Reba Perlitz remembers, "It was so hard, since she was real and it was like it was my baby and somebody else had it." Karen Kuschner adds, "You know how you always stare at the picture? I felt this bond going across the ocean. We wondered what she was doing, even though she was a baby. I just thought about her all the time." Karen began to trace their intersecting destinies as soon as she got the referral, by checking the calendar to see what she had been doing the day her daughter was born. I did the same, and I thought it very propitious that both my daughters were born while I was giving lectures. The first was on women in contemporary Sweden and included, oddly enough, a segment on unwed motherhood. The second was a meditation on Psalm 39 about coming to terms with the end of one's life. What a thrill to learn that another life was just beginning and would soon entwine itself with mine.

No matter how long it lasts, the child's absence leaves an emotional void. On one bad day, I commented in my journal, "It feels like she's been here and gone, leaving her mother with no sense of direction." A few lucky parents are able to correspond with their children if they are older and literate, or with the director of the child's orphanage, if it is a small one and the director has time to pay personal attention to each child. Sending clothing, medicine, and baby formula helps a parent ease anxiety about the child's well-being. The rest of us have had to fill the void with our imaginations and with the business of getting ready. Bill MacNamara teases his wife Mary by claiming that she painted their son's bedroom twice in the three months before he arrived. It is not far from the truth, Mary admits:

> We didn't get the referral till January, and he came at the end of March. We set up a crib in his bedroom in November. Every week I'd go in and change the sheets in there and dust and sit in the rocking chair and squint my eyes and stare. I did it with our daughter too. I'd sit in that room and squint my eyes in the dark and stare at the crib and imagine a baby in there. It felt like my upper arms hurt, like a muscle spasm, because I wanted to hold him so bad.

Many parents describe holidays that go by with still no child to share in the celebration as lonely and depressing, but there are other moments that keep the spirits buoyant and mark the passage of time. For parents who travel to their child's birth country, it is learning that all their paperwork is completed and no more is required of them until they get the call to make plane reservations. For those whose children are escorted, "visa clearance" is the last hurdle. Once the child is legally approved for entry into the United States, the waiting begins in earnest. I opened my mailbox one day and found a note saying that a registered letter was waiting at the post office. When I went to claim it, the postal clerk looked at the return address—the Immigration and Naturalization Service—smiled knowingly, and asked, "Is this a visa clearance for an adoption?" "Yes," I answered, surprised. "I have three Korean children," he announced. "You'll never regret it." Focused as you are on your child-to-be, it begins to seem as though every other person you meet has adopted children.

Unexpected, and sometimes unexplained, delays are not at all uncommon. The waiting period seldom passes without a hitch, though some hitches are slight and others trip the parents up for quite some time. The complications that turned up in both my adoptions were greatly frustrating but, ultimately, very instructive. In early June of 1980 we received a referral for a "healthy and lovely girl" relinquished at her birth in late March in Seoul, Korea. Her name was Keun Young, translated as "root of a flower." "I hope that is a sign of what she will be," I wrote in my journal. "Delicate and gentle to the world around her, but firmly attached to the ground. To us, she will also be Grace, because she is an undeserved benevolence." I kept her pictures in my purse or my pocket at all times, not just to have them ready to show off, but because they were a tangible symbol of my optimism about the future. Everywhere I went, I carried her with me in spirit. I sat at the edge of the lake with her and imagined her picking wild strawberries in the woods. When the sparrows perched on the sill outside my study window, I wanted to watch her excitement. At night I had dreams about children wandering in unexpectedly, or disappearing mysteriously, or disintegrating in my arms as I rushed to find help. They were only "parental anxiety dreams," my friends who were already parents assured me.

Visa clearance came on July 16, delayed about ten days because the Minnesota Commissioner of Public Welfare had been on vacation. That evening, the first family in our preadoptive counseling group to finish all the preliminary requirements went to the airport to get their baby. We could expect to do the same in three to six weeks. The very next day, however, brought troubling news. Our social worker called to say that the Korean government's quota on foreign adoptions had been filled for the year, and we would have to wait until a decision was made to lift the quota. That had been the routine the past few years, and she expected the problem would be resolved by fall. Everything else that happened that day was an irritation. A phone call from a student who wanted me to read her dissertation proposal unnerved me. How unfair for other people to go on with their lives like that. A week later, on a very anxiety-ridden day, I wrote, "There is nothing more to do. It is a peculiar state to be in—'limbo' is the word usually applied to it, but in limbo all human experience is suspended. In this case, life goes on, emotions fluctuate, and the luxury of suspension isn't affordable." By mid-August, I was referring to the baby most of the time as "Keun Young" or as "the kid." I had become superstitious about using the name Grace, afraid she would never know this identity that we had anticipated for her.

I was clipping news articles about Korea, as I had begun to do as soon as we applied for a Korean adoption, and it became increasingly clear what was delaying her arrival. President Park Chung Hee had been assassinated the year before and the military leader Chun Doo Hwan had just installed himself in power. Chun had undertaken a purge of the government bureaucracy that had brought much of its work to a standstill. By fall, the agency confirmed that no one in Korea had assumed responsibility for reevaluating the quota or for issuing passports to orphaned children, unless they were in immediate need of medical care. All through the summer, Kim Dae Jung, the leader of the democratic opposition, had been in prison awaiting trial for his part in the anti-Chun demonstrations that preceded the Kwangju uprising in May. In September, Kim was sentenced to death by hanging, but granted a two-month stay of execution pending appeal.

I watched these developments with my allegiances badly torn. If Kim Dae Jung were executed, there would be more uprisings surpassing Kwangju in intensity. There might even be full-scale revolution. As someone who styled herself a justice-seeking world citizen, I had identified with the democratic opposition and hoped for an end to military dictatorship. Now, though, I found myself wishing for enough political stability to allow the government to function smoothly, which meant, I guess, consolidating Chun's power. This test of my convictions left me feeling very selfish. I began to tell myself that Keun Young would never come, just to prepare myself for that eventuality. I imagined her at age twenty, living in a democratic Korea, and wondered how much she would know about the fate that had almost been hers.

At the end of September, the social worker called to say that she had received an update on Keun Young. She was doing everything babies were expected to do at six months and was thriving in a foster home, where she was "cared for with sincerity." The photographs that came with it were absolutely beautiful and gave her reality again, but there was still no word on when she would come. When I look back in my journals from fall and early winter, I am surprised by how awful the delay was to bear, since the intervening years have soothed the memory of it. I was, as a friend put it, "on emotional hold," and it made me a physical wreck. My husband's reaction was to set aside problems over which he had no control and not waste his time in needless worry. Every now and then, though, he would erupt in anger that quickly got displaced onto some other object. Our very different coping styles were a source of added tension.

On January 22, 1981, Grace Keun Young arrived by Northwest jumbo-jet at the Minneapolis airport. The very same day, Kim Dae Jung's death sentence was commuted under pressure from the U. S. government, to smooth the way for President Chun's visit to Washington. The day before, the hostages held at the American Embassy in Teheran, Iran, were sent home. Grace's arrival seemed to me of the same magnitude as these events, worthy of a banner headline. She was not the tiny, malleable being we had expected in July, but an alert and active ten-month-old with a full-blown personality and a vocabulary of three Korean words. She was healthy, happy, and obviously well cared for. The delay had served her very well.

Our second experience of prolonged waiting was considerably shorter, but even more frightening. The preliminary process had gone very quickly. We received a referral on March 3 for a baby born in January whom we planned to name Maria, though we usually referred to her as "the baby" or "the second one" or "Grace's baby sister." Visa clearance came just two weeks later, and by the first week in April, we were informed that she was tentatively scheduled for the next flight. There were, however, some problems left to resolve, and our social worker recommended "measured anticipation." I felt sure I could manage that, since I had gotten along so far without the nervousness that characterized the wait for Grace. By April 13, that had changed:

> I am beginning to feel impatient at the delay in the baby's arrival. Every time the phone rings, I jump. I really had expected a call by midweek. I assume the silence means that she won't be here this week. Her six-to-nine-month size clothes are lying in a pile on the vanity. I hope I haven't jinxed it all by being too prepared.

The next day brought word that Eun Sook, as I now called her, was being held back deliberately because of concern about her development. She was underweight and had spent time in the Angels' Baby Home being treated for diarrhea. There were other problems, too, but they were not specified. A few days later we received new pictures of a very pretty, but cross-eyed baby, and close-up color pictures of the lines on her fingertips. I took them to the pediatrician, who said that the lines did not look like the stigmata associated with Down's syndrome, a possibility I hadn't even considered. The major delay in her development was poor control of her neck, a symptom that might suggest cerebral palsy. Also, her head appeared to be growing faster than her body. He helped me devise a list of questions to ask of the Korean agency and then spoke frankly about what we ought to do if our fears were realized. "It's good and moral and altruistic to say that handicaps don't make a difference," he acknowledged, "but it's also a burden for a lifetime." The social worker, too, advised us not to feel obligated to take Eun Sook. They could find us another baby if we wished. But she was already our baby. Her pictures had been propped on the mantel since the day we picked them up, but now I found myself trying not to look at them as I walked by. I was afraid to make her too real or to get too firmly attached. Without more conclusive information about her, it was hard to think clearly about the awesome decision we might have to make:

If she is retarded and not really conscious of her surroundings, including the people who take care of her, would there be any benefit in bringing her here? How would her life be maintained in Korea? If she has a troubling, undiagnosed health problem, do we have her sent in for examination there, to "work the kinks out," as we would on a new car? Or do we bring her here immediately for tests, taking the chance that it might be something life-threatening? If the problem is identified and uncorrectable, how willing are we to accept her as is? And what if everything remains uncertain—even mysterious—as it feels right now? On what basis do we decide what to do?

I have real moral qualms about asking for a new referral. If there is clearly no benefit to her in being part of our family, then I must not let myself be motivated by guilt to bring her here anyway. But I don't really expect the issues to be clear. I suspect we will have to decide whether we will take a risk or whether we want a different child whose prospects look better. It would be very fallacious to think that any child comes with a no-risk guarantee, but are we, as prospective parents, morally obligated to accept a child whose health is more precarious than average? Being such a child myself, I am inclined at first to say, Yes, of course. But then I ask myself whether I want to volunteer for heartache, whether I am prepared to nurse her through poor health. Biological parents don't get this choice, so why should we have it? Are adoptive parents entitled to be selective, as people who have offered themselves as parents to children neither nature nor the law compels them to take? I don't know.

I have also anticipated the strange form of grief we might experience cutting ourselves off from Eun Sook. During that long half-year before Gracie came, I imagined going through life wondering whatever happened to that girl whose baby pictures I carried in my purse. My fate would have been bound forever to Keun Young, somewhere out of touch in the world. I also wonder whether giving her up would affect our relationship with the new baby. Would we see her as a substitute? Or as a third child? Could we call her Maria? European mothers who lost children in infancy, like our great-grandmothers, saved the names for re-use.

There are so many things to think about. [My husband] says he is postponing it all until he has some information to go on, but the only way I can handle anxiety is to let it run its course, then write it down.

We were never driven to the point of decision. Hyun Sook Han of Children's Home Society was making a trip to Korea, and she examined Eun Sook and pronounced her healthy, but a bit slow in developing. I wonder often what we would have decided had she had cerebral palsy. I like to think that I would have said yes, but the situation is still only hypothetical.

Maria Eun Sook arrived, as re-scheduled, on May 12, 1983, just one week short of four months old. We drove to the airport thinking ourselves prepared for anything. But I was certainly not prepared for the plumpest, rosiest cheeks I had ever seen in my life, the bright eyes, and the hair as long and thick as a two-year-old's. This was truly a happy ending. But suppose it had turned out differently? Would we have found happiness in watching her grow and develop as best she could?

It is interesting to think back, ten years later, to that initial selection process. Given the opportunity to specify what kind of child we would like, my husband and I sketched out a fantasy child: intelligent, musically talented, verbal, beautiful, confident, nice as can be. Amazingly enough, Grace seemed made-to-order. It is not an unmixed blessing. There are times when I am tempted to confine my "root of a flower" to the pot that molds her to that perfect shape. But when she cracks the clay and sends off stray shoots of her own, I have learned to stand back in admiration and watch them blossom. We were far less specific, and certainly less demanding, the second time around. By the time of Maria's arrival, my attitude had become "surprise me." And what a surprise she was and is. I am continually amazed at her creative imagination and her fanciful sense of humor. She is my glorious right-brained child, who remembers colors not by their names but by their positions in the rainbow. I wouldn't even have known how to ask for one like her.

4

Coming Together

January 22 and May 12 are holidays at our house. These are Grace and Maria's "arrival days," the anniversary of our coming together, in person, to continue on as a family. We do not celebrate arrival day as festively as a birthday, but we do take note of the day's special meaning, and we make an occasion of looking at the photo albums that record each girl's arrival at the Minneapolis–St. Paul Airport. Every year, as an arrival day approaches, I have intentions of celebrating it at the airport to relive that joyous event, but always I realize in time that there is no satisfying way to relive it, except to do it again.

Recently, I was among the friends and family members waiting for Lata, a one-year-old girl, to arrive from India to join Ginny, a single, first-time mother. We were a big crowd that didn't stand still long enough to be counted. I remembered the phone call from my social worker the day before Maria's arrival in which she relayed to me, without much enthusiasm, the airline's request that we limit our group to six people so as not to obstruct the flow of passengers at the gate. Twenty-seven friends and relatives showed up. Who could I refuse a first glimpse of my new baby and a share in the excitement? Ginny's group seemed as large and as animated and Ginny herself was buzzing around on adrenalin, just as I had.

When Lata's plane, the last in a flight from Calcutta to Bangkok to Tokyo to Seattle to Minneapolis, pulled up at the gate, part of the crowd pressed up against the railing, while the rest of us spread out behind on tiptoe. Cameras were focused and film advanced into place. But nothing happened. The jetway, the chute that the disembarking passengers walk down into the terminal, would not connect with the door of the plane. We could hear the sound of pneumatic machinery and insistent banging against the side of the plane. One try, then another and another. Anticipatory tension relaxed into laughter. She had made it halfway around the world, and now they couldn't get her off the plane. As we all crowded closer to witness this failure of modern technology, an elderly couple squeezed in next to me and asked, "Is there somebody famous on this plane? Who is everybody waiting for?" I explained what was happening and pointed Ginny out to them. "So *that's* why all these children of different races are here," they nodded. I hadn't noticed until then how many of us well-wishers were internationally adoptive families ourselves.

After fifteen or twenty minutes, the problem was fixed, and the passengers began filing off the plane: white and black Americans, and Asians of many nationalities, including a three-generation Hmong family obviously new to this land of exile. There was a short hiatus and then three women came out, each carrying a baby. Ginny had told us to watch for a blue dress or a yellow dress that she had sent to the orphanage for the trip, but there was the child in the photographs dressed in a pink sleeper. "Is this Lata?" Ginny asked the woman carrying her. "No, I don't think so," she said, and she read some other name off the papers in her hand. Another friend and I had leapt to Ginny's side and were now insisting, "It's *her*, Ginny. Just look at her. It's Lata." It *was* Lata, and the name the woman had read turned out to be her birthplace, mistyped. The moment of confusion was not unusual. My very first view of Grace, from behind, revealed an unexpected bald spot on the back of her head, and she was smaller than I thought a ten-month-old baby would be. As soon as the flight aide handed her to me, she snuggled her face into my shoulder, which certainly eased *my* apprehension. With her thumb in her mouth besides, she wasn't totally recognizable. It was hours later, in the middle of the night, that I saw, full front, the face in the photographs that I had memorized. Momentary uncertainty seems appropriate to the occasion. After waiting so long, with emotions suspended, you hardly dare trust reality. How could Lata suddenly be here, in the flesh, after Ginny had become so inured to living in anticipation?

It was a wonderful, awesome, joyous meeting of mother and child, and I would be thrilled to go through it again with other friends who adopt internationally. The joy is infectious. As I gathered my kids and walked away from the gate to go home, I saw the elderly couple looking on and smiling. They had stayed to welcome the famous passenger.

Mary MacNamara's summation of arrival day captures both its emotional quality and its import:

It was so exciting. My husband even said to me once, "You know, getting married was the biggest day of my life. But I have to tell you, the happiest day was the day those children came." That was really wonderful. It feels like you are in the twilight zone when you go to the airport. You're just sort of oblivious to everything that's going on around you. It's just such pure, unadultered joy—well, a little bit of fear mixed in, too. You go into that airport a couple and you come out forevermore a family. Things change totally. You'll never have that same life again.

Every adoptive family has its own memories of arrival day and its own special way of narrating the sequence of events. Not all of them go like this. In some cases, going to the airport alone is more appropriate to the situation. Many parents, of course, travel to the countries of their children's birth to pick them up. Other versions of the story will be told here, as well.

Those who have witnessed an arrival like Lata's are left with an image of the jet plane as stork, delivering a happy, bouncing baby to its eager parents. Infants do generally weather the transition quite well. Among the families I interviewed, the "mild" and "contented" baby was the rule—to quote adjectives used frequently in Korean referral papers to describe the baby's personality. Many, perhaps most, parents receiving infants observe virtually no trauma, hardly even any adjusting, to their surprise and relief. I was amazed at how quickly Grace settled in. As soon as we got into the car at the airport, she pulled my hair and reached for my glasses, laughing and babbling. We did go through jet lag for a week as she reordered her days and nights. The first night, I sat with her in front of a full-length mirror, to keep her entertained. She looked at my reflection, then at me, then at my reflection again, and said, "Um-ma, Um-ma," the Korean word for "Mom." I was flabbergasted. She already knew who I was to be in her life. It felt as though all the bonds were sealed at that moment, and I had never imagined it would happen so quickly and smoothly. A few weeks later, however, I noticed that some of her habits had changed. She was sucking her thumb less frequently and with less vigor. She no longer whimpered in her sleep, and her cry had changed from a wail of "Ai-ai-ai" to the kind of cry I was used to hearing from a hungry or wet baby. The first few weeks, there were several moments when she would get a faraway look in her eyes and shudder. When this, too, stopped, I realized that she had, in fact, been showing signs of grief or fear. When Ginny described to me how Lata sometimes shuddered, I was ready to acknowledge that flying across the ocean to a new home is not a painless change, even for a baby.

The MacNamara children were each about five months of age when they arrived. After experiencing a smooth transition with her first child, Mary was very alert to the difficulty her second child was having:

I don't believe Katie smiled for the first eight months she was with us. She seemed to be grieving. She had lived with her birthmother for almost two months. The parents had been living together, and before Katie was born, the mother discovered that the father had been unfaithful to her. So she moved out and moved back with her mother, and then the birthmother and the grandmother were going to raise Katie. Well, after a couple of months they realized that that wasn't going to be possible for them, so then she was placed in foster care a couple of months, and then she came to me. So in less than five months, she'd been in three homes, and she was feeling kind of scared, I guess. I don't know how an infant would feel. I know it seems weird, but I know she felt something. She felt afraid or something, because she wasn't real cuddly. She didn't like me to hold her real close. She just wasn't a real happy baby.

But her brother adored her from the first day she came. Billy was sixteen months, and he just thought she was as fine as frog hair. That was a big help, because he liked to rub her leg or pat her arm, and she seemed to like that. When we would be holding her to feed her, Billy would come up and touch her arm or her leg and she would make happy noises, and that was about the only time she ever really did. I don't know why she had such a hard time, but we figured, we'll just keep on being physically affectionate with her and smile at her, and sooner or later, she's going to warm up to us. I felt bonded to both of my kids before they even came. It was immediate. But I don't think that Katie, especially, felt bonded to us for a long time. But I always felt that it was worth the wait, and we would just keep plugging away at it, and sooner or later she would. It worked.

The child's adjustment may depend a great deal on temperament or on physical comfort, so it is difficult to generalize even by age or developmental stage. My daughter Maria had already gone from one foster home to the agency's convalescent hospital to a second foster home. Nevertheless, she was one of the cheeriest babies I have ever seen.

Among adoptive parents, it has become commonplace to call the child's arrival in the family "coming home," as in "John came home from Chile on November 13." This makes me squirm a bit. It implies that the child has been away, on alien territory, or living in a vacuum, with no attachment to people or a place that could be identified as "home." Infants and toddlers living in foster care certainly do not understand that they are there only temporarily. The ever-present woman who attends to the child's needs is mother, with no qualifiers. Children in orphanages may have special affection for a staff person or for certain other children in the group. Even streetchildren are not living in isolation. Armando Jordan, 19, who was adopted from Colombia at 9, remembers a younger boy he befriended:

> I was just walking one evening and someone said, "Do you have a dollar?" in Spanish. I turned around, and he was just a beautiful little kid, and he had nothing on but underwear. I just wanted to take him to a hotel and say, Here, sleep the night, but I didn't have any money myself, so I took him to where I was sleeping. We were living outside. I had built my own little house and put blankets under. I was creative. I kept myself warm. I put him in there and brought food in there. He loved it. He was just like my little brother. I was taking good care of him and I'd take him everywhere. And he just loved me. I told him I was going to be right back with something to eat for him, and I never came back. Until this day, I think of him still. I just cry, because I don't know whatever happened to him. I hope he's all right, but he was a smart kid.

The flight to the United States does take children away from the people they have learned to depend on and to long for and transplants them into a new situation that does not immediately feel like home. Even a child happily anticipating adoption can never really be prepared for how vast the changes will be. The scene at the airport may not fill the arriving child with joy. The people look strange and different. The sounds and smells are unfamiliar. It must be a little like landing on another planet. Here is how Michael Carroll, a sixth-grader, recalled his flight from Korea four years earlier in an essay published in the magazine *Roots and Wings:*

> My flight to the United States from Korea was very unpleasant, mostly because I felt perplexed and at the same time, I felt frightened. One

of the reasons was that I was so homesick. I was homesick because I missed the orphanage. I was also sad from thinking of the orphanage. I wanted to scream in agony, but if I did, I would have felt embarrassed. When I looked around the plane, I noticed that I looked different than the other people in the plane. I felt so strange because I looked different and could not speak the same language. . . . I was worried that my new parents would not like me because I looked different than the other people I saw on the plane. (Winter 1989, p. 13)

For older children conscious of being transplanted, an exuberant airport welcome would be overwhelming and thus insensitive. Linda and Fred Truman understood that and kept their first meetings with their new daughters subdued. That turned out to be wise, because there were problems in the transition that they could not have anticipated. When they first decided to adopt, they applied for siblings and were assigned two sisters, ages six and two, who had been relinquished to the care of an orphanage by their grandmother. During the waiting period, Fred and Linda sent over photographs and small gifts for the girls, to acquaint them with their home-to-be. The day of the arrival, the Trumans got a last minute phone call informing them that the older girl was not on the plane because of an error in her passport. They met the younger girl as scheduled and expected to go to the airport again in a few days to pick up her sister. Weeks passed with no word and finally, the agency told them that they had lost track of her. She was apparently not returned to the orphanage, and there was no word on whether she had gone back to her grandmother. The family connection they had hoped to preserve by adopting siblings had been broken. Sixteen years later, they still have no idea what became of the sister.

Although they had not expected Jonna to be in excellent physical shape, they were not prepared for the degree of malnutrition she had suffered. They had been warned only about lice, and so the first event upon arriving home from the airport was a bath and shampoo, which Linda laughs about in retrospect as an awful initiation into a new family: "You throw her in this bathtub and the poor kid's screaming her head off. She was really scared: 'What are these people doing to me?' But that was something that you just did, right away." According to the birthdate on her documents, Jonna was three months older than the Trumans' son, but he was a full head taller. Linda describes her appearance this way:

She was tiny. She had little stick legs and a big, protruding belly. She looked like a bird. And to walk up the steps she had to put her hands on her knees and push. She had very little strength—just these tiny little bones.

The big belly and the stomach pains that woke her up screaming in the middle of the night were caused by intestinal parasites. The physicians the Trumans consulted were not accustomed to seeing such cases and reacted with some skepticism. But finally the parasites were cleared up and Jonna began to grow:

She was able to gain weight, and her body changed to normal shape. She grew ten inches the first year she was here. You could just about see her growing. And then she started losing her teeth. And in nursery school, the teacher said that her fine motor development was far above the level that would be expected for a two-and-a-half-year-old. And she'd sing songs. We've got tapes of her singing little Korean songs.

A thorough physical examination suggested that Jonna was not two but at least five years old. The Trumans realized that she was aware enough to remember aspects of her life in Korea, and, with an interpreter's help, they understood that she had been crying for her grandmother and her sister. Linda suspects that Jonna's grandmother might have falsified the ages—the older girl was supposed to have been six—to make them more appealing to prospective parents. This is ironic, since the Trumans had requested older children in the first place. They decided to have Jonna's age legally declared as four, to allow her some time to catch up before entering kindergarten. It was jarring to have to change their perspective so suddenly and begin treating her as an older child.

In retrospect, Fred and Linda believe they made the right decision and that Jonna's aptitude and behavior have been appropriate to the age they established for her. Although the disparity between Jonna's estimated and actual age was larger than in most cases like this, misstatements of age are not uncommon. Many malnourished children whose birthdates are unknown do have to have their ages adjusted after a balanced diet spurs their growth or the attention they receive in their new homes stimulates their intellectual and motor development.

While the Truman family was making adjustment upon adjustment, they also welcomed a second daughter, a nine-year-old whom they had selected from a photo album of waiting children very soon after learning that Jonna's sister would not be coming. Linda describes her arrival:

Of course, she was this big kid. You didn't pick her up and hold her in your lap. It was fun and exciting, and I liked seeing how she was reacting. With an older child, it's more like another real person, instead of you controlling everything and sweeping this little thing off her feet. You have to wait and see what's going to happen and handle it as it happens, rather than having your plan and going about it.

By that time we had picked up a few Korean things we could say, like Are you hungry? Do you hurt? Do you have to go to the bathroom? They had a Korean-speaking woman at the airport who explained to Soon Hee what was going on and that we were going to be her family. On the airplane, Soon Hee had been given the care of a younger child because they only had so many escorts, and here was a capable nine-year-old. Soon Hee thought the child was going with her, so when they took the child away, she was even more confused. She just kind of sat in the car and was very quiet, very quiet. Later she told us it was months before she realized that Jonna was Korean. By that time, Jonna had gone through several periods—first she chattered in Korean, then there was a time when she didn't talk at all and she was just very quiet, and then she spoke English. So she was not speaking Korean when Soon Hee came. It was really funny, because we thought for sure these two would be able to communicate, but there wasn't that kind of attempt at all.

Soon Hee did not settle easily into her new home. She quickly grew defiant, stole money, broke family rules, and bullied the other children. This behavior brought the Trumans into family counseling, which did not ease the situation very much. At age 23, Soon Hee's memories of her adoption are fragmented and puzzling. She knows that she lived with her Korean parents and four older siblings until her father died.

It seems like everything went so fast—faster than it did. It seemed like he died and then all of a sudden I was in an orphanage home. They were taking my picture and cutting my hair and checking to see if I had lice. And then after that, I went back home for a while to see my family. I remember them buying me nice clothes—the nicest clothes I'd ever gotten. And then the next thing I remember

was, I was at the airport, and then I was on the airplane. They
didn't really say goodbye to me, you know. Nobody ever told me
where I was going.

Of her arrival in the United States, she remembers how frightened
she was to be separated from the other little girl, and how fascinated
she was by the doors in the airport terminal that opened automatically.
She followed along with her new parents, not fully understanding who
they were, despite the interpreter's explanation. Now married, with a
child of her own, she looks back on this period of her life as a time of
unmanageable frustration. She was angry with her Korean family for
giving her away. "That's how I saw it: them just giving me away."
And she was angry with her adoptive parents, as well. "I kind of blamed
them then, because I figured, well, if they didn't adopt me, I would
never be here. I thought because they wanted me, that's why my mother
gave me away."

Leaving a familiar environment, no matter how impoverished, for a
new one in which life seems beyond mastery would be frightening for
almost any child of Soon Hee's age. Jessica Martinson's first year with
her nine-year-old daughter Anita, who had spent two years in an orphanage in Guatemala, proved to be the most stressful year of her life:

> She was very angry, very, very withdrawn, and very depressed. She
> went through a very difficult grieving process. All those things about
> loss and separation are *real*. Even though intellectually I could separate
> from what was happening, her mood affected this entire household,
> and there were months that I think I really, really learned what
> despair is like. I'm sure it gets worse, but the intensity of her depression
> just permeated everything.

Jessica describes Anita's behavior as a kind of testing prompted by distrust.
Anita's previous experience with adults had been abusive, and she anticipated abuse and rejection from Jessica, as well: "As it was explained
to me, kids in her situation don't trust anybody, don't believe anybody's
ever going to keep them, so why not be the worst person you can be
and just get it over with and get this person to give you away?" Jessica's
gentle tolerance only confused Anita and increased the tension between
them. Feeling in danger of losing her patience, Jessica sought counseling
for both of them, together and individually:

I had never experienced not liking somebody, especially a child. And this was my kid! I didn't like my kid! The crazy thing is, it's real safe for me not to like my son, and sometimes I don't like him, but I've always known I loved him, that I've grown to love him. One counselor said to me, "Look, babies come and there's nothing to dislike about a baby. There's no personality there or anything. A nine-year-old kid has developed all kinds of yucky habits that you can dislike." When they're younger, you have the illusion that they're turning out to be what you want them to be. They're fulfilling all your expectations. But, see, Anita wasn't fulfilling my expectations.

Parents who have waited long and eagerly for the child's arrival, studying the referral picture and making plans for the future, certainly do build expectations, and these may not be compatible with what the child is experiencing. Jessica believes that the agency could not have prepared her much better for the emotional upheaval that she and Anita went through: "I'm not certain that I would have heard it. I think that there's a romanticism that all of us get into at the time we're adopting, that you really don't understand what they're talking about." Jessica had to ease up on her own expectations and focus on Anita's need for support through a grieving process that she learned was not unusual:

She was in therapy with a group of kids, all of them having the same kinds of experiences, all of them coming from backgrounds of deprivation and neglect. They did special exercises with those kids. They got to write letters and say good-bye to people that they never got a chance to say good-bye to, and they were very sad. It gave them a real safe place to work through some of those things. It wasn't individual therapy. It wasn't just Anita. They didn't feel like they were the ones that had been the bad person. That was really a turning point for her.

During the preadoptive counseling they kept talking about bonding and attachment. I never understood what that meant until it didn't happen for Anita and me. It was scary to admit that, but I knew that I'd do everything I could for her. I was going to keep at it, and I was committed to her. I realized after the second year that I had started giving her goofy nicknames and all of that. All of a sudden our relationship took on an affection that just wasn't there before.

For the first time, I really felt love towards her. I also think, for her, that she was feeling some of that back. She just wasn't as mad at me anymore. She trusted me finally.

Parents who adopt older American children, particularly children whose family status has been in flux for some time, are likely to anticipate and gear themselves for a difficult adjustment period. That is not always true of internationally adoptive parents. When the child comes from a less technologically developed country, and particularly from an institution or a situation of severe poverty, the public perception is that the child is lucky and sure to be thrilled with the abundant food, the comfortable home, and the brand new toys and clothes. Some adoptive parents, as well, engage in this kind of thinking, mostly in a wishful sense: Having everything ready and nice should make the arrival easier, and displaying their love in this way should quickly win the child's heart. How surprised they are, then, when the child hoards food in dresser drawers, rejects gifts, and behaves in self-protective ways.

It is virtually impossible to overestimate the degree of culture shock that an older child coming to the United States for adoption is likely to experience, particularly one who is also catapulted from barefoot poverty to a throw-away consumer economy. First, there are the obvious differences in customs. Soon Hee Truman remembers her surprise when her new family walked into the house with their shoes still on. Beyond that, there are very significant differences in values, in orientation toward possessions and toward relationships with people, and in the limits on acceptable behavior. Parents who have little knowledge about their child's birth culture and have never been immersed in a culture other than their own cannot fully imagine how disruptive this change must be to their child's sense of security. Silvia Kowalski explains:

Culture shock is one thing when you travel, when you're a tourist, but it's another thing when you know that this is where you are going to be the rest of your life, most likely. The first thing that made an impact on me about American culture was that everything was clean. It seemed like Americans were so clean. Right after that it was how wasteful the American culture was. I had thoughts about so much poverty in Colombia, and then to see how much was wasted here. I alienated myself from it and didn't want to be part of it.

Another thing was, I was raised Catholic, and I experienced a real sense of conflict with morals. For example, I was 12 years old and I had never seen an adult female undressed. To suddenly see my mother—I thought she was totally disrespectful to *me*. The Hispanic culture is very private, and that was the ultimate to me. I was just in shock.

To steel themselves against the impact of this alien culture, Silvia and her sister at first refused to learn English. They would speak Spanish together, and when their parents or other people understood some of what they were saying, they just talked faster. "We would play a little game," she says.

The difference in language is emblematic of the other cultural differences. Communication with the newly arrived child is reduced to the basics of gesture and facial expression, and even these may have different meanings in different cultures. At the same time that Soon Hee and Anita were testing their new families with hostile behavior, they were also enduring a frustrating trial-and-error approach to learning English. Both families had difficulty arranging tutorial help at school. Anita suffered the humiliation of failing a test of her competency in Spanish, her native language. It took the intervention of an adoption worker with experience in Latin America to determine that she had been tested in Castilian Spanish, which is quite different from Guatemalan vernacular. Because Silvia wanted an education so badly, she was finally persuaded to learn English, and it came easily because she was accustomed to studying, having completed the sixth grade in Colombia. Anita, like many of the children who have lived on their own, had only attended school regularly for one year prior to her arrival, so she was behind in other subjects as well. What finally smoothed her transition to school was enrollment in a special program for non-English-speaking students that had been set up for Southeast Asian refugee children, who were arriving in such numbers that their presence in the classroom taxed the resources of the regular teachers.

For children younger than eight or so, the barrier of language seems a bit easier to overcome than it was for Soon Hee and Anita. The pattern that Jonna Truman's language took—speaking Korean, then withdrawing in silence, and then speaking English exclusively—is a fairly common one. One mother told me that her five-year-old son was very loquacious in Korean when he first arrived. Then, in apparent frustration at not being understood, he went for six weeks without making a sound, which naturally made his new parents anxious about his emotional well-being. One day, he abruptly started speaking again—in perfect English sentences.

I certainly do not want to leave the impression that all families who adopt older children go through a year-long trial by fire. Many children do adjust quickly and show every sign of being content in their new home. How well prepared they are in advance and how thoroughly they understand the change they are about to undergo makes a substantial difference. Simply being told about the move may not be sufficient, if they can't comprehend geographical distance or permanence. Armando Jordan knew he was going to "los Estados Unidos" but, having never been to school, he had no idea it was a different country where people spoke another language. Ease of adjustment probably depends, as well, on how much benefit the children see for themselves in joining an American family. Two of the children whose parents reported very smooth transitions—Steven Duval and Randi Solberg, both six at the time of arrival—experienced discrimination in Korea. Steven is Amerasian and Randi is physically handicapped. Though they are not in the mainstream in this culture, either, their difference from the norm is less striking in a more heterogeneous society.

As the number of children coming to the United States for adoption has increased, support services have emerged in response to their unique needs. Adoption agencies, child welfare workers, and family therapists are seeing the value of peer groups like the one Anita Martinson took part in. There are more pediatricians familiar with racially specific illnesses and Third World health issues. The University of Minnesota has a widely known International Adoption Clinic that serves its own special-ized clientele, as well as educating health professionals in how to assess normal development in children born in other areas of the world and how to treat illnesses that they would otherwise seldom encounter. Bilin-gual education for Spanish-speaking students and English as a Second Language classes help ease children into this difficult new language in which they are now expected to function day-to-day.

Many of us who choose to adopt infants make that decision, in part, to avoid the extra measures required to integrate an older child into the family. Never having tested my capacity to love a child of my own—either adopted or biological, I wanted to start fresh with a baby who would have no prior allegiances and no memory of previous hurts. Laurie Means, who has given birth to two babies and adopted a five-year-old girl, testifies that there is, indeed, a difference in how bonding takes place:

There's a whole different set of stages that you go through with an older child. You don't have the advantage of this cuddly baby that you bond to, and you put it down and it stays in the bassinet. An older child has a whole set of demands, an agenda. You don't have that sense of control that you do with a baby, and you can begin to somewhat resent this. You know, it's a full-blown person who really doesn't owe any allegiance to you and isn't going to love you unconditionally in the same way that a twelve-month-old does. They have to earn your love almost, and you have to earn their love. I think about this as a whole different way of bringing a child into your family. But there are advantages to it, and one of the advantages is forcing us as a family to look at cultural issues and to look at the idea of parenting—that we really don't own our children.

Infants do, nevertheless, make some significant changes in habit when they arrive to join their new families. Sleeping in a crib may be a new experience and a frightening one if the crib is in a single bedroom, out of sight of the rest of the family. Or, imagine the sensation of being laid down in a prone position if you have always slept on your back. Grace's bald spot was explained to me as evidence that her foster mother had kept her on her back so that her head would flatten out to fit Korean standards of beauty. Feeding habits and schedules, subject to ever-changing trends in child development theory in this country, also vary cross-culturally. Parents of Korean infants often describe their babies as plump and assume that the foster family fattened the baby up to make a good impression. Breaking the baby's nighttime feeding habit may be one of the biggest struggles. Is your baby sleeping through the night yet? is one of the first questions that new American parents eager to share their experiences ask each other. Getting up in the middle of the night, preparing a bottle for a crying baby, then lifting the baby out of its crib and sitting down to feed it is regarded as something of a nuisance, especially if the child doesn't really need the extra nutrition. In Korea, the baby sleeps on the floor next to the mother, so nighttime feedings are less disruptive. If the adoption agency provides a big enough supply of formula, then a model Korean foster mother will indulge the baby's demand for food and not withhold it.

A major change for infants and young toddlers who have been in foster care in Asia or Latin America is the decrease in actual body contact that they experience when they come here. In cultures where the family sleeps together in one room, where the mother carries the child strapped to her back as she goes about her work, and where there are grandparents or siblings available to hold the child, the warmth of another human body is a constant source of security. Does the child accustomed to foster care grieve this loss on coming to the United States, where babies ride in carseats, get wheeled around in strollers, and put in playpens out of reach of dangerous objects?

Elsbeth and Edward Saunders' fourth son arrived from India at age two. They had found him through a private connection with the director of a boarding school in India that occasionally takes in orphaned or abandoned children. The director had not yet placed children for adoption internationally, and the school had to be licensed for that purpose, which took much longer than anticipated. In the meantime, Raj lived in the director's home as a foster child and was cared for by her adult daughter. Elsbeth describes the daughter's sari as "his security blanket—just a thing he was attached to all the time."

> If it was cold, she'd wrap him up in it. If he was standing up doing something, he would hold onto it. He was rocked to sleep in the sari. So for two years he really got the kind of cuddling that I don't think any baby gets here. She took a year off work just to stay home and take care of Raj. Then the next year she went back to teaching school but took him with her every day. So the hardest thing for him has been coming into a family where we encourage independence and have to, just because both of us have worked and been real active. The kids have been in daycare since birth. The biggest adjustment for him has been moving from a private doting situation, one on one, to being part of a crowd.

Both the Saunders family and the foster family in India were intent on making Raj's transition to his new home as easy as possible. The young woman accompanied him to the United States and spent two weeks living at the Saunders home. She planned to help him transfer his allegiance by coaxing him to show affection to his new parents. Her presence caused only confusion and distress, so she moved out but stayed in touch for another week before returning to India. Even telephone conversations proved to be upsetting. "All of a sudden he was totally removed from us," Elsbeth remembers. "He talked to her for a while and then he cried for ten minutes straight and then he was just withdrawn." The Saunders consulted an adoption counselor and a child psychologist, both of whom advised them to break the contact immediately. "What needed to be clarified in his mind was that he was no longer going back to India. No one is returning. We are his parents, period." After that break, Raj seemed more at ease, though he had difficulty adjusting to his new independence. Because he had been carried much of the time, his large motor development was not on a par with other children his age.

Witnessing her child's affection for the foster mother and seeing herself as the instigator of confusion and grief left Elsbeth with ambivalent feelings. She believes, on the one hand, that her son was overindulged—what Americans call "spoiled"—and that this complicated the move:

> When it is hard to shift him from his old patterns to the current ones, there's a kind of resentment that forms toward the people that took care of him before. Generally, you're totally appreciative because they went over and above their call of duty to do this. Even though you appreciate it totally, you also resent the fact that they pampered him so much. I think it's easier when you adopt if you don't know the people that took care of him for that time, because there's just so many levels of guilt and a sense of obligation. I almost feel like I need to report. I feel like, I don't want to be reporting to you. It's not your business anymore. However, I appreciate the fact that he now has a landing place in India when he wants to renew connections with his country, and we will probably go there as a family and visit.

On the other hand, Elsbeth is convinced that the Indian family's intentions were good ones. A baby girl whom they had assigned to the Saunders had died shortly after coming into their custody. This experience must have made them very solicitous of Raj's welfare.

The Saunders family was directly confronted with the fact that their son was going through a major separation: leaving home as well as coming home. We who receive our children from an unfamiliar flight aide or escort in the joyous chaos at the airport are spared that reality and the ambivalent feelings it is likely to engender. This experience left Elsbeth and her husband with an acute sense of what Raj lost in gaining a permanent family, and some concern about not compensating enough for the loss. Elsbeth speculates, "It would have been easier for Raj if he had been in an institution for a couple years. Then this would have come off as a move up, but in all it ended up netting him just a lot less attention." In the long run, though, his attachment to the foster mother will probably serve him well. Child psychologists observe that children who learn to depend on a loving adult in infancy have an easier time forming close relationships as they go through life. It is also important to remember that the foster mother, who was single and employed, would probably not have managed to care for him had there not been a family waiting to adopt him very soon.

Parents who travel to pick up their children also see the separation firsthand, not only the separation from caretakers but from the culture as well. There are very good arguments for going through this experience if the time and expense can be managed. The Frazee family has welcomed children both ways. After a very trying trip to India in the company of a woman whose baby died shortly after they got there, Donna Frazee felt, nevertheless, "like I missed out on something not going to Colombia to get my other children. Going to India really provided that special, immediate bond with that child. It really helped us to understand something about the culture she came from. It just provided a real good first beginning."

In some cases, seeing the child's temporary home helps to explain behavior that might otherwise be puzzling and frustrating. As soon as Rita Garman met her son Noah at two-and-a-half, at an orphanage in Brazil, she realized that he was going to be more of a challenge than her other five children. Seeing the conditions in which he had been living helped her to understand his hyperactivity. Because the orphanage was crowded and understaffed, he had spent nearly all his time there confined to one long, narrow room. Within that space, he had been free to act out with little restraint. Rita knew that establishing firm boundaries—both spatial and behavioral—would be critical in helping Noah adjust to life in their family. She describes their two weeks alone together in Brazil as a "very intense" period in which she cuddled and held him much of the time, a luxury they would not have enjoyed at home with the other children vying for attention. "I think that really facilitated it. According to all the bonding studies, he should have been an unattached child, but he wasn't. He bonded very easily with me."

Virginia Corey's trip to India to pick up her infant son began as a nightmare but ended up as "the most extraordinary experience I have ever had." She was shocked to find him severely malnourished, feverish with pneumonia, and unresponsive. "He was one pound over birthweight at four months. I held him, literally, in the palms of my hands, he was so tiny." Naturally, Virginia was both frightened and angry at finding him in this condition. Her reaction was tempered, however, by what she learned and experienced in the three weeks that she was compelled to stay on while he recovered enough to risk the long journey to the United States. Had she stayed home waiting for reports on his health, she would have thought the people who arranged the adoption remiss for housing him in an orphanage not under their control and then rarely checking on him. Going to India showed her the lay of the land in that region and the difficulty of traveling from one town to the next. Stopping in at other orphanages showed her the tremendous need for people and resources to care for homeless children. Since getting the referral, Virginia had been sending money to supply her son with formula that ought to have kept him well nourished. Had she stayed home, she might have suspected the agency of fraudulently diverting the money to other uses. Though she was, indeed, angry that the orphanage had not taken better care of her child, she could understand why her effort to provide formula had not worked:

> The money I sent was probably simply divided up. I don't know how many outside sources of support these children had, so that I think whatever I sent for the individual use of my son became a communal fund. You have to put yourself back into the context, and from their standpoint, it would make sense. I think a can of formula costs about twenty-five rupees. Now if you think that seventeen rupees a day is an average wage laborer's salary, that is a really expensive purchase. It had to have been terribly, terribly difficult.

Virginia was very impressed with the kindness and generosity of the people who helped nurse her son to health. The woman who arranged the adoption took personal responsibility, found a relative willing to invite Virginia and the baby to stay at her house, and hired a nursemaid to help. The four women took turns feeding him on a two-hour schedule around the clock, which relieved Virginia of her fears:

> I had had no contact with babies prior to that. I am an only child with no close relatives. I was still learning how to give him the bottle, which I didn't do initially because I was really too afraid. He was so tiny that he was hard to touch. They taught me how to care for a baby while I was there, and that was a very useful experience.

After this, she had enough confidence in the people who had assisted in the adoption to apply to them for a second child.

Becoming acquainted with people and seeing how they lived and worked demystified a culture that Virginia had thought of as quite alien. Initially she had hoped to adopt from Latin America, because it seemed culturally less remote, but, of the programs she checked into, the one in India imposed the fewest restrictions on single parents. "I had not given India much thought," she says, "because I felt that I had no background in Indian culture, that I was, if anything, overwhelmed by the kinds of problems that existed in India, the mass of people, and the seeming inability of anybody to cope with those problems." The impression she carried home along with her new son, which she can use as a backdrop in telling her children the stories of their adoptions, is of the beauty of the coastal landscape, the vitality and diversity of the people, and the rich impact of the atmosphere on the senses:

> It was raining cats and dogs when I came out of the airport in Bombay. It was one of the strongest sensual experiences I've ever had in terms of the heat, the darkness, and the smell. It was as if you had emptied all of the spice jars.

Seeing your child well cared for certainly does humanize a setting that might otherwise seem strange and intimidating. Traveling to adopt a child is a more enlightening experience than, for example, vacationing in a resort populated by other North American tourists. Reba and Michael Perlitz remember their trip to Colombia to get their daughter as "an exciting adventure." Michael begins the story:

> We each spoke a little bit of Spanish, but we had never been further south than Mexico. We went to Colombia with great trepidation, and we landed in the town where the welfare office was, which is a fairly small town. God, what are we doing here? was the first thought. We were frightened. It was at night. A woman who had been assigned to us as our interpreter picked us up and took us to our hotel. The next morning she came by and we went right up to the welfare office, and they gave us the address of a house out in a small village that you could take a cab to. There were cows and goats roaming the streets, and it was a little adobe house.

Reba continues,

> I felt really weird going there, because it was like, Oh, here come those rich Americans to take this baby away. And they did not tell the foster mother we were coming, because they had had some very bad experiences where the foster mothers got real attached to the

kids, and when they heard the adoptive parents were coming, they hid the babies. Mariana, the foster mother, wasn't like that at all. She had another little foster child and two boys of her own who were older. She lived in an adobe house with a dirt floor. It was spotless. She was obviously a smart, competent woman. They forbade us to give her any money. They didn't want the foster mothers to expect that they were going to get a lot of money from America. We brought her some gifts and that's what they said was the right thing to do.

She gave us a meal and then we went upstairs. Leah was sleeping upstairs. She was in the corner of this bed with pillows all around her and covered over with blankets. Mariana picked her up and gave her to us. I felt like I should feel some way that I didn't—that I should have this overwhelming feeling, but I was just sort of in shock. She was beautiful. She was just beautiful. Mariana actually came back to the hotel with us, just to look over our stuff and make sure everything was OK. She also came to the plane to say good-bye.

Michael describes himself as feeling "like a babysitter" initially. The newness of parenthood, coupled with seeing their child nestled in at the home of an experienced and loving mother, could easily account for that. Leah, who was six months old, showed no signs of upset either during the rest of their stay in a hotel in Bogotá, nor on the flight to the United States, nor on arrival. "She never missed a nap" is the way both Reba and Michael characterize her passage from foster home to permanent home. Their trepidation at being in an unfamiliar Spanish-speaking country was eased by meeting people and having time to see something of the culture while they waited for the legal process to be completed. Michael admits to being impatient initially with the very different work pace:

We dealt directly with a woman at the government welfare agency in the town where Leah was born—a very nice woman who at one time said to me in a not very nice situation, "We consider our children our national resource, and this is how we do it. Listen, this is all we have. We're giving up our children and it hurts to do this." It was because I had finally been pushed a little too far by the red tape. I recognized her feelings immediately and backed right off. That was the only time I ever responded in a way that I felt was kind of "Ugly American," and her response was fully correct.

The Perlitzes returned home with sound impressions of Colombia and great respect for the woman who cared for their daughter, and they have kept in touch with her over the seven years since. "We feel that a lot of Leah's smile and her spirit and fire come from Mariana and the fact that she was really well cared for," Michael says.

They had hoped to adopt a second Colombian baby and to house the child with the same foster mother. As it turned out, new regulations instituted by the Colombian government put them above the age limit for adopting an infant, and Reba didn't feel skilled enough yet as a mother to adopt an older child. They turned to Honduras instead and embarked on a new adventure that was a marked contrast to their Colombian experience. While the Colombian government was cautiously refining its policy on international adoption and tightening procedures, Honduras was, in Reba's words, "a free-for-all." The Honduran counterpart to the conscientious Colombian welfare worker who had set Michael straight was a lawyer obviously earning a large income on international adoptions. The foster care was not of the same quality. On the first of the two required trips to Honduras, they found their baby in ill health and very tiny for his age. As it turned out, he was a different baby from the one whose referral they had been given, and the lawyer had neglected to tell them about the change. The explanation itself was troubling because it raised questions about how and why children become available for adoption.

> The birthmother of that baby got worried and she started taking him back. Some mothers take the baby back and then go to another lawyer and get some money and then go to another lawyer and get some money, and she was threatening to do that. So they substituted a different baby.

The International Alliance for Professional Accountability in Latin American Adoptions made reference in its October 1989 newsletter to similar incidents and offered this explanation:

> . . . A common practice among certain Honduran attorneys is to offer several agencies a particular child. The agency that gets its documents in first lands the child—the other agencies are told the birth mother changed her mind or some other excuse. This creates a real emotional hardship for the family that is expecting the referral is theirs, only to discover that the child is "no longer available."

The bureaucratic procedure that the Perlitzes went through seemed to them arbitrary and inefficient. Michael feels that his impatience with the Honduran process, unlike his reaction in Colombia, was justified.

As an example, you have to meet with the director of welfare. This person is kind of a bottleneck. You have two interviews, a week apart. And the interview consists of asking you about fourteen questions from one side of a piece of paper and a week later turning over the piece of paper and asking you fourteen questions from the back side, which means obviously that the week in between was a week in a hotel. It could have been done in an hour. And people have had that second interview cancelled on whim. You can go there and wait for two hours, and the person who does it may show up or may not. In Honduras, I genuinely felt that at any given time everything was going to fall through.

Michael did not believe that the procedural requirements were primarily meant to serve the children's interests.

It is set up as social welfare, but there's so much graft and corruption. The same system is applied to everybody, but the costs are not the same for everybody. The foster care for the child prior to adoption is not evaluated, not controlled, not standardized. The legal services are not standardized. An attorney can get whatever he wants from whatever the couple is willing to pay.

The Perlitzes learned, as Virginia Corey did in India, that influencing government officials, either with monetary rewards or by drawing on personal connections, is fairly standard procedure in making the system work efficiently. In their own vocabulary, "bribery" is not a nice word. There has, of course, been much discussion about whether U. S. citizens conducting business internationally can legitimately violate their own rules of fairness and "do as the Romans do." Adoptive parents who find themselves partaking in such a practice are morally troubled, confused, and frightened of consequences. Michael says, "You never know if you should be bribing this judge or not, and you can get in trouble if you bribe the wrong judge. It's a very difficult situation. You have to totally trust your attorney."

After two weeks in Honduras, during which David was in their custody, the Perlitzes had to return him to foster care and go back to the United States to wait for three months while more legal procedures were completed. Asked what it was like to leave David, Reba answered, "Horrible. I think it is so awful, because then it's a real baby, it's your baby, and you're leaving him. I think what they are trying to do is get you to stay down there for four months." When word came that David was about ready to emigrate, Reba went back to Honduras alone expecting to stay for a week. The final steps in the legal process dragged out to six weeks, in which time she got to know other adoptive parents who make up what she came to see as a specialized tourist industry. The longer the parents have to stay, she maintains, the more money is generated for hotels, restaurants, interpreters, and other services. She found her time there extremely frustrating on the one hand, because she did not know from one week to the next what additional documentation would be required and how long it might take to secure it. On the other hand, it was precious time to get to know her new son. "Whoever gets six weeks with a second child," she asks rhetorically, "without your first child there being weird?"

Hearing the Perlitzes describe their experience in Honduras was troubling and I didn't really want to believe them, but I have heard other stories that corroborate their testimony. Honduras is a very impoverished country—the second poorest, after Haiti, in the Western hemisphere. International adoption offers a new source of revenue, at least to the country's professional elite. There are, of course, people in Honduras who are genuinely concerned about the welfare of children and about the hardships that compel parents to relinquish children to adoption lawyers. There are also principled lawyers who understand their clients' anxiety about getting through the process. But at the time of this writing, to judge from both direct testimony and published accounts, those who see adoption as a way to make money seem to have the upper hand. This naturally angers some Honduran citizens who think of adoption as selling away their nation's children. National uncertainty about the wisdom of international adoption is projected onto adoptive parents by subjecting them to what seems like a very arbitrary procedure.

Whatever ambivalence Reba Perlitz was feeling about the ethics of the situation, it was resolved by a very rare and meaningful coincidence. One day, she and her son's birthmother happened to be in the lawyer's waiting room at the same time:

It was very, very difficult, I think, for both of us. The attorney, in his totally tactless way—there were fifteen people sitting in his office—said, "Oh, there's David's mother." I went over and asked if she wanted to hold him. She was very shy. She had four other boys, and she had a three-year-old. Her husband had divorced her because he wanted to marry someone else, and he had accused her of adultery. She was pregnant at the time. All the children wanted to be with her. She was just incredibly poor, and she just felt that he would have a better life. I saw her about four times, and the day I left, she asked the attorney to translate to me that she wanted me to know that she wasn't doing it for money, and that she was only doing it because she loved him and she wanted him to have a good life. Tears were running down both of our faces. And she wanted me to treat him as if he were my own. And I said, "He is." I had no trouble bonding to him. It was instant.

Michael remembers Reba relating the mother's words just a bit differently:

She said, "I'm not doing this for money. I only want to know that you will love my son and accept him as your blood." That's a quote, to which Reba could say yes. It's like, "Here, with love, take this child and care for it because I can't." And Reba could say, "I will." There was a sense of closure that existed there, which I think maybe no adoptive parents ever get to have. That's very special.

The shared tears in the attorney's office confirmed the paradoxical nature of adoption. The Perlitzes were made concretely aware of the birthmother's poverty and her sorrow, but at the same time, they received her affirmation of David's adoption into their family.

Ideally, when parents who have traveled abroad "come home" with their children—the term is very appropriate in this case—it is with a newfound respect for the child's place of origin. Roy Brower sees this as a matter of basic fairness that also applies to families who simply meet their children at the airport:

By becoming parents of adoptive kids, you have become a cross-cultural family, and that means there needs to be equal appreciation for those other cultures. It's not only, How well can this child adjust to this culture? That's the biggest mistake that's made. I really think that, as much as possible, there needs to be an appreciation for all that the child comes from and represents.

What if the parent's experience in the child's birth country is disillusioning? How, then, do you come to feel an appreciation for the culture? Reba draws a distinction between the Honduran people and the government:

The people on the street in Honduras were wonderful. I never saw
a hand raised against a child. I never saw a child being yelled at.
People would stop me on the street and say, "What a beautiful baby
you have. How old is he? He's so lucky that he's going to the United
States. You're so wonderful to do this."—teenagers, men, women,
everyone. Men make fools of themselves over little kids and they
have no self-consciousness about it at all. The resistance and the
hostility were in the government.

Michael puts the situation they witnessed into a larger historical and
economic context. Describing Honduras as "a real banana republic,"
he says:

The country's been raped—by Spanish conquistadors and by
Americans, primarily, and by American corporate interests specifically.
It's amazing that it survives. I give Honduras a lot of credit for still
being there under the conditions it has to be under. Tegucigalpa is
not really David's place of origin. That's where he was conceived,
but it's not his origin. The ethnic part of him is Miskito Indian,
and you can't get to that culture. That's a sad thing about Central
and South American adoptions. The original cultural and ethnic base
of those geographical locations is gone.

I asked the Perlitzes that question because I was perplexed by it myself.
How would I talk to my daughters about South Korea, a country I
knew, mainly from the newspaper, as an oppressive military dictatorship?
What little information I had about the underlying causes of Korean
adoption yielded an image of a highly patriarchal, class-conscious society
that did not tolerate deviations from a very rigid norm. How could I
begin my relationship with my daughters from a position of respect for
their birth culture?

The year that Grace turned eight and Maria turned five, I took a
brief but intense trip to Korea to meet with people involved in international adoption. I stayed in a home in a neighborhood well away from
the tourist hotels, bought groceries at the market, joined the daily hikers
on their way up a mountainside at 5:30 A.M., attended a church service.
It was not total immersion, however. People spoke English to me, and
my hostess had taken up the fashion for Western furniture, including
beds with mattresses and box springs. I was fortunate to witness the
intangible qualities of Korean life that do not get reported in the Western

press: generosity, courtesy, good humor, easy laughter, and an openness and trust among strangers that you do not see on city streets in the United States. I left Korea feeling great admiration for the people working in adoption agencies, who do so out of a genuine commitment to the welfare of children. Yes, South Korea is, with United States aid, a very militarized country, but the level of personal violence is well below that which Americans tolerate. Yes, it is a highly structured patriarchal society, but the women I met were no shrinking violets.

My most memorable experience in Korea occurred on the very first morning I was there. Arriving at Eastern Child Welfare Society, I was ushered into a large, desk-lined room. Sitting on a couch along the opposite wall was a woman so familiar it was like recognizing an old friend in a crowd of strangers. "This is your daughter's foster mother," the social worker who accompanied her across the room informed me. I had seen her face, a little younger and considerably thinner, on a two-by-three-inch photograph taken the day Grace Keun Young left for the United States. When I compare that photo with the more recent ones, I am surprised that I knew her at all, but the recognition was immediate and certain. We stood together awkwardly, smiling but unable to speak across the language barrier, while we waited for an interpreter and a van that would take us to her house. Her first two questions were "Didn't you bring Grace along?" and "Can she speak Korean?" I was afraid my visit would only disappoint her.

After a long drive to a part of Seoul that I would never find on my own, the van pulled into a narrow side street and parked. The foster mother, who had a name now—Mrs. Cha—led us up a steep brick pathway to the top of a hill. As I followed behind, I imagined my little baby tied on her back with a quilt as she carried groceries home those long months that I spent worrying whether Grace would ever arrive. She lived in a small, traditional house on a courtyard with a watchdog, kim chi pots, and geraniums just like the illustrations in the Korean children's books we have. Clearly, she was not as well off materially as our family is, but there was no cause for either pity or guilt. This was home. The best surprise was waiting inside: an 88-year-old grandmother with deep laugh lines who held my hands and would not let go. "Your daughter received much love in this house," she assured me. We sat on the linoleum floor where Grace learned to crawl, and I made a point of looking out the window, to see what she saw when she pulled herself up for the first time. The conversation consisted mostly of interpreted "thank yous" and expressions of happiness: "I am so happy you came to see us." "I am so happy to meet the people who took care of my daughter."

Had I personally taken Grace out of Mrs. Cha's hands, it would have been a very humbling experience. How would I ever match the nurturing that she and her family had provided? Seven years later, I could show pictures to prove that Grace was still thriving under my care. It obviously gave them great satisfaction to see that. Since then, we have exchanged brief letters, still relying on interpreters. The picture I took of Mrs. Cha and her mother-in-law is enlarged and framed and hangs on our dining room wall along with the photographs of my parents and grandparents. The language barrier allows me to romanticize a bit, of course. If we could talk freely, we might disagree on everything but our love for this one child. No matter. I do feel tremendous gratitude and respect for the care that Korean foster mothers in general provide to children about to be adopted abroad. I had several opportunities to watch them meeting with the social workers or waiting for the doctor at the agency's clinic. The affection bestowed on those babies was very much worthy of notice. I don't think I have seen such enthusiasm for children in an American waiting room. I asked the interpreter who the foster mothers are and she described them as mostly poor women who have finished raising their own children and want to do something for needy children. The money they receive doesn't compensate them for their work. "They wouldn't call themselves poor, though," she explained. "They would call themselves just ordinary people."

Meeting Mrs. Cha and filling part of the void in Grace's history showed me the arrogance of using the words "coming home" for the child's arrival. Grace had just as surely left home to make that journey. When we came home together, from the airport, it was to the task of creating a home on entirely new and mutually beneficial terms.

5

Becoming a Family

When Sally and Gordon Anderson received a referral for an infant girl relinquished at birth in India, they began to do what any other expectant parents would do: mull over the names they might give to this child. They settled on Meena Kathleen, the first an Indian name that would be easy to pronounce, and the second, the name of Sally's older sister. Because of a lengthy legal process, the baby spent her first year in an orphanage, where she became the favorite of one of the staff members. There she was called by a different name, which the staff member asked Sally and Gordon to keep. Sally wanted to show her gratitude for the special care her daughter had received, but she didn't like the other name. There was a principle involved, too, she felt. "I didn't want to say no, but she's our child. We can share, but not to that extent."

The name this little girl would bear was not a matter of indifference, either to Sally or to the woman at the orphanage. To name a child is to claim it as your own. Without the genetic ties that bind most families together, gestures that announce "this is my child" are very important. Choosing a name for a child adopted from another country is by no means trivial, since names can also signal ethnicity. Yes, there certainly are parents who call their newly arrived children Lindsay or Ryan without much thought to the names' significance. Like the Shirleys of the 1930s and the Debbies of the 1950s, these children become living records of American popular culture. However, if their names are Lindsay Hee Ae and Ryan Luis, they tell a different story. For very many parents, the child's name is a symbol of how they intend to negotiate the cultural distance between the child's past and future.

The way in which my children were named is a good illustration. It is not considered propitious in Korea for a child to go nameless for very long. Children abandoned at police stations or relinquished in maternity hospitals are very quickly named, most often by a social worker.

95

A birthparent's family name, if known, or an assigned, common name, such as Kim or Lee, comes first. This is followed by a combination of two monosyllabic names, which must have a special meaning that confers good fortune on the child or suggests desirable traits of character. Despite being accustomed to names that simply sound nice and mean nothing, the adoptive parents sometimes take the meaning of their child's Korean name as an omen or as evidence that fate has brought this particular child to their family. An adoption worker I interviewed in Korea chuckled when he told me how tedious this naming process can get. Sometimes the social workers just open the Seoul telephone directory and point. I laughed, too, but this did not shake my conviction that my own daughters' names are of profound symbolic import. Fate must have guided the social worker's finger.

Before we learned who Grace was, we had her name ready. It was, to begin with, my grandmother's name, and passing it on to my child was a way of placing her in my family lineage. I could have named her Alma after my other grandmother, but Grace had extra appeal. Being allowed to raise a child not of our own making was, after all, a gift of grace. Grace also seemed less culturally specific than other names we might have chosen. The concept of an undeserved blessing, divinely bestowed, has a name at least in every culture where Christianity is represented. As a personal attribute of beauty and charm, "grace" has a counterpart in many other languages. As Grace, my daughter would thus transcend cultural divisions and be, quite simply, a member of the human family. Her Korean name, Keun Young, means "root of a flower," the perfect metaphor for the qualities we hoped she would possess: hardiness, vitality, and the potential to blossom again and again. There was no doubt that we would keep Keun Young as her middle name. We thought of it, rather, as a coequal name, to be used if she ever chose to reclaim her Korean identity. Maria's naming was a variation on the theme: a paternal grandmother's name—one that has been assimilated into many languages—followed by the name she was given at birth, Eun Sook. By fateful coincidence, this means "pure benefit," that is to say, "grace."

With the encouragement of adoption placement workers, parents of Korean-born children now commonly do retain a part of the original name as a middle name or as a third given name. They may use the personal name, as I did, or the birthparent's family name, as a way of preserving that connection. Other children, too, bear middle names, and sometimes first names, that indicate their national origins. Some agencies in India require that parents give their children at least one Indian name in order to maintain a tie to the culture of their birth.

Yet, even older Korean children are likely to be renamed on their arrival in the United States. I have felt some discomfort on behalf of those who get stamped with cute, faddish names that obscure their heritage. Yet, I can appreciate that such names may offer at least temporary solace to children who are self-conscious about being different from their peers. Having to explain to English-speaking children with no intercultural experience that your name is, indeed, Byung Ook, can be very awkward. On the other hand, some children may think it worth the effort to preserve their original identity. Fred and Linda Truman gave nine-year-old Soon Hee the choice of keeping her name or taking another that they had in mind for her. She felt, "I was Korean, and I should have a Korean name. An American name didn't really suit me. It's not because I didn't like the name, but it just wasn't me." Children from Spanish-speaking countries can more easily use the name that denotes "me," because the increasing numbers of Hispanic-Americans have made names like Miguel and Rosario more familiar. Anglicized to Michael and Rosie, they obscure ethnic origins but retain individual identity. As more Asian people immigrate to the United States, it may be more feasible to preserve the names of children adopted from Asian countries. My children pronounce the names of their Hmong and Cambodian classmates with no sense of strangeness.

Besides conferring an individual identity on the child, a name can also signify family membership. If the child is given the name of one of the parent's relatives, the act of naming implants the child in the family lineage. Mary and Bill MacNamara were pleased to learn that their son's birthmother herself had chosen to give him the same name as his birthfather, who had participated in the decision to place him for adoption. Now Billy bears the name of his adoptive father, as well, so his full name acknowledges his attachment to two families. Giving a family name to an adopted child also makes a statement to the extended family: The parent is claiming the right to share the family heritage with a child who is not a blood relative. The constant use of the child's name thus serves as a reminder that the family accepts the child as one of its own. In some families, unfortunately, this claim is disputed. Tina and George Molinari named their first son, born in Korea, after both their fathers. When Tina later gave birth to a son, one of her uncles was angry that she had not saved the names for this child, the "first-born," to whom, in his opinion, they rightfully belonged.

Whether it is intentional or simply uncomprehending, a relative's failure to accept a child as a genuine member of the family strains extended family relationships. Often, refusal to accept the children is indicative of deeper rifts in the family. Chuck Stensrud had been trying to heal old wounds in his relationship with his father when he and Margo Speiser adopted their children from Korea, but he has given up since learning that the children's pictures are not allowed among the other family portraits. In this case, it may be race rather than adoption itself that is at issue. The two domestically adopted grandchildren are acknowledged. The hurt is greatest when the children ask why they so seldom see this set of grandparents, while they get to visit Margo's parents for several days at a time.

Seeing your beloved child rejected for as mindless a reason as race or a different set of genes is cause for sorrow and anger that can turn into life-long resentment. Frequently, though, the resistance is short-lived. I have heard many stories about skeptical grandparents who were won over as soon as they saw the child. It happens often enough that it is held out as a hope to prospective parents who aren't sure whether to proceed against their own parents' wishes. Rita Garman offers her father as an example:

> There's always some good that can come out of everything, even if it's just a development inside the person—a capacity to relate and deal with other people, to have empathy or sympathy. My Dad just about shocked me. He was the most resistant to our adoptions. He is not one to speak out on any matter, but once we were sitting at the table and the subject of baby Louise, the test-tube baby in England, came up. He said, "Look at all the children in the world who need homes. What are people doing that for?" I thought, Why, you rascal. You're the one who gave me the most headaches about adoption. And here he was totally reversing his viewpoint. I could tell he had integrated the children into his family.

Sometimes, the family's resistance is not really rejection but poorly articulated worry about how well they can manage the confusion or the racial hostility the child might encounter. Sally Anderson was offended when her mother, who presumably understood how eager she was to adopt children, suggested that she wait for one that wasn't so dark. Her father-in-law was better able to distinguish between his own feelings and his concerns about what the child might experience.

> I remember him saying, "You'll never know how people in the outside world will treat him. He will probably not always be accepted, but he'll be sure to be accepted in the family." That was real assurance that everything was going to be just fine.

Integration into the extended family takes more than a kind reception or simple tolerance of the child's racial difference, however. Constant awareness of difference has to give way to affection for the child's individual character before full family membership is achieved. When Grace first arrived, my parents were very eager to show off the cute little Korean baby and to tell the story of her adoption. I was happy to see them so excited, but I am more content now that the novelty has worn off and they treat the girls as honest-to-goodness grandchildren. Though I had not intended Grace's name as a test of the family's openness to an internationally adopted child, their reaction to it gives continuing proof that the children have been welcomed into the family, with all the rights that confers on them. Some of my relatives seem honored, even, that I have passed on my grandmother's name and thus preserved the cherished memories it evokes. For example, when Grace showed my aunt a quilted pillow that she had made, my aunt said to her, "Your Grandma Grace would have loved to see this. She used to make those, too."

The quilted pillow is just one example of a very common tendency in adoptive families: to look for resemblances and affinities that confirm the child's "fit" in the family. Pointing out similarities benefits the children, as well, as Mary MacNamara explains:

> If Katie's said something hurtful to me and she's feeling remorseful afterwards, I tell her about the bad things I felt about my mother as a kid, so that she'll know it's not just her. I say things like, "You know, you're just like me," or "You're just like your Dad. He used to do that, too." I think that's good for them. It bonds them within the family, and it's the truth. My son's personality is so like my husband's it's amazing.

It is not only a matter of matching virtues. Traits thought of as negative can work as well. Commenting on Katie's sometimes recalcitrant behavior, her father says, "She and Mary go at it real well. They're both stubborn. They're very much alike." When Jessica Martinson was at her wits' end with Anita's moody withdrawal, her parents reminded her how moody and withdrawn she had been at Anita's age. Suddenly moodiness was not just a problem but a shared trait of character to help bridge the distance between them.

In the absence of such similarities, parents have to be cautious not to make their child feel like a misfit. Although Rachel Storber has had a smooth relationship with her 15-year-old daughter ever since she arrived from Vietnam in infancy and feels entirely bonded with her, she is conscious of fundamental differences in their personalities. Rachel and her husband are both talkative, outgoing people who place high value on having friends. Suzanne is quiet, enjoys solitude, and prefers keeping her feelings private. Citing studies that claim that environment counts for more than 50 percent of a child's personality, Rachel says, "But there's that other percentage. I always wonder what it is that makes her do this or that, and how she will turn out. Even to this day, I worry about pushing my own personality on her." Research into the force of genetics, such as the widely reported studies of identical twins raised apart, leaves adoptive parents feeling uncertain about how much influence they have over their children's behavior. There is a risk that differences in character, especially those the parents find troublesome, will be too easily attributed to heredity, with a fatalism that makes the child feel excluded, or even responsible, for being not quite right. In some cases, personality traits may be falsely attributed to race or ethnic origin, compounding the mystery: "Are all Korean children this stubborn?" a frustrated parent asked at a workshop I attended. A wise parent, confronted with a puzzle of a child, watches in awe-filled anticipation as the pieces fall into place, aware that every child is ultimately one-of-a-kind. Such patience is required with birthchildren, as well. Betty Ringstad, the mother of two adopted and two birthchildren, all but one of them grown, is surprised to see the strongest reflection of herself in her Korean-born daughter.

It makes sense that parents adopting across racial lines would focus on similarities in personality traits. In placing white infants with childless white couples, adoption agencies used to match the physical characteristics of the two sets of parents as closely as they could. Telling the new parents, "Oh, your baby looks just like you," offered them simultaneous congratulations and reassurance. This is not the first comment one would think to make to a parent who has adopted a child from another country.

Eventually, however, it may be appropriate, to many parents' surprise. Very shortly, the awareness of difference that many of us expected to have all our lives gives way to familiarity with our own unique child. We simply "forget" that our children don't look like us. When strangers ask where they came from, we are honestly taken aback. Mary MacNamara says,

> I remember when my kids were babies, thinking, How do they know this baby is Korean? It's really dumb. My son has black, black hair and darker-than-average skin. How could they not know? When he was about three years old, my husband put him on the bike and was riding up and down the street. I remember that his hair was blowing back and he looked like that kid in the Peanuts cartoon whose mom rides him up and down. I saw him from a distance and didn't realize at first that it was my husband and son. Suddenly, I thought, That's my son? He's so dark. It just amazed me.

What parents notice first when we look at our children is not black hair or dark skin or "slanted" eyes, which look nothing like the caricatures of Asian eyes anyway, but how they laugh through their noses or knit their eyebrows when they are telling us something serious. Some of these may, in fact, be family traits. Proximity seems to breed similarity. Our children pick up our vocabularies and imitate our gestures and facial expressions. In surprisingly many cases, this gives rise to a physical resemblance obvious even to people outside the family. The first time I saw Steven Duval standing next to his father, I thought he was the other son, the one born into the family. Their matching postures and facial expressions were more striking than the difference in their coloring and their eye shape. Betty Ringstad's daughter, her match in personality, also resembles her physically. People they know in the local Korean community also comment on how much Kathy looks like her mother.

Skeptics might dismiss this enumeration of similarities as an attempt to gloss over the fact of the child's adoption and the racial difference between parent and child. I probably would have thought that myself prior to 1981. But now, with some experience, I agree with Mary MacNamara that pointing out likenesses "bonds them within the family, *and it's the truth.*" Many parents, no matter what their expectations, come to feel that their particular children were "meant to be" theirs. Some similarities crop up too early to be learned. Others are uncanny enough to give you the shivers. When Grace turned out to be a very verbal

child, friends joked, "Well, it's in the genes." When she learned to
read as if by magic, as I had, they asked, "Are you sure she's adopted?"
The day she brought her school directory home from first grade and
showed me the check marks she had made by the names of all the
children she knew, I thought, This *is* my kid! Maria and I share a
penchant for fantasy, while Grace is very literal and concrete, but otherwise I have thought of Maria more as a character unto herself. When
my Danish grandmother died at age 96, I skimmed through the family
mentally, thinking what a loss it was that none of us had inherited
her playfulness, her whimsical humor, her dramatic flair, her passionate
emotional range—until I landed on Maria. A treasured memory took
on greater significance: Wheeling my grandma through the nursing home
with Maria on her lap. "Where did you get that beautiful baby, Alma?"
someone called out. "Oh, I had to go a lo-o-ong way to find *this* one."

Evidence that affirms a child's "rightness" for the family is eagerly
taken to heart. When Reba and Michael Perlitz received a referral for
a boy, it was an easy decision to name him after Reba's father, who
was terminally ill. Her father was very honored by the choice, especially
since his own son and namesake had been killed in the Vietnam War.
By the time they went to Honduras to meet David, Reba's father had
died. There they learned that the child assigned to them had been
replaced by another, born six weeks later—born, in fact, on the very
day of his adoptive grandfather's death. Reba took this as a sign that
"he was really meant to be ours." Michael attributes to Reba a spiritual
understanding of adoption: "She considers it basically a correction of a
mistake at birth. This child was born to be ours, but was born in the
wrong place. We and his birthparents act as a team." Mary MacNamara
says much the same thing: "Maybe God had to take a real circuitous
route, but He got my children to me in the best way. I think they
were destined to be my children, and they always will be."

Whether or not they attribute the match to God or to fate or to coincidence, many parents sense an inevitability about their relationship with
their children. This feeling, again, could be dismissed as justification,
were it not so real to the parents who experience it. To many of us, it
comes as an entire surprise. We may have intended, from the beginning,
to treat our adopted children as if they were our own, to behave within
our family as if it were as natural and normal as a family formed by
birth. What we find, instead, is that "as if" falls by the wayside. There
is no need for pretense or for effort, because the children *are* our own,

our families *are* natural and normal. Our understanding of "family" shifts, by force of experience, from a biologically based entity to one bonded in spirit. Even if our children can be seen, objectively, as replacements for the genetic heirs to whom we planned to give birth, they become irreplaceable themselves. Their birth situations and their adoptions are no longer anomalous but essential. Mary MacNamara puts it very well:

> It's always been important to me for my kids to know that I love their birthmothers, because their mothers are part of them. That's the way it is. I may want to change that, but if I changed that, they wouldn't be who they are, and they wouldn't be Korean. I wouldn't want them to be anything other than what they are, and I wouldn't want any other children than the ones I have.

This is a message that Mary, like many of us, wants to convey to her children over and over until they have no doubt about being wanted and accepted unconditionally. Her daughter Katie was complaining one day about having parents slightly older than those of her classmates: "Why did you wait so long to adopt us?" she asked. "When I get to be thirty, you're going to be so old you might not even be alive." Mary's answer was quick and confident: "I told her it was her fault because I had to wait for her to get born." A woman from India whose family runs an orphanage there told me of her amazement that American parents seemed open to any child at all, despite skin color, mother's religion, or illegitimate status. For most of us—though, to be sure, not all of us—"any child at all" becomes, by some miracle of fate or human psychology, exactly the right child.

How jarring it is, then, to be wheeling your grocery cart through the produce section, feeling for all the world like a real parent in search of vegetables palatable to your own children, and to hear an unfamiliar voice ask, "Are those kids yours?" The initial, but usually unvoiced, response is incredulity that anyone would question the relationship. "How can they not be my children," Mary MacNamara thinks, "if they're more important to me than my siblings or any other so-called blood relative? How can they not be my kids, if they're the ones I would die for?" Nearly all the parents I talked with find situations like this awkward, but virtually no one chooses to address the issue of entitlement with a complete stranger. Most of us will simply say yes, hoping that will end the inquiry. It seldom does. Other questions typically follow: Did you adopt them? Where are they from? How long have you had them? Do they speak English? Are they really sisters? A few of the curious delve further into the family's circumstances: Do you know anything about his background? What happened to his real parents? Do you have any children of your own? Can't you?

The situation is complicated because the questions are usually asked with a friendly smile and no ill intent. In fact, many people stand ready to congratulate us for doing a humanitarian deed. "Aren't those children lucky?" a woman in the restaurant booth next to ours exclaimed to her companion. "I suppose you can learn to love them just like regular children." The questions and comments betray ignorance about how adoption works and the day-to-day experience of adoptive families, not to mention insensitivity to the children themselves. Sally Anderson sums it up: "We don't get negative comments, but we sure hear a lot of dumb things." Given that internationally adoptive families are both numerically rare and wrongly perceived, many parents feel an obligation to help educate the public. Even if they don't welcome the questions, they use them as an opportunity to explain and advocate for international adoption. Betty Ringstad advises,

> If you're going to get mad at people and huff at them or put them down, then you don't accomplish anything. I think each one of us has to accomplish a little bit with people we come in contact with in our world. If we do that, we'll help make the world a better place. You have to respect the fact that people are at all different levels of enlightenment.

This requires tact, of course, and tact is not always easy to maintain, especially if the questions feel intrusive. Tina Molinari, visibly pregnant, was holding her son by the hand when someone walked up and said, "What's the matter? Didn't you know you could have kids?" Tina gets tired of hearing the unsubstantiated but popular belief that adoption is a remedy for infertility. The implication that the child's presence in the family is only a means to a more desirable end is very hurtful. On the contrary, Patti Cronin felt that her children were quite sufficient and that infertility "just didn't matter any more." Getting pregnant after all was a bonus, but bearing a child was no greater joy than picking one up at the airport. "The love is the same," she says, and other parents of both adopted and birthchildren corroborate that.

Having the relationship between siblings questioned within their hearing is also troubling, as Mary MacNamara explains,

The hardest thing was, people used to come up and say to me all the time, "Are they really brother and sister?" I felt really uncomfortable. I didn't want to lie, and yet, I didn't want to say no, because my little kids were looking up at me to see what I'm going to say, and if I said no, the damage to their sense of family would have been terrible. And yet it wasn't important information to this total stranger who was asking me this awful question, who I'm sure never realized how harmful it was. They would walk away and never remember it. So finally, after some weeks of hassling with myself over it, I decided that I don't owe them anything, but I do my children. So I'd say yes. And even then I'd get people who'd say, "Oh, you know what I mean." And I'd say sternly, "Yes, I know exactly what you mean." And then they'd get the idea that maybe they had offended me.

I used to answer "Are they really sisters?" with "They are now," but having to add a qualifier was still troubling. After much experience, I've come around to an answer that implicitly questions how siblinghood is determined. "Well, they fight in the backseat of the car," I say.

The most compelling reason for tact is not to kill rudeness with kindness, but to spare our children from hurt. "It's a really dangerous situation," Mary MacNamara claims. "If I got angry, would my children then think, 'What's the matter with me that Mom gets mad when people want to talk about me?' " I tried, for a while, to mask my irritation with the added force of pride: "Yes, these are my two beautiful daughters, and I'm so glad they are." I hoped it would put my children at ease, but instead it made me uncomfortable. My answer objectified them just as much as the question did. So then I tried passing some of the questions on to Grace, who was four at the time, to demonstrate that she could indeed hear and understand English. When I heard her answer a simple "Hi, how are you?" with "I was born in Korea and so was my sister," I decided it was not fair to put her on the spot. From then on I have given short, unembellished, and sometimes misleading answers— "How long have you had them?" "Oh, forever."—and then averted my eyes to discourage any more questions. Once Grace asked, in a stage whisper, "Do you like that?" That was the cue that I needed to explain my feelings and check on hers. Now we make jokes like "Where'dja git those kids? At K-Mart?" and Maria pinches the dog's face and says, "Ooooh, you got such chubby cheeks."

Avoiding the questions is less helpful to the children than demonstrating how best to answer them. Children do, indeed, get questioned themselves, mostly by their peers. Beth Larsen, at nine, is accustomed to explaining her family make-up to curious friends who want to know what happened to her "real" mother:

> Usually, they can't understand. I say, "Well, my real mother lives with me," and they say, "Yes, but you lived in Korea." And I say, "Yes, my birthmother lived in Korea, and she still does." And they say, "Well, isn't she your real mother?" and I say, "No, my real mother is the person who's raising me." People ask me questions especially about if my sister is my natural sister, and I say, "No, but usually it just doesn't matter, because it's just like she was born after me. She'd be just the same. It wouldn't make any difference to me."

Having been through five more years of such questioning than Beth has, Amy Andrews has grown weary of it.

> At first I just answered, but then after a while I said, "Why must you know all this about me? Does this make me different from you or something? You should look at my personality, not my background." But then I got used to it again, and I just blurted out the same answers. They didn't mean me any harm. They were just curious. I've never been able to say, You're being rude, but I've been thinking to myself, I wish they'd stop asking these questions.

Answering questions is a sensitive matter for Anita Martinson, because her history of abuse and her life as a streetchild might set her apart from her classmates. Her mother has advised her not to answer if she doesn't feel like it, to say she doesn't know the answer, or even to make up a story—to say that her birthparents died, for example. "It's a real fine line," Jessica says, "because I don't want her to be ashamed of her past. But she thought she *had* to tell everybody."

The sight of Asian children with white parents seems to prompt the most direct inquiries. Parents of Latin American children report a more subtle kind of testing. Someone who saw the Martinsons together commented, "This is your daughter? She doesn't look like you," to which Jessica responded, "Oh, don't you think so?" Anita was upset at the comment, but pleased with her mother's quick thinking. Sometimes even ordinary compliments like "She's so cute" are offered with a look and in a tone of voice that seems to demand explanation. "You know exactly what's going through their minds," Roy Brower says, "and I'll be damned if I'm going to give in to it. So we just say thank you." A social worker told me a story about a client of hers who was in the grocery store with her four-year-old birthdaughter and her one-year-old Hispanic son. A woman approached and asked pointedly, "What does their father look like?" With no hesitation, the little girl answered, "He looks like a frog."

This is not paranoia, nor is it shame at being exposed as second-class parents, not fortunate enough to have children of our own. On the contrary, we are a very proud lot. We do get pleasure out of watching people genuinely admire our children, as any parent would. A good share of us came to international adoption as seasoned nonconformists, thinking ourselves well suited to build families in some way other than the norm. As a general rule, we welcome attention from strangers that is offered with kindness, understanding, and above all, sensitivity to our children's need for family security. What we dislike is being called to account, in the presence of our children, at the whim of anyone whose curiosity is aroused by our difference. Being treated as a sideshow freak, available for gawking at, is an experience familiar to people of minority status, who do not relish it either. What stranger would ask a white parent with a white baby, Did you give birth to that baby yourself or did you hire a surrogate? It is obvious difference that must be justified.

On occasion, ignorant comments may cross the line into racism. Mary MacNamara told of an obnoxious and profane man, mad at the world, who swore at her "Chink kids." Ron Josephson and Gwen Ryan endured a tirade, while eating in a restaurant, from a deranged man who spotted their baby and insisted that Asians had a shorter gestation period and were overpopulating the world. The other examples I heard could also be dismissed as isolated instances of mad raving. Stony silence and stares are more disturbing. Several parents told me of traveling with their children in parts of the country where international adoption is very rare and feeling as though a direct question would have eased the tension. Elsbeth Saunders has noticed a difference in the way people react to her two adopted children. The son from India draws attention and questions, but when she is alone with her biracial black-white son in a crowd of white people, they are met with silence and sometimes disapproving expressions. "You can just see them putting us in a category: multiracial kid, single parent, food stamps." When her husband is with them, the curiosity *is* voiced and the faces are friendlier.

When the questions come from children, it is easier to take them at face value. Children usually ask directly for the exact information they want, with no judgment implied. The first time it happened to me was when an African-American child in the park asked, "Are you her mom? Then how come you're white and she's tan?" This child was obviously learning the social meaning of skin color and having to reckon with a situation that didn't fit the scheme. I took as much time as he would give me to explain international adoption. Parents also tend to read the comments differently when they come from members of the child's ethnic group or other people of color. Even "What a wonderful thing you have done for this child" is tolerable when it is based on first-hand knowledge of the conditions in which the child would otherwise have lived. People of the same ethnicity are more likely to regard the children as small human beings than as novelty items. Black adults who approach Elsbeth and her son usually speak directly to him, and she welcomes that as positive reinforcement of his African-American identity. I feel the same way when a Korean adult pats Maria's cheeks. I know that she is being admired by someone with a deeply ingrained appreciation for round-faced beauty.

A few of the parents I interviewed had run headlong into the debate about the propriety of international adoption. There were critical comments from African-American people who oppose transracial adoption, and questions from Vietnamese immigrants puzzled about the adoption of children from other Asian countries. How will he learn his own language? and Why isn't he living with his own kind? arise out of a firm definition of cultural boundaries in which cross-cultural family allegiances make no sense. Most parents, though, reported positive reactions from people of color. Since her son's arrival from Korea, Debbie Whelan finds herself being greeted more openly by black people in her racially mixed neighborhood.

> The barriers have sort of tumbled down. My guess is that there's a
> recognizable symbol that you are open-minded in your attitudes toward
> people of different races. There's just a different acceptance of you.
> I have some black friends who also guess that this is the case.

I must admit to curiosity about how Korean adults perceive us as a family. It matters a great deal to me that they affirm our being together. If the waitress in a Korean restaurant, in talking to the girls, refers to me as "your mom," I am ready for whatever challenges we face on the way down the street.

How effectively parents answer the questions and comments depends in large part on how firmly bonded we believe we are: we with our children and our children with us. Most of the parents I talked with felt that their children were truly at home in their families, but this is certainly not always the case. There are parents who continue to see their children as strangers to a degree and to treat them as exotic little objects. They may even make a display of the child's difference and invite conversation that equates international adoption with American noblesse oblige. Silvia Kowalski felt hurt every time her mother referred to her son as "my baby Jason" and then to Silvia and her sister as "my Colombian daughters." "She wouldn't say, 'This is my white American baby,' " Silvia points out. Her separate status in the family was reinforced by the role she was assigned as a curiosity in the small town where the family lived. "It was in the town's newspaper about how the Kowalskis adopted from Colombia. People knew me simply because of how I looked and said, 'Oh, you're the Kowalski kid who's adopted from Colombia.' "

Recently, much has been said, in both the professional and popular media, about children who remain—to use the current therapeutic term—"unattached" to their adoptive families or to anyone else. The parents of these children have to be particularly sensitive to comments that set them apart. Some families are caught, from the time of the child's arrival, in an exhausting struggle to find harmony. Others nearly come undone during the child's adolescence, a period of life when the resilience of family ties is, and ought to be, tested. Some of the parents I talked with whose children are beyond adolescence were surprised to find that the strain had actually tightened the ties. In relatively few cases, there is so little compatibility between parent and child that the only recourse the parents see is to "disrupt" the adoption—legally terminate the relationship. Usually, this is a very sad solution to a pattern of behavior that threatens the family's very stability: cases in which the child sexually abuses siblings or threatens the parents with violence, for example.

So-called unattached children are more likely to have been adopted after toddlerhood, and the psychological dynamics that inhibit family bonding seem most often due to the child's previous experience. Just what constitutes abuse varies from one culture to another, but children who feel abused respond in similar ways. Whether they are adopted domestically or internationally, children who have learned to distrust adults commonly protect themselves by keeping a safe emotional distance. Observing Anita's behavior, Jessica Martinson has concluded that attachment can be learned, but it requires knowing one's needs and being able to depend on others to satisfy them, something that was foreign to Anita's experience.

She didn't know you had choices about these things. She didn't know that you could tell someone that your shoes didn't fit anymore. She grew so rapidly after she came, and she would stuff her feet into the smallest shoes she could, but who in her life had she ever been able to tell? She could not understand why I wanted to look at her school papers. Why would I care about her school papers? Now if I don't look at them, I'm in trouble, but I bet that took a year before she really understood that I wanted to see how she was doing. She thought that was really crazy, that I cared about that.

Bonding is not necessarily a reciprocal matter. Parents may feel very much attached to a child and thoroughly committed to the child's welfare even as the child stays isolated in self-protection or anger or sorrow. If the parents have the emotional maturity and the intercultural sensitivity to empathize with the child's feelings, they are better able to make such an attachment. Nevertheless, the child, lacking an aerial view of the forest of human experience, may remain intimidated by the size of the trees, no matter how much guidance the parents offer. Parents also have the advantage of power to form or break the attachment and can thus choose to hold on, no matter what. The bonds look more tenuous from the perspective of a child who has little voice in the matter and speaks another language besides.

The fact that an older child does not form an emotional attachment to the new family does not necessarily mean that the child is lacking in the capacity to love. Silvia Kowalski believes that true bonding may be too much to expect in some situations.

I think my sister and I were beyond that age where the bond between parents and children forms. To me, they're not my Mom and Dad, not emotionally. To an infant they would be. I have known ten mothers, all of which I had to call Mother whether I wanted to or not, and then to suddenly be forced to call yet another couple Mom and Dad— To this day, I thank them so much for the chance that they have given me, and I regret a lot of the grief I caused them. Now we're able to talk on an adult basis, and they understand more where a lot of my acts came out of. If I have an issue, I will turn to them. I don't always turn to them, but I know they are there.

Despite the fact that she does not feel emotionally bonded to her parents, Silvia realizes that her children, if she has any, will feel affection for them as grandparents. The detached, but cordial, nature of her relationship with them will not impede that.

Grief at the loss of the birth family can make it especially difficult for a child to become attached to the adoptive family. It is even harder if the parents see adoption in the United States as salvation for a child of poverty and fail to recognize that the child has experienced a great loss. The adoptive family must be prepared to wait out the grieving process, especially if the child, feeling alone in sorrow, resists the new parents' sympathy as an encroachment. Armando Jordan was nine years old when his mother was severely disabled in an accident. "She went into a coma, and that caused a terrible tragedy. She lost her memory, so she became crazy. They took her away from me, and my sister left me, and I had to sleep in the streets." Within a year, after being taken to an orphanage by a compassionate stranger, he was placed with an American couple in their fifties. "I asked them how far away I was from home, and they told me it was miles and miles and miles away and it was over the ocean. I yelled out, 'Why did you let them do that to me?'" After nine years, he is still mourning the loss of his mother, whom he remembers—and quite naturally idealizes—as young and very loving. He dreams of finding her again, even if she is lying comatose in a hospital. Talking to his parents about his grief has not been helpful, because they only admonish him to forget the past, which would mean giving up his memories of being genuinely loved. Without those memories, his life seems of less value. If he cannot bring his past with him into the family, he cannot be a part of it himself. Besides human nature, culture also figures here. Armando's strong filial devotion to his mother and her memory is very much in keeping with his early Latin upbringing.

Soon Hee Truman initially felt more anger than sorrow about her separation from her birthparents, and she expressed it by refusing to show any affection to her new parents. "I didn't want to call them Mom and Dad, but one day I was in the bathroom and I had a bloody nose. I remember calling her Mom for the first time because I was so scared." It was only in retrospect, after leaving home in adulthood, that Soon Hee realized that she had a firm place in her family. Linda, her mother, tells how surprised Soon Hee was that her parents would want to stay in touch and hear news about her life, especially after her turbulent adolescence. This new sense of belonging has brought her grief about her birth family into focus and also helped to relieve it.

> You know, it does get better. You begin to realize that, whatever the reason that you got adopted, at least the parents who adopted you obviously wanted you and wanted to raise you. Sometimes I think to myself, God, I'm so happy—I'm so lucky to have a family. I can't imagine being adopted by anybody else.

Children adopted in infancy have no reason to question their family relationships until they observe that most children tend to look like their parents. If they don't notice that themselves, others will certainly draw it to their attention. Some younger children ease into this new awareness by underscoring the ways they do resemble their parents. According to her mother, Michelle Gaartner likes to pick out matching clothes to wear, so that she and her mother will "look like twins." Adding a bit of wishful thinking to the fact that her parents' hair is greying, eight-year-old Margaret Chatten doubts that her classmates know she's adopted because "my mom and dad's hair used to be my color."

Several, but by no means all, of the parents I interviewed reported that their children use "You're not my real mom" as a manipulative device within the family, but it is neither intended nor heard as a threat to family bonds. It's just the handiest weapon to wield when things don't go their way. If other children question them about their "real" parents, they give answers similar to Beth Larsen's. Children, as well as parents, affirm their family's normality when the need arises. Beth Larsen is surprised that "some of my friends think it makes a big difference in my life just because I'm adopted. It doesn't to me, but because they don't have the experience, they think that." Asked how she would explain the adoption experience to them, she answered:

> I'd say it's just practically the exact same as living with your birthparents. There's only about two things that are different. One thing is that you probably don't look much like your parents. You

might, though. You could end up looking like them, and people would say, "You know, you look like your parents that you live with now a lot more than you probably did your birthparents." And another thing is that you wouldn't just sort of come from a hospital and know where the hospital is. But it's mostly just the same. You act like their children. They act like parents. You go to school and they pick you up from school.

It is easy for parents to lure ourselves into thinking that the test of our family bonds is the degree of our children's serenity. We would like our kids always to feel in their hearts what Beth tells her friends in the fourth grade. In fact, even firmly attached children can have explosive moments and phases in which they seem alienated. Bonding, however it works, does not give us absolute power to steer our children away from unhappy feelings. Amy Andrews was adopted in infancy by parents whom she depicts as loving, knowledgeable about Korean culture, concerned for her welfare, and worthy of her respect. At age ten, after a peaceful childhood, she suddenly turned "mean" as she describes it, told her parents she hated them and refused them the place in her life they had occupied until then. A counselor who worked with her focused on abandonment as the probable cause, though there were no clues in Amy's own mind to help her name the source of her rage. At fourteen, she talks in the past tense about this difficult period in her life, and the family is intact.

There is an interesting dimension to Amy's story: She writes fiction and often writes in the first person about a Korean immigrant girl living with her parents and an older brother. "I've just wished that I had a Korean family," she says, "and that I was birth and that we moved to America, but I never think of that person that's my birthmom. I just wish I had a Korean family." This reminded me of a wish that Grace expressed one time when she was about seven: "I wish that you looked like us, and that you were Korean, and we were born in your tummy." The longing was not for a different family, but for an even firmer attachment to *this* family. And, to my relief, she did not say, "I wish I looked like you." In our case, Mom is the one who doesn't match.

Amy is an only child, and an important part of the Korean family fiction is the brother: "I've always wished I had an older adopted brother who could go through something with me and help me and stuff."

Many parents are sensitive to the possibility that their child might feel lonely in an otherwise all-white family, especially if the other children were born into it. Betty Ringstad recalls,

> Once our older daughter said, before we had adopted our son, "Isn't it interesting that Kathy is the only one in our family who isn't related by blood." The good Lord must have put the thoughts into me, because I said, "Well, I don't know about that. Daddy and I aren't related by blood. So I guess Daddy and Kathy and I are the only ones in this family that aren't related by blood." It completely diffused the issue. After that, we talked about, We're a family because we decided to be a family. I felt inspired, I really did, because my instant thought was, Oh, it's going to hurt Kathy.

The risk of exclusion is frequently cited as the reason for a second international adoption. Laurie Means and her husband plan to adopt another child to "diffuse the otherness of Melanie," their Korean-born daughter:

> Right now she is a kind of otherness in our family. There's the Caucasian and the other. There is that sense, even though you don't articulate it and you wouldn't ever treat anyone as an other, it still is there, just because it's there. So if there were another culture— black or Indian—that would say, There's three different cultures in this family. No one is an other.

When Donna Frazee and her husband agreed to accept three siblings, rather than the single child they had requested, the comfort-in-numbers argument was influential in their change of mind. The Frazee children do fall into natural subgroups: The birthdaughter and the Caucasian adopted son, who were the only children for seven years; the three children from Colombia, who have a shared history; and the "little squirt," from India, whom everyone dotes on. In other families, temperament may be a stronger affinity than national origin. When Marlene and Dan Duval selected their daughter from an album of waiting children, they had in mind a Korean sibling for their son and a sister for their birthdaughter. Their family of four would thus include two sets of pairs: the boys and the girls, the white birthchildren and the Asian adopted children. What happened instead is that a strong alliance developed between Pam, the birthdaughter and Steven, the adopted son. She was the one who fended off comments by making clear that he was her brother, and in family disputes, it was usually the two of them against either their older brother or their younger sister.

Living in an internationally adoptive family also affects the way in which the family's birthchildren experience "family." Psychologists and sociologists have identified typical problems for siblings of adopted children, such as feelings of displacement; concern about fairness when an older adopted child is given more behavioral leeway; jealousy of siblings who presumably were "chosen" rather than accidents of nature, and so on. These reactions are common in both domestically and internationally adoptive families.

There are, however, some additional concerns for the siblings of internationally or interracially adopted children. Marlene Duval believes, for example, that the relationship between sisters Pam and Anne was in some ways strained by their racial difference. Anne, as a rarity, attracted more attention, which made Pam feel inadequate.

> What I was seeing was that together they were beautiful sisters, because they were so contrasting. But when Pam and Anne would walk down the street, Pam always felt that everybody was looking at Anne, because she was the pretty one. Well, Anne didn't feel like the pretty one. She felt like the outsider.

The extra attention that a minority child draws certainly can be painful for the birthchild, or for an adopted Caucasian child, who thus fades into the background. It can be an ongoing source of tension. Young siblings have some interesting and creative ways of coping with that kind of exclusion. Mark Truman insisted until he was well into elementary school that he was Korean like his sisters. His mother guesses that he honestly believed that, because the family attended Korean school on Saturdays and ate Korean food to make Soon Hee more comfortable. Bob and Rita Garman's seven-year-old daughter gets angry when anyone refers to her as white. Her family's dominant skin color is tan, and that is how she sees herself. In both these cases, *belonging* according to the family norm is the crucial matter.

For older siblings, the rivalry is more openly expressed, and it may be more important to establish and defend uniqueness. Like many families who seek out activities related to their children's birth culture, the Molinaris all participate, because the parents believe that the family shares in the heritage of all its members. After a week at Korean culture camp, during which he was in the minority for a change, nine-year-old Paul walked around the house singing Bruce Springsteen's "Born in the U.S.A." as a taunt. Ten-year-old Daniel chanted back "Born in Korea" and the volume rose. Their mother sees this as one more example of a basic competitiveness that exists between the two boys, who have been brothers ever since Paul's birth. The point is not whether they can get along smoothly. They may not even like each other very much. What matters is that they can express anger, as well as love, without jeopardizing either one's membership in the family. Displays of sibling rivalry can be read as a positive sign that the family bonds are secure. Without certainty that the ties will hold, children who are conscious that adoption is not the "natural" way might be afraid to test them. Sibling rivalry expressed in terms of ethnic difference may be evidence that the family's unusual make-up is not a taboo subject. My favorite example of this came serendipitously one Saturday at Maria's dance class. A girl about eight who had been doting over Maria came up to me and asked, "Is she adopted?" "Yes," I said. "She was adopted from Korea." "So was I," she said. Then, gesturing at her younger sister, who was obviously their mother's offspring, she added, "She was adopted from Mars."

Becoming comfortable as an unusual family is easier if we are not entirely alone. Many of us seek support and a sense of community from other internationally adoptive families, either on our own or through adoptive parent organizations. This subculture of racially mixed families is an important source of practical advice on child-raising, and offers opportunities to socialize with other families like ours. The experience of adoptive parent support groups over time seems to show that affinity is strongest among newly formed families. As the children grow and find their own interests, and as family life settles into a normal course, the fact of international adoption is not enough of a bond on which to continue to build new friendships. The ones that survive are those where the families have other shared interests, too. Though parents perceive this community as very important to their children's sense of identity and family security, the children themselves do not always feel that need. After Melissa Woodrow arrived from India as a toddler, her family was very active in a parent group and often hosted social gatherings at their house. They no longer do that, because Melissa, now 12, finds these events boring and would rather spend the time playing on her athletic teams. Beth Larsen's parents still get together with other families with children from Korea. "I know them, and I play with them," Beth says, "but it seems that I'm more comfortable with my own friends. It doesn't make any difference to me, and usually it doesn't make any difference to them either." It may, nevertheless, be the very presence of those families that enables Beth to feel blasé about them. Knowing others who deviate from the norm shifts the norm itself. One morning, I overheard Maria playing house with two friends, one Korean and one a Germanic blonde. "Breanne's our daughter," Katie said, "and she's Korean, too, but something went wrong with her hair." "No, no," Maria objected. "We adopted her."

In illustrating how "real" the ties that bind the internationally adoptive family are, it is not necessary to obscure or minimize difference. To say "My brother was adopted from India" doesn't diminish the relationship but merely describes how it came to be. Nor is it necessary to portray our families as idyllic. In fact, one sure test of our normality is that we are subject to the same stresses that disrupt the lives of other families. No matter how thoughtfully and deliberately we proceeded with adoption, nor how much care we take to address problems as they arise, no family achieves immunity to adolescent rebellion, temporary or permanent alienation, mental illness, chemical dependency, divorce, or death.

Making our way through these thickets, we need to see whether or not racial difference and adoption make them more entangled. One family I talked with had a daughter who became chemically dependent as a teenager. During this time, she was also alienated from the family and was particularly hostile to her mother. Once in treatment, she discovered a well of anger against her birthmother, who had abandoned her under conditions that would probably not separate mother and child in the United States. Since she couldn't contain the anger and had no legitimate outlet for it, she had transferred it to her adoptive mother. Her mother readily accepted this explanation and was eager to forgive her, but did not really appreciate the depth of her daughter's feeling until an experience of her own helped her empathize:

After my mother died, I had some real feelings of abandonment. I guess it's because my relationship with my mother was not what I wanted it to be, and I realized after my mother was dead that it never was going to be. In many instances, she was very childlike, and I learned to take care of her and her feelings rather than my feelings. I called my daughter and said, "I never really understood what your feelings must have been about this mother who gave you life but isn't going to have a relationship with you." I apologized for being insensitive about that, not deliberately but I just didn't know and didn't understand. She cried and said, "Mom, I'm really glad you called to tell me that." Things don't change, but you can get an insight into someone else's pain. It made me realize how precious it is to have a caring relationship between mother and daughter and to really treasure that and not let other garbage interfere.

Recognizing anger at abandonment and displacement and learning to see the birthparents' actions in a specific cultural context can help clear away barriers between adoptive parent and child.

Much has been written about parent–child conflict in adoptive families, but little has been said about conflict between parents. In another family, the daughter's misbehavior became a source of tension between her mother and father. For one thing, she learned to control their relationship by acting out. "The first and only time my husband and I went away overnight by ourselves and left the kids with the grandparents," her mother recalls, "she went to the discount store, shoplifted, and got picked up. So right away she taught us never to leave." The mother sought counseling, which the father chose not to participate in. She guessed that the daughter's behavior had to do with the loss of her birthparents and the sudden transplantation to a new culture, and she felt sympathy with that, even when the relationship was at its worst. The father saw this focus on separation as a "crutch" used to excuse bad behavior and opted for strict discipline instead. Being caught between father and daughter was very stressful for the mother: "I was afraid of doing the wrong thing. She would yell at me, and if she didn't, he would. I was on eggshells for years, never knowing which one was going to be upset." The daughter is now grown and has some insight into her behavior that has improved her relationship with her parents. The parents, however, have yet to reconcile the incompatible perspectives on human behavior and on child-raising that the experience brought to light.

There is a myth that couples who have survived an adoption agency's scrutiny are a sure bet for lifelong commitment. In fact, having agency approval only heightens the embarrassment when divorce occurs. Even families that handle the perils of international adoption very well may succumb to other, more ordinary hazards. My marriage ended when my children were just four years old and eighteen months. We practiced joint custody until their father moved away nine months later. The girls and I are thriving as a family, and I am confident of my motherly abilities, yet I am aware of the irony that Korean policy would not allow me to adopt them in my present circumstances. In a country with a poor and unstable economy and a stigma against single motherhood, I might even be driven to abandon them. This is very sobering to think about.

There are, as yet, more questions than answers about whether divorce has a special impact on children adopted from other countries: Do children who have already been relinquished by birthparents see divorce as yet another abandonment and begin to expect others? Will they be angry about not being placed in a more stable household? How do children who have been displaced from one family to another and one country to another experience moving back and forth between homes in shared custody? Without genetic ties, what is the children's relationship to an adoptive parent who is absent from their lives? How do children feel if a parent forms a new family that includes birthchildren? What if the parents disagree about whether and how to foster the child's ethnic identity? The next generation will have to supply the answers.

Even death may have special implications for the internationally adoptive family. When I hear of parents dying, I find myself thinking, They came all this way only to be orphaned again, as if the loss is greater for adopted children than it is for birthchildren. One of the families I interviewed had lost their teenage daughter, adopted in infancy, in an automobile accident. Thoughts of "If only . . ." are a natural reaction to accidental death. For an adoptive family to think, If only we hadn't brought her here, to these new dangers, seems inevitable. This family's religious faith eased the self-blame and offered them the certainty of reunion in an afterlife. Nevertheless, people awkward at expressing sympathy did ask if they would have adopted their daughter, had they known what pain was in store, which they answered "resoundingly, yes."

To put it succinctly, internationally adoptive families are like genetically linked families, only different. Sometimes the differences are critical, and sometimes they are irrelevant. When they matter, there is no shame in acknowledging them. By highlighting the differences as warranted, we can stretch popular definitions and show that the conventions we use to describe "the family" as an entity do not always fit. One pervasive metaphor, which virtually all families must confront at some time during their children's schooling, is the family tree. What do we do when the teacher assigns our child the task of tracing the family's twigs and branches back toward their common root? Positing Adam and Eve as forebears is an option for Latin American children born to Catholic parents, but it would require a huge sheet of paper. Children from Asian cultures even have different mythological progenitors. The easiest way out is simply to do the parents' genealogy. Tina Molinari sees a benefit in this for younger children, because "they're dependent on your roots for their security. And that's who I want them to bond with—the grandmas and grandpas on both sides." For teenagers, she thinks it's important to include biological ancestors. "That question would be there, so why not break the silence about it when they are doing their identity searching?"

If a family tree is a genetic chart, then simply plugging in an adopted child is inaccurate, unless we use the "grafted tree" image that appears in some adoption literature. If the family tree is a record of the family's history, then adoption should be acknowledged as a vital factor in that history, and there should be some symbol to suggest that children adopted into the family come with a history of their own, played out in another part of the world. For second grade, Grace and I came up with a clever solution to the family tree dilemma. We were forced to try an alternative not just by adoption but by divorce and remarriage. What we did was reconstruct our family as a peony bush. We probably took some liberties with horticulture to make the metaphor work, but here is how it goes: Each member of the family is a peony bulb with roots that go down into the soil and perhaps entwine with the roots of other bulbs. Grace's and Maria's roots are marked with the word "birthparents" and a South Korean flag. We marked the other family members' ethnic roots, too, making ourselves a multiheritage family. The bulbs are clustered together, nestling against the bulbs with whom they share the closest relationships. Our peony bush is different from the standard variety in that the bulbs do not all produce the same color of blossom. The peony bush was not an arbitrary choice. It was suggested, first, by the name Keun Young, and was already an operative symbol of my family's continuity. After my grandmother Grace's death, some of her children and grandchildren dug up peony bulbs in her yard and transplanted them in our own as a memorial. Grace and I turned in the assignment feeling quite proud of our ingenuity. I was also very satisfied with the metaphorical import of the family-as-peony-bush. Planted separately, we would probably thrive all right, but planted together in common ground we bloom in greater abundance and splendor.

6

Telling the Story

Lucas and Cesar are brothers, 15 and 14, both from Colombia. They have been brothers since Cesar joined the Connor family at age seven. Lucas had come three years earlier, at age five, and they have an older sister who was adopted as a baby in the United States. Their parents have also taken in foster children awaiting placement in adoptive homes. Adoption, then, is the Connor family norm, an experience that the children share. Yet, they have not experienced it in identical ways, nor do they give it equal significance in the shaping of their lives.

"There's not much to tell," Lucas warns as he begins the life story I have asked him for. "I really don't remember much about my early years, and then I was adopted when I was five. I just kind of totally forgot my Spanish and everything." He knows that he lived in an orphanage, but he can call up only one memory from that time: "I was little and I wet my bed. So the person that takes care of me wakes me up in the middle of the night and gives me a whack on the butt and has me take a cold shower." Not a pleasant memory, but he chuckles as he tells it. His parents tell stories about his arrival and adjustment, but he himself has no memory of the incidents they relate. They have told him what they know about his history, but there is no information about his birthparents. Asked if he ever wonders how his life happened to take this course, he says yes, but quickly adds his own explanation: "It's kind of like a second life, I guess. The first life didn't go well, so I got adopted and got a better life." In Lucas's opinion, the second life can be lived satisfactorily without much understanding of the first life. "You just let life go on. You shouldn't take it badly and feel wrong about it. Just keep on living your life and make the best of it."

I realize that Lucas's terse answers to my questions could be a signal that he has better things to do than sit still for an interview. His response, however, is true to the character description given by his sister, who put me in touch with the family. He is easygoing, fits in well with kids his age, doesn't reflect a lot on being adopted or being Hispanic. With his dark hair and tan skin, he could be taken for Southern European as well as Latin American.

Lucas's brother Cesar is his opposite in both appearance and demeanor. He has Indian facial features, and he speaks with a slight accent. This in itself is intriguing, because children who acquire a new language before age 10 or 12 generally master its sounds completely. Cesar's life story is rich with anecdotes told in sensual detail: sights, sounds, smells, the nearness of the forest, the shape and feel of a spinning top he played with. He also has a sense of the social context in which these memories took shape:

> We had a big cornfield that wrapped all the way around the house almost. We owned part of it, but the person who owned all of it was this one lady. I can't remember her name, but she would visit my father and me and see what was going on. I would help out packing the corn and also taking it down and burning it. Just outside to the back of the forest, there was a big bean harvest. People from the town came to help out. They would go in with potato sacks, collect it, take it home and go to the market and get money for it.

Cesar's early experience is so well recorded in his memory that it is easily evoked by reminders in the present. The sound of his feet turning the rocks on a gravel road transports him to the road that led to his house in Colombia. The singing of certain birds and the smell of spices bring back familiar scenes and sensations.

> Everytime I hear, smell, taste, or see something and my brain likes whatever I see, that brings back Colombia. I'll be looking at something and it reminds me of Colombia. It's just like my brain goes back and sees something else. It'll take three or four minutes.

The richness of Cesar's storytelling suggests that he is unusually observant, with all his senses alert. I asked him if he is artistic and he blushed and shrugged it off, "I can memorize. If I could go to Colombia, I could go to every place I was and I would still know it." This capacity for memory is both blessing and curse. With the memories of place and time come the feelings that Cesar experienced in an early life marked by emotional turmoil. Abandoned in infancy by his birthmother, he was adopted by a childless couple who, though illiterate and poor by

North American standards, had steady agricultural work. They lived in a two-room house with an adjoining room for chickens and did not go hungry. Their mode of child-raising mixed harsh physical punishment with indulgent love, and their own relationship showed the same extremes:

> My dad would beat up my mom. One morning I was in the room sleeping, and they were already fighting, in that same room where we slept. My mother was crying. My father was yelling and screaming and hitting. I would catch this about every other argument that they had. When they weren't fighting, they would be having a joyous time together.

In the most turbulent times, Cesar would run away from home, young as he was, and join the children living on the streets for a while. "When I came back, I was welcomed like I was the loved one." On the street, he learned behavior that his parents would not accept, and he became more resistant to their discipline. What upset his mother most of all was some precocious sexual play, an acting out of sexual abuse he experienced outside the family from age three or four. "My mother got tired of that," he says matter-of-factly, "so she decided to hand me over to the orphanage."

These remembered incidents demand interpretation. As Cesar describes it, "I guess the problem with me is I have a lot of controversies in my head. I kind of get angry at myself and regret a lot of things." As he sorts through the memories, he feels anger at his mother for sending him away and then anger at himself for provoking her to do so. "I just keep thinking that if I had been smarter, I wouldn't be in a big mess, kind of like I don't know where to go." Cesar is getting counseling to help him with these feelings and with the consequences of sexual abuse. His family wants to see the problems resolved and has his well-being at heart.

Yet, Cesar feels that his habit of remembering is a source of conflict with his parents. "I get two different signals. I get a message that they want me to forget about Colombia, and another message is, they want to remind me of Colombia." The reminders come in the form of comparisons, meant to illustrate how his life has improved. The overt message is "to forget the past and look ahead." His father is afraid that dwelling on the past will make Cesar nostalgic and cast Colombia in a better light than his actual experience warrants. Cesar believes this advice is meant to help him, but he disagrees: "If I forget about the past, it would be kind of like losing my heritage as well. To me, Colombia is a precious place. Colombia is still the place that is home." Moreover, counseling keeps the past in focus, as the source of explanations for his personality traits and habits of behavior. This has spurred rather than stilled his memories. "I guess every year I keep on wondering about Colombia more and more. It keeps on egging me on, not really knowing what's there, and wondering how much has changed, and really wondering about my parents." To Cesar, looking ahead doesn't mean forgetting the past. It means reconnecting with the past and testing the memories by traveling to Colombia when he finishes his education.

A standard comparison of these two brothers would cast Lucas in the role of the well-adjusted child who shows no ill effects of adoption and transplantation to a new country, while Cesar continues to have difficulty bonding and becoming acculturated after several years. Yet, to mark Cesar as a "problem child" would be a grave mistake. His alert senses and his habit of endowing mundane events with personal import suggests a rich capacity for living and a constitutional rootedness that may serve him very well in the years beyond adolescence, whether they are spent in the United States, or in Colombia, or in a new place altogether. Hearing him talk about the "precious place" that is still "home" reminded me of how fundamentally secure I feel at the sight of cattails in a marsh and the sound of red-wing blackbirds. The experience of the present moment is deeply enhanced by vivid memories from the past. For a child like Cesar, forgetting the past might diminish the present and rob the future of enchantment.

Though my sensibilities resonate with Cesar's, I have no qualms about Lucas's easy adjustment. I know, from watching my two daughters grow, that there is deep-seated individual variation in how human beings come to terms with a life of uncertainty. Indifference, or even repression, may be as damaging or as fruitful as remembering. It is not memory itself but coherence and continuity that matter here. Memory may or may not be the key to redressing the incoherence and lack of continuity that are the sensitive core of life for adopted children.

I am always surprised and saddened when I hear about parents who show no interest in their child's memories or who even discourage them. I can understand that parents with a child who persistently balks at accepting present reality might urge "forget the past" in helpless frustration. If the child seems weighted down by painful memories, parents powerless to help may see no recourse but forgetting. Jessica Martinson speaks to that:

> It's so hard to accept that a child has been really damaged. You can love them to death, but that's not going to make what happened to them better and it's not going to take it away. Being the kind of controlling person that I am, that was one of the most difficult things to accept. There were lots of things in her life that she was just going to have to come to terms with herself. I was never going to be able to put a bandage on or kiss it and make it go away.

Regardless of the parents' intentions, to a child struggling to understand how the past led to the present or how the future might restore the features of the past that the child longs for, "forget the past" conveys a selfish and unloving parental message: "The life you lived without me is of no value. You are only what I make you." We do not re-create our children when we adopt them, much as we might like to. The more we try to claim that awesome power, the more they have to draw on their independent memories in order to develop into autonomous human beings.

In our joyful anticipation of the new child, we parents can easily forget that adoption begins in tragedy. The primary bond between parent and child is broken. But the life that preceded this tragedy may not have been tragic in itself and may have left pleasant memories that intensify the sense of loss. Joan Schumack, adopted from Greece at age five and now a public speaker on adoption, compares it to amputation in that "a part of your existence has been severed." Children adopted internationally undergo an additional rupture, like that experienced by immigrants of any age. Those who carry vivid memories of a very different place, where thoughts and feelings were expressed in another language, may see adoption not only as amputation, but as exile.

In choosing to adopt older children, Linda Truman was relying on the persistence of memory to heal over the rupture. "It was real important to me that the children have some memory of their own of Korea. I felt that they should have something that was theirs, that I couldn't give them and I couldn't take away from them." This "something that was theirs" would give them the personal momentum to achieve continuity even as they changed families and cultures. Ironically, memory has not served either of her daughters in that way. When Jonna listens to the tape recording of herself singing in Korean, she marvels that she ever knew that language. The memories she brought with her faded quickly. All she knows is the life she has lived in the United States, and she is, to all appearances, at ease with that.

Memory might have helped Soon Hee find order in the chaos she felt as a teenager, but it proved unreliable. She has a small store of what Ruth Kim Schmidt, also from Korea, calls "snapshot memories." "Everything is very vague," Soon Hee says. She remembers sneaking along with friends to cut open a watermelon in a patch nearby, and she remembers hearing her mother and her older brother fighting. "I remember that because it would scare me." Speaking of her father, whose death led to her adoption at age nine, she says, "It's funny, because sometimes in my dreams I can picture him, but I can't picture his face when I'm awake, even when I try." She doesn't remember him being around much of the time, and that confuses her. "I wonder if they were even married. Maybe he's not even my father. Who knows?" Having facts to complete the life history where memory fails could ease the self-blame that Soon Hee carries with her:

> Sometimes I wonder if it was even hard for my mother to give me away. Sure, everybody tells you it was because it was best for you and they were just thinking about you. But I wonder. That's what they say, but maybe there was something else besides that, because I wasn't exactly an angel, either, when I was in Korea. I think all adopted kids wonder why.

"All adopted kids wonder why." Like all generalizations, it bears exception, but parents are advised to keep this truth in mind throughout the process of raising their children. "Never underestimate the magnitude of the rejection your children feel," Joan Schumack urges. "Someone did not want us for the simple fact that we existed. We know that we were given away." Helping our children to understand why is the most critical task of adoptive parenthood. Without a plausible explanation, the child's life history remains severed in an irreconcilable before and after, lived in entirely different parts of the world.

The majority of internationally adopted children, however, arrive as infants or toddlers and thus have a short and unremembered "first life," to use Lucas Connor's term. For some, having no memories makes life in the American family sufficient in itself, and the gap in their personal histories is not worrisome. Debbie Balcom, now 18, seldom asked any questions about why she was adopted. "It was never a big curiosity of mine. I was here and I was happy." On the verge of leaving home, she has begun to wonder, and she anticipates traveling to Korea to find answers in about ten years. For other children, curiosity looms early on. If left unsatisfied, it can feed feelings of rejection and displacement.

Knowing that the child's interest in adoption can follow either course, many parents begin laying the groundwork for understanding even before the children arrive. The question What should we tell our child? is addressed in preadoptive counseling sessions, and reluctance to tell the story is reason enough not to adopt, especially if the child's physical appearance makes the fact of adoption evident to all. In effect, we who have adopted children with no memories have the responsibility of constructing a past for them—a past that incorporates both personal data and cultural knowledge. It can be constructed deliberately, with special care to make it liveable—a past that causes no shame or lasting regret, even if it has elements of tragedy. Or it can be a clumsy structure, made of the scrap lumber of ill-considered comments and assumptions made in ignorance.

Telling the story from the point where the adoptive parents join it is the easiest part of the task. It is also an important and natural place to begin, because children's first questions usually have to do with how they came into their families. The photo albums that my daughters periodically heft along to school for show-and-tell open with their referral pictures. The text gives basic, public data about the little baby born in Seoul. The tenor of the pictures and captions conveys the joy and thrill of receiving a new child and becoming a family. This "life book," as literature on adoption calls it, offers what younger children seem to need most: the security of being welcomed and loved by the adults whom they know as their parents. Divorce has made looking through the albums somewhat bittersweet for my children, but they still turn to them often for evidence of "me when I was a baby."

Photographs and stories about the arrival seem to give this moment mythical import in the younger child's personal history of the world. Some children claim to remember it. Sally Anderson's daughter Meena insists that she came off the plane, at ten months, saying, "Where's my mommy? Where's my mommy?" Joy Egholm, who came from Korea at 18 months, used to tell people, when she was about six, that she remembered coloring on the airplane, and when she dropped her crayon, a little boy picked it up and gave it to her. Her mother would intervene with a sing-song reminder, "Joy-oy, that never happened." She wanted so much to be able to talk about her trip, she says, that she had to make something up. Some children make a ritual of reenacting the arrival. Chuck Stensrud tells about a game his daughter Susan played for more than a year at three and four:

> She would lie down at the end of the bed, and Margo and I would be in bed, and then she would make a noise like an airplane. That would be our cue that we were supposed to do our role. Our role was a mom and dad who wanted to have a baby, and it was coming pretty soon, and wouldn't it hurry up and get here? The airplane noise would get louder and louder. Then we would say, "Oh, here's an airplane. I wonder if that's the one. I wonder if that's the one our baby is on." She'd make little crying noises and we'd get real excited and say, "Oh yes! That's the one! That must be ours!" And then she'd pop up over the end of the bed and snuggle in between us and be in our family. It was great fun. I don't know if she thought of it or if Margo thought of it, but I used to think, Wow, what a neat way of teaching this.

As children become conscious of racial diversity and hear other people questioning their parents about their origins, they begin to realize that their mode of joining the family is not the norm. Wondering "why" gradually takes precedence over rehearsing the "how." Telling them from the beginning that they were adopted and that they were born in another country, as most parents do, doesn't insure understanding. At six, Sarah Larsen, Beth's sister, explains adoption in a rather sketchy fashion:

> Adopted is having a mother that can't take care of you. Somebody gets married, and they want a baby, but not out of their tummy, so they go to this place, and they tell somebody something, and then somebody gives them a picture of he or she or both, and then they say something, and then they get it.

The sense that children make of our explanations depends on how much they truly understand about reproduction. My favorite illustration of how a child comprehends the getting of children takes shape in a series of journal entries recorded when Grace was three and a half:

August 20, 1983

Everytime we pass the t-shirt store on Fiftieth Street, Grace looks at the infant shirt in the window and says, "We should get one like that for Maria." Today I pointed out that she has probably gotten too big. "We could give it to somebody else then," she suggested. "Ya, we could give it to Rivie's baby," I offered. "I don't know what she looks like," Grace said. "Neither do I. We don't even know if it's a she. We'll find out in January when the baby comes." You could almost see the lightbulb pop on: "Maybe we can go to the airport!" I paused a minute before quashing her excitement. "Rivie's baby isn't coming to the airport. It's coming to the hospital." There was no response. I'll wait until the questions come—no point in answering them before she knows enough to ask.

November 30, 1983

Last night at Mary's house, we had the first reproductive moment-of-truth. Grace asked Mary why she had her Christmas decorations up already, and Mary said it was because they were having a baby soon and they would be too busy after that. On the way out, Grace asked, "Where's their baby now?" I thought to myself, Be truthful but brief. "In Mary's tummy," I said. I have never seen Grace at a loss for words. She fell back against the door jamb and just looked and looked at me. "In her tummy??" she said. "What's it doing in *there?*" I hedged a bit: "That's how lots of people get their babies. Not everybody goes to the airport." "I thought babies just came when it was dark"—a non-sequitur or a recollection of the airport experience? We were waiting to cross rush hour traffic on Lyndale when she asked the next big one, "How does the baby get out?" "There's a place in the mother's bottom where it comes out. Mary will go to the hospital to have the doctor help her because it's kind of tricky." She was silent for five blocks, until we reached our corner: "If our baby was in your tummy, that would be pretty funny." "No, our baby wasn't in my tummy," I explained, "because we got her at the airport from Korea." "I wouldn't like to be in your tummy," she offered. "Mary's baby is too little still to be noticing that," I said. On the way into the house, she sang, "Three French hens, two Easter eggs, and four shiny men in my tummy." There were no more questions.

December 1, 1983

I decided last night at bedtime to lay the groundwork for the truth
about adoption, rather than having the questions sprung on me in
the grocery store. So I told her a story about a young woman in
Korea with a baby in her tummy who just wasn't ready to be a mom.
Maybe she was too young. Maybe she was all alone. Maybe she didn't
have enough money to raise a baby. Maybe she didn't have a place
to live. "Why?" Grace asked, and I could only say, "We don't really
know why. We don't know that much about her." Then I told how
she came to the hospital when it was time for the baby to come out
and asked the nurses if they would find a mom and dad for the baby,
who was so pretty and nice that it made her very sad she couldn't
take care of her herself. The social worker at the hospital named
the baby Keun Young and the story proceeded from there in familiar
terms. Grace was uncharacteristically quiet for a moment, then picked
a magazine up off the table, shoved it at me, and said, "Read this."
When I put her to bed she was even more affectionate than usual.
She hugged me and wouldn't let go.

December 27, 1983

After lullabies on Christmas night, Grace asked, "Does God make
people or do people make people?" "Little babies grow in women's
tummies," I answered, avoiding the theological issues. "And then
do they put them on the airplane?" "Some babies," I said. "You
and Maria and Annie Soon and Rachel—" "Did I grow in your tummy?"
"No, I've never had a baby in my tummy. You and Maria came to
us on an airplane." I would have continued, a step at a time, but
she rolled over to sleep.

January 7, 1984

We got a call this morning that Rivie had gone into the hospital.
"Is she sick?" Grace asked. "No, she went in to have the baby,"
her dad explained. There was a long pause, and then Grace looked
up with a grin on her face and said in a knowing little sing-song: "I
bet she isn't Korean."

Needless to say, I was greatly impressed with my daughter's amazing
logic. She had put the evidence together and come up with a stunning
conclusion. Of course, the conclusion still left room for misunderstanding,

which came to light a couple of years later when she learned that one of her Caucasian playmates was adopted. "Usually when you're adopted, you look Chinese or something," she said. "Adopted," it seemed, showed in physical signs that set you apart from the majority, who were white or black and born into their families. It was clearly a matter of difference. It is not uncommon for children to equate being adopted with being of their own ethnicity. "Look! He's adopted!" Karen Kuschner's preschool daughter shouted when they passed an Asian man on the street. Adoption and ethnicity are not easily untangled if the only people they know who resemble them are other adopted children. I remember Grace's comment as we pulled into the parking lot at a Korean cultural event: "Hey! That family even has a Korean mom!"

Although I raised the presence of a birthmother and apparently stirred the waters in doing so, the birthmother did not soon become the object of Grace's curiosity, nor of Maria's. The first "why" questions focused not on reasons for separation but on my motives for wanting children who were not born to me—namely, for wanting them. At least we do not lack for knowledge in giving our children that information. Judgment is the tricky part, especially in cases where the parents are infertile. There is a vast difference between "We really wanted children and couldn't have any of our own, so we adopted you instead" and "We knew we couldn't have children by birth, and adoption was the best way to have the child we wanted." As for explaining the international dimension, there is a difference between saying, "There weren't enough American babies so we had to go all the way to India to find you," and "Here we were in the United States, hoping for a baby, and there you were in India, needing a family, and I'm so glad we got matched up." Explanations that shrink the world and make boundaries more permeable are better than those that turn the child's birth country into a distant and exotic land.

For a long time, the story generally told to adopted children was that their parents had chosen them, specifically, out of all the children available. This has been eased out of fashion in preference for truth telling and because of the moral pressure it places on the child. Joan Schumack warns of the disillusion that comes with learning that you really are interchangeable, that another child would have received as jubilant a welcome. A variation on the "chosen child" theme is still practiced by some families and it carries some of the same risks. It portrays international adoption as a rescue mission and thus pegs the child as a lucky survivor.

Ruth Kim Schmidt, now 30, was adopted from Korea at age 4. Her father is a minister, and her parents came to adoption with a special concern for the plight of Amerasian children that was motivated by their religious faith. Ruth's mother took on, as her personal ministry, the task of finding homes for the many children awaiting adoption, and she and Ruth made the rounds of church groups. Ruth would wear her Korean dress and sing a song or two and then she would go play in another room while her mother showed slides of the orphanage. Feeling banished, Ruth assumed that the slides must be awful to look at. Adding on the audience's comments about what a wonderful Christian thing her parents were doing, Ruth acquired what she calls "a heavy burden of specialness." The message was, "Isn't it fortunate that your parents rescued you from that horrible country and the destitute life that you surely would have lived if you had stayed?" She felt that she had to keep proving herself worthy of that, "to make everybody happy that they had done this." Ruth is careful to point out that her parents did not make their love conditional on her behavior. Nevertheless, she didn't risk putting it to the test. If the truth be told, there *is* an element of rescue in Ruth's adoption. Amerasian children living in Korea in the years just after the war were treated cruelly and, as adults, they still face discrimination. The Hofbauers, Ruth's parents, already had all the children they had planned on raising.

Parents who are not infertile *are* accomplishing a rescue by opting for an existing child in need rather than bringing another baby into the world. The challenge these parents face is interpreting their choice to the child without making themselves look noble and making the child feel unworthy. During a heated argument with their daughter Anne, in one of the most trying phases of her adolescent rebellion, Dan Duval objected to the way she was treating her mother and said, "She loves you, and if she didn't love you, you wouldn't be part of our family, and you need to think about that." The implication of the statement made Marlene uncomfortable: "It was almost like he was giving me credit for adopting her. I don't like that, because I feel like it was the work of the Holy Spirit. It was like the seed was planted in my heart and it really bloomed."

Parents who have an active religious faith do often explain their actions in terms of that faith, setting individual motive aside in favor of a divine power at work in human life. That is how Bill and Mary MacNamara, who are Catholic, explain to their children how their family came to be:

We would sit down at the dinner table and really discuss how God puts people together, and it doesn't matter what country you're from or who your parents are. If God has meant you to be with these people, in this house and this family, that's your family. It doesn't necessarily have to be a birth from the tummy and the whole business.

The Garmans, who are evangelical Christians, have a more structured theological framework within which they interpret adoption. According to their faith, God's plan for humanity is adoption through rebirth. "We've been adopted into God's family," Bob Garman says, "so what's so unusual about us adopting kids into our family?" Rita adds that they "have tried to teach them that this is part of God's plan in their life, to work out their life for their best and for His glory in the best way possible." They do see adopted children as "chosen," but by God rather than by their parents, and they want their children to see adoption as empowering:

Why did God choose you as maybe one out of a thousand to have this opportunity? (I'm thinking of the thousands and thousands of gamines in Colombia and Brazil and other South American countries.) This was not just an accident that happened to you. You are not a victim. You are a special, unique creation of God, and He has a plan for each person's life.

The parents are very instrumental in this plan, though not the instigators of it. In the Garmans' view, making the decision to adopt was simply following God's will for their lives and their children's.

In telling the story this way, the Garmans are also conveying to their children the beliefs and values that they want them to live by. All of us do that, though not always so consciously, since few of us have such a perceptible worldview in which to give meaning to our actions or those of the birthparents. No matter how we tell our own family stories, most parents do want to be deliberate about how we portray adoption itself as a way of forming families. Often, we become aware of this when we find ourselves having to counter messages about adoption that our children get from situation comedies on television. What I keep stressing to my girls is that no matter what led me to adoption, the fact is that the children I have are exactly the ones I want. They find ways to test that: "What if you did have a baby? What if you had gotten Annie Soon and Matthew instead? Wouldn't you love them? What if you never knew us?" I tell them that I probably would have loved any baby, but I can't imagine loving anybody more than I love them. The adoption story is full of "what ifs," but there is no longer any "if" about my part in it. The step I took is one I will never regret.

Confidence about our own values and judgments is essential in helping our children understand why they are not being raised by their birthparents. That means, first, being aware of how we ourselves feel toward their birthparents and the actions they took. To get at that, we can pay close attention to the times when the birthparents enter our consciousness—what evokes their presence and how that leaves us feeling. Margo Speiser describes one such moment:

> Tony and I were sitting on the steps last night waiting for Chuck, and Tony walked out to the end of the sidewalk, then jumped over and ran up the hill. That was a great accomplishment. He was so cute, with those little legs dangling down. He's a little boy now— no longer a toddler. Again, I have this wave of sadness for whoever it is that did not see this, that had to give up this privilege. And I can't help but think that they would think it was a privilege also, because I think it is.

I, too, feel sorrow about the birthparents' loss, and I want my children to know that it is cause for sorrow. Because of that, I fully expected that they would feel the hurt of their own separation early on. Instead, their overt awareness of the birthmothers' existence in the world has come and gone and come again, is sometimes emotionally laden and sometimes matter-of-fact. Gearing my storytelling to their sporadic interest rather than my consistent desire to explain and interpret and clarify has been hard work. There has been no one time in which it seemed appropriate to tell the whole story intact. Pieces of it emerge as they need information to gauge their lives by—"Will I be as tall as you when I grow up?"—or to figure out how the mysterious adult world works—"If my birthmother and birthfather had that much of a relationship, why didn't they just get married?" Questions like these could prompt me to tell the whole story, if only the audience would sit still for it. Peggy and Jack Gaartner have had a similar experience with their seven-year-old daughter Michelle. As Peggy tells it, "We haven't gotten into it yet because the questions haven't come. She just isn't old enough to grasp some of it yet, but we're expecting it." Their daughter, like mine, will quickly change the subject after a brief answer that leaves the parents hungry for more conversation. Peggy goes on,

I'm real quick to read stuff in. I'm quick to decide, Oh, that means a psychological thing. But she does that with everything. Her mind just goes, "click," and it moves on. She'll hang on if she's not satisfied with the answer. She'll keep bugging you and bugging you until she gets it. If she moves to another subject, that means, well, that's over. I've got more to say, but she's done—that's all I wanted for now, thanks. I think she just has a good way of knowing what she needs at the time, and that's enough.

Even if parents do get to tell the story in one sitting, there is no guarantee that the child will store it up for future interpretation. Asked if she could tell me something about when she was a baby in Korea, Sarah Larsen answered, "I don't know. That was a long time ago." Her mother had told her quite a bit, but, Sarah admitted, "I forgot."

The social worker who saw Bill and Mary MacNamara through both of their adoptions advised them that there is, indeed, a proper moment for telling the story: the very day the child arrives. In Mary's words,

He said, "I know that's ridiculous. They're not going to understand any of it anyway. But you tell that story over and over, and they're going to know it by heart. When they get old enough to realize what it really means, it's not going to be a big shock to them." So I did that, just about every day. I'd tell them everything I knew. When they were about three or four years old, it clicked that that meant there was another mother, and she was still in Korea, and they weren't born to me like all the other kids were. That was really painful for them. My son even cried. He said he was worried about her—was she OK? Was she lonely? I felt such sorrow for the kids, but there wasn't anything I could do to make it easier for them. I remember thinking at the time, I'm so grateful that my social worker told me to do that, because if I had waited till they were seven and laid that on them, I couldn't have borne the pain they would have felt. At least this way it's a realization rather than a big shock.

There is another advantage to telling the story over and over, or "keeping it alive at all times," as another mother, Debbie Whelan, describes it. The more familiar the parents are with the details, and the more practiced they are at telling them, the more comfortable they will be transmitting the sensitive information that the children have lost someone very important. Watching the children's responses to the story change as they mature and can interpret it in more subtle ways keeps the parents from being undone by explosive reactions. Katie MacNamara, for example, was quick to put the birthmother's existence to use as a manipulative tool. She has a repertoire of sentences beginning, "My *real* mother would never . . ." "Katie was real mad at me once," Mary says, "and she told me that she missed her Korean mother, but not her Korean dad, because Daddy was just fine. You know what she meant. She meant, You stink, old woman." At other times, Mary says, missing her Korean mother seems to be a very genuine sorrow for Katie:

> She goes in and out of phases. A year ago, when she was eight, she was having a real hard time with it. She felt abandoned by her birthmother. When she would meet Korean women, she'd just latch on to them. I think she was sort of projecting them to be her mother— her *real* mother. I can remember feeling kind of hurt by it, that she would just latch on to them, but I thought it was important, too, to help her work it out. So I never tried to intervene or anything, and actively tried to give her access to Korean women, and it's worked out OK. Now she's in a period where she's not having any problems with being adopted.

Mary seems well equipped to mother her children through these sensitive phases. She acknowledges feeling hurt but can keep those feelings— very natural ones—in check while giving primacy to her daughter's need for affection from someone who resembles the lost mother she has presumably seen in her imagination. Katie is fortunate to have such a remedy available for the feelings of rejection that arise from time to time. Her example makes a good argument for getting to know adults of the children's nationality. In telling the story over and over, Mary keeps reminding herself of the birthmothers' existence and clarifying her feelings toward them. They are, for her, very real people with whom she shares a remarkable fate.

> I feel a sisterhood with those women. I feel extraordinarily grateful to them, and I hope that they're OK. I really care a lot about their welfare, because I know they love these children, and so do I. Gee, you know, that's a pretty strong bond. If I love my child, I love every part of them, and that includes their biological parents and the country they're from. I've always made it clear that it's a subject I'm comfortable talking about. And sometimes they'll say to me, "Does this hurt your feelings if we talk about this, if we care about them?" "No, no, don't ever think that," I tell them.

It is a rare parent who tries to keep the children unaware of birthparents elsewhere in the world. Yet, many parents do take comfort in the fact that the birthparents are far away and difficult to trace and thus pose no threat to the family relationship. Peggy Gaartner says,

> The parent is so remote, they're so far away, and you don't know who they are, and the dad can't be found. That feels more secure to me, that somehow my daughter can't be taken away. It's less likely than if she had a set of parents that she could just look up in Iowa and go establish a relationship with later. If that were the case, I would, of course, want her to have that if she wanted that. But I don't know whether I want it for me. I wouldn't stand in the way of her having that experience, but I want her just to be my kid.

None of us is altogether free of this fear of losing our children's loyalty. "I anticipate a broken heart," Margo Speiser admits. The fear is not unique to adoptive parents, either, but shared with all parents who worry about the attraction of other ways of life with values different from their own. However, if we indulge this fear and keep the birthparents distant to protect ourselves, we risk portraying them to our children as alien and mysterious. Unless the birthparents take on full humanity in our imaginations, we cannot tell the story convincingly enough to ease our children's feelings of loss or rejection.

I have spoken of telling "the whole story," when in fact, the story is seldom whole. The piece of it most likely to be missing is motive. Why did my mother give me away? is a question to which very, very few of us can deliver *the* truest answer. Of the parents I interviewed, only Reba Perlitz was lucky enough to hear why from the birthmother herself. Motives have to be inferred from other knowledge and the experience we have of such matters. Lacking any more precise explanation, a great many parents opt for some version of She did it because she loves you. Though it is intended to assuage feelings of rejection, this is confusing to a child who has no sense of paradox. Their adoptive parents love them, too, but have not given them away. Following the idea through a logical course can be very unsettling: Suddenly parental love offers no promise of permanence. The Gaartners believed that they had communicated this message of love to their daughter by reiterating it at every opportunity. How surprised they were then when they overheard her explaining the situation to a new friend who asked why she wasn't living with her "real" parents: "I guess they just didn't want to take care of me." Since then, they have been more careful to stress the circumstances of life that made keeping a child—*any* child—virtually impossible.

Explaining why comes hardest to parents whose children were found abandoned, rather than handed over in person to hospital or orphanage personnel. "Parents unknown" offers no basis from which to infer personal motives. The mother of a Colombian-born daughter wrote in *OURS* magazine of her anguish at learning, eight years after the adoption, that her daughter had been found abandoned about one month after birth.

> The thought of my so dearly loved child being deserted on a city street and found by some strange woman was overwhelming. I was grateful that my children were still in school and that my closest friend, who is also an adoptive mother, was visiting when I received the mail that day. I read the documents and cried . . . When my husband returned from work that evening, we discussed what we had learned. Our big problem now was what and when—if ever—to tell Heather what we knew. What would she think of herself in relation to her biological mother, of whom I had always painted such a loving picture? . . . Her biological mother had abandoned her on a city street. If her father and I found that news distressing, how would she react to it? (January/February 1989, p. 25)

They decided not only to tell their daughter, but to let her read the papers herself.

> We spent the next three hours crying, hugging, and talking. I told her that she was bright, beautiful, and mature. That the short beginning of her life in Bogotá was over. That her life is here and now. That her dad and I were her "real" parents even though we did not give her life.

It certainly is distressing to imagine the children we love lying alone on the ground or wandering, terrified, through a crowd of strange faces looking for the parents who left them behind. Yet this mother's reaction to the fact of abandonment is an unfortunate example of how easily the child's past can be misconstrued and then dismissed as having no value. It is also a case of the adoptive parents distancing themselves from the birthparents and perceiving their actions as alien and incomprehensible. There is a glaring omission in this piece of storytelling—an understanding of the cultural context in which the child was abandoned. Another *OURS* reader supplied some of that in a succeeding issue:

> I wonder if this child, who was supposedly in good condition when found, was not "abandoned" as such, but instead had a mother who loved her enough to take her to a place where she would be found and cared for by a family with more resources. Since Colombian law restricts adoptions of children with known families, she may have found a friend or relative willing to take the child to the authorities and to give this improbable story so the mother could not be traced. (September/October 1989, p. 5)

Relatively few countries have a bureaucratically structured, governmentally regulated system of adoption as extensive as that in the United States. The severing of family ties and the transfer of children from one family to another are unthinkable in many cultures. In some countries from which children are being adopted, it is a crime to attempt to give away one's child. When social and economic circumstances make it impossible for parents to raise the children to whom they give birth, means are found to do what is necessary but not allowed. There may be tacitly understood signals—like leaving the child in a certain kind of place—that mean the parents want the child to be adopted; this was the case in South Korea before relinquishment was legalized. Some of the buildings housing government child welfare offices in India have a niche in the wall with a basket where infants can be left anonymously, without penalty to the parents. In these settings, abandonment is no more likely to be an act of callous disregard for the child's well-being than is an American birthmother's decision, after weeks of professional counseling, to place her child for adoption through a licensed agency.

In the absence of actual, unbiased evidence to the contrary, it is most reassuring for our children to assume that their birthparents had their interests at heart. To answer How could she do this to me? in a salutary way, we cannot ourselves be troubled by How could she do this to my child? What Melissa Woodrow's parents have told her about her abandonment is clear from the way she explains it: "My mom and dad couldn't take care of me, and they wanted me to have a good place, so instead of dumping me off on the streets, they left me on the doorstep of a hospital." It is important to do justice to the people who are, after all, our children's progenitors and thus the source of much that we love about them. Margo Speiser sums it up:

Why were they given up? We don't know. We'll never know the particulars probably, but the most likely thing is that it was a tremendous act of love, and that it had to be very, very difficult, no matter what the culture was dictating. It can never be easy to give up a child.

Joy Egholm, who knows that her life as an Amerasian in Korea would have been difficult, respects her birthmother's generosity in letting her go:

I think about my son, and I think, OK, let's say I was a single mother. I thought about this when he was a year old, about the time that she gave me up. I thought, I have this little boy. He's a year old. Could I give him up to somebody? That just takes a special person. You know how they always say that it takes special people to adopt? But I think it takes just as special a person to give a child up, to be that unselfish to know that it would be better for the child. I guess I like to think that she loved me as much as I love my son now, but she just knew it was better for me. There's no way I could just give Brian up right now, no matter how poor I was. I think that would be the hardest thing in the world to do.

Even when we do know the particulars of the separation, they will not always satisfy the children's need to know why. What will they make of "Your parents couldn't raise you because they were poor," when poor people in the United States do not give up their children voluntarily? They may have their children taken away to foster care if they are also drug dependent or imprisoned or charged with child abuse, but poverty alone does not usually break family ties. Will they assume that their parents were unworthy to raise children? What will they make of "Your mother couldn't raise you because she wasn't married," when the number of single teenage mothers is on the increase in this country? And what comfort does that give a child adopted by a single parent or one whose parents have divorced? If we offer poverty or unwed status as the insurmountable problem that motivated their parents to give them for adoption, we have to help them understand how those circum- stances influence personal behavior. This requires knowledge about the birth culture as well as an intercultural sensitivity that we may not, in fact, possess. Nevertheless, we need to begin the inquiry, drawing on all the resources available to direct us away from the common pit- falls.

When Yoonju Park, director of the Korean Institute of Minnesota and a social worker, began meeting with a group of Korean-born teenagers to discuss adoption issues, she was surprised to hear them portray Korea as a primitive, underdeveloped country. Probing for the source of this misperception, she learned that some of the parents had told their children that they had been placed for adoption because their birthparents were poor. The children had interpreted "poor" not only as an economic condition but as a cultural impoverishment and had extended it to cover Korean people generally. She cautions families to use the term "poor" advisedly and to keep it relative.

To children ensconced in middle-class life—to many adults for that matter—poverty is a mystery for which some simple explanation must be found. Susan Speiser asked her father if Korean people were lazy. "No, they're hardworking people," he answered. "Well then, why don't they have enough money?" she asked. "Why didn't my mom have enough money to feed me?" To a child who knows nothing about economics, poverty appears to be a personal failing, or even an inherent attribute that sets the poor apart from "us." One way I have sought to demystify poverty for my children is by volunteering as a family at a free dinner served to people in need, some of them also homeless. After several months of this, I was taken aback to hear Grace and Maria talk solemnly about "helping The Poor People," as though they were a different species. It struck me as ironic, also, and I could have come on strong with something like, There, but for adoption, go you. That would have been a quick solution, but a very arrogant and insensitive one. Instead, I talked about the safeguards that keep our own family from hunger and homelessness: a father who pays child support, unlike most noncustodial fathers; access to state-funded health insurance so that we are not impoverished by my chronic illness; and relatives who would help out if we came upon hard times.

If American poverty is an alien condition, how much harder it must be for our children to identify with pictures of the shanty towns that ring Latin American cities or of beggars on the streets of Calcutta. How do we endow birthparents living in these situations with a recognizable humanity? Roy Brower has the good fortune of a job that allows him to travel to Third World countries and occasionally take his family along. The children have not been back to Colombia, but have seen poverty up close in Central America. Visitors from other countries whom they meet through their father's work are involved in the issues of human rights and economic justice. Roy says,

We don't address those as issues *particularly* that often. We try to
reflect the values in the way we deal with our experiences in the
Third World, the people that we know, the people they meet when
they are with us, the relationship we have with refugees, so that
they begin to sense our valuing of people who come out of situations
of poverty and political oppression, and they begin to understand
the causes of that. And then, when they ask about their own upbringing
and they talk about it, we just let them fantasize a little bit: "Well,
what do you imagine your birthmother to be like?" I think both of
them assume that she is in a situation of poverty. We try to develop
an appreciation and understanding of people who are in that situation.

First-hand familiarity and a demonstrated ease among people living in
poverty would certainly make the life stories we offer our children more
vivid and convincing.

    With unwed motherhood, we run headlong into social stigma. The
risk of portraying the birthparents as unworthy is even greater than it
is in the case of poverty. Often, of course, these two circumstances
are intertwined. Our responsibility here is to explain stigma without
stamping its marks on our children's images of their parents. "Your
mother wasn't married," suffices only until children get some inkling
about the role of sex in reproduction. The young daughter of a friend
of mine posed a very typical question for children of six or seven or
eight, "How could my birthparents have a baby if they weren't married?"
My friend paused before answering, "Well, they had sex." Her daughter's
mouth dropped and she shook her head. "You shouldn't have told me
that," she said. My friend read that response two ways: Her daughter
had already learned that sex is to be kept private, and she didn't really
want to hear anything about her birthparents that seemed improper or
even "gross."

    Our attempts to explain how unwed parenthood leads to adoption
are culturally encumbered by the history of sexual puritanism in the
United States and the frantic and confusing "revolution" against it,
which has obscured sexuality in suggestive car commercials and perfect,
unblemished bodies interlocked on a movie screen. There are a few
parents who judge their children's birthmothers by the puritanical standards, finding them indecent or even sinful. One of the many cottage
industries started by adoptive parents to supply the demand for baby
announcements and gift items sells a printed version of a poem that
contains these disturbing lines:

Some would gather money along the path of life,
Some would gather roses and rest from worldly strife.
But we would gather children from among the thorns of sin.
We would seek dark almond eyes and a carefree toothless grin.

Even if we try hard to avoid such ethnocentric self-righteousness, children confused by our society's conflicting messages about sex may yet be troubled by the circumstances of their birth. A mother long experienced in international adoption who had made every effort to instill ethnic pride in her children told me that, to her surprise, the greatest difficulty her teenage daughter experienced had to do with her birthmother's sexual behavior and its possible implications for her own sexuality.

Sex may not have been the critical issue for the birthmother herself, however, and the society in which she lives may not see bearing a child out of wedlock as a sexual transgression. Stigma results when basic cultural mores are violated, but these may not be sexual ones primarily. There is a double sexual standard in Korea, and men prefer virgin wives, but the greater harm in unwed childbearing is that it violates the integrity of the family, which is the very foundation of Korean society. In Latin America, where families are more commonly formed and re-formed without marriage, the boundaries of social class are kept inviolate. A wealthy man may have a "little family" with a mistress he regularly visits or even regard his household servants as readily available sexual partners, but the children born to them are not entitled to his paternity in the same way his wife's children are. This is the setting into which the teenage girl mentioned above was born. In explaining how stigma operates, we have to be careful not to leave our children thinking that their existence is a violation of morality or that their birthparents are evildoers. I want to talk to my children about the injustice and the sorrow of their birthmothers' situation, even as I try to understand its cultural underpinnings.

Some parents use the word "choice" in explaining the birthmother's act of abandoning or relinquishing her child. We Americans believe ourselves to be self-reliant individuals who exercise free will and constantly make choices by weighing options. It is easy for us to slip this image onto the birthparents as well, especially given the current discussion of reproductive choice which poses motherhood, adoption, and abortion as alternatives for pregnant women. These options may not be equally available to our children's birthmothers, nor do they have the economic resources to act on them. Moreover, individual *choice* may matter less to them, given the culture in which they were raised, than their *obligation* to family or community, even if fulfilling the obligation requires a painful sacrifice. Telling our children that their birthmothers "could not" raise them or "had no choice" but to abandon them may bring us closer to the truth than describing their actions as an exercise of free will.

It would, of course, be much easier to explain these complex matters to our children if we could offer them personal testimony from the birthmothers themselves, as the Perlitzes can do in talking with David. Parents of children born to American birthmothers have access to published resources that look at adoption from the birthparents' point of view, and, as adoption in the United States becomes more open, more children have the opportunity to correspond with birthparents or even have face-to-face meetings. In other cultures, there are strong reasons not to risk the exposure that a letter or a meeting might entail. What is needed is a safe medium in which birthparents can make their motives and feelings known to the children and the families who adopt them. The staff of the Ae Ran Won Home for unwed mothers in Seoul has begun collecting personal stories from the residents and translating them into English to make them available to adoptive families. These first-person accounts make clear not only how painful the decision to relinquish a newborn baby is, but also how difficult life would be for both mother and child if they were to stay together. "The more I thought about you, the more I knew adoption was the only way," one mother writes. "When I came to that conclusion I ached all over. I believe that you will be a credit to your adoptive family, more than I was to mine."

So far, the word "birthmother" has appeared far more often than "birthfather," and that is an accurate reflection of my conversations with both parents and children. In most cases, the birthfather does not figure explicitly in the story of how the child came to be adopted. Even if he is named on the referral papers, he may well have left the scene before the child's birth. In speculating about our children's heritage or in anticipating their feelings when they realize they have been "given away," it is usually the mother whom we focus on. There seems to be consensus that the maternal bond is the primal and thus the stronger one. We are neither as puzzled nor as moved to emotion when fathers leave their children. Children, too, generally show more curiosity about their mothers than their fathers. Of the adopted people I interviewed, only Joy Egholm and Brad Crosby, both of whose fathers were in the U. S. military, mentioned having birthfather fantasies. In both cases, they were of the knight-in-shining-armor type that even birthchildren sometimes entertain. "I used to think that my father was a millionaire," Joy says, "and that he would have this special trust fund for me when I found him." Brad's fantasy is similar:

Someday I'd come home from school and there would be a limousine parked out in front of my house, and there'd be a trustee ready to hand me the papers, and that would be a gift from my real parents. The way I am, I should have money. That's got to be a trait I inherited from my father, because I know my mother didn't have money. If you're going to dream, dream big.

Boys may be a bit more interested in their fathers than girls are, because they can expect to resemble them. It would be interesting to know whether children whose fathers assume a large share of the child care, as Bill MacNamara and Ron Josephson do, have more questions or do more fantasizing about their birthfathers. Seth Josephson, at seven, has begun to ask for basic information about "my dad in Korea," which his parents unfortunately cannot supply.

It was only after she was married and had children that Ruth Kim Schmidt began to think seriously about her birthfather's existence in the world. She prefaces the account by saying, "I had a revelation about adoption and my own personal life experiences that hit me like a thunderbolt." It had to do with her dating habits and her attraction to men somewhat older than herself:

It was the classic, Oh, you're looking for a father figure. But I had a really good relationship with my adoptive father, so that never really quite fit for me. But then I hit it on the head. It's not your adoptive father, it's your birthfather and that unfinished piece of business— the feeling of true abandonment by a male. I had never allowed myself to think about that very much. I had never really fantasized about him. Maybe once in a blue moon it would flit through my head that I even had a birthfather. Now I found myself getting really angry and I thought, Why am I so upset about this?

To me, the really sad and tragic thing is, I feel like I'm a good person and that I've done some positive things with my life, and he doesn't even know that. It's really too bad for him, you know. He's got a family that either he's not aware of or . . . I felt angry, but I felt real sad that there was a piece of his life that he isn't involved with or doesn't understand. The feeling is really new for me, and it's hard.

I guess I look, too, from a broader perspective on males in general and our social attitudes around men and their responsibilities as far as children are concerned. I have a real concern about that politically, that there are so many Amerasian children who are from very similar situations as myself, and that our country allows that kind of irresponsibility. It strikes me on several different levels—the abandonment by men of children.

In the current version of her life story, Ruth's sorrow at abandonment centers around the figure of her birthfather. As for her birthmother, she has, as she puts it, "forgiven that situation."

I harbor no ill feelings towards her. I guess being a woman and having children of my own and knowing how difficult that is, and having a child that is biracial and would be discriminated against, and the cultural and economic times, etc., etc. I guess I've built myself a story and an understanding of that that makes it real easy for me.

A very significant event that helped the story take that direction was a reunion with the foster family that took care of Ruth between ages two and four. Her foster mother explained how difficult life was for Korean women who had relationships with American soldiers and bore biracial children. "Maybe her motive in telling me these things was for me to be forgiving and understanding," Ruth says. Ruth also learned on this visit that the foster family had tried to adopt her but that the policy in operation was to resettle Amerasian children in the United States. Seeing the family again restored memories of living in their home, and they were pleasant ones.

I had a real consistent, stable, caring environment. I look to that as one of the reasons why I have the mental health that I do. I think there's a real important need to be wanted, to know that there were other people who cared about me, and very early on. There's a real stability in that.

Feeling that stability has helped Ruth "reckon with" her abandonment. "There is a kind of hole," she recognizes, "but I don't have any really driving need to fill that in." She had a rare opportunity, also, to hear someone who knew her then describe what she was like as a child. Still, she has enough experience of living with the void to make her "obsessed with saving my own children's childhood for them."

My husband says, "Can't we get rid of some of this stuff?" and I say, "No!! I have to have every article of clothing they ever wore." My children will never have to say that they don't have pictures of themselves as babies to bring to school because we have volumes of them.

Ruth's meeting with her foster family is instructive for those of us who can offer our children actual evidence that someone cared for them in their birth countries. This is one way we can provide some continuity to their life stories. Without being terribly effusive about it, Grace has shown her foster mother's photograph to her friends and she keeps a letter from the family, written in Korean, among her guarded treasures. Judy Pollard is hard put to fill the void because she has conflicting information about where her daughter was before she entered her life so abruptly at age two. She has extrapolated a past from her daughter's behavior: "I know she was loved. She's a loving child—a warm child. So wherever she was, she was cared for to a degree and loved." For children who arrive at an older age with memories of their own, building continuity can mean helping to keep the happier memories alive. In Anita Martinson's case, it is life at the orphanage where she was taken after her rescue from the beating. "It was a wonderful place for her," her mother says. "It gave her the first security and stability she had had in her life." My daughter Maria has made her own distinctive use of the information I can give her about her early care. Hearing that she spent some time hospitalized in the Angels' Baby Home, she conjured up an angel who took care of her in that early phase of babyhood that neither her birthparents nor her adoptive parents witnessed.

Fantasy is, in fact, the most accessible tool that children have for filling the gaps in the story. What we, as parents, offer to the construction of a liveable past ought to be accurate, truthful, and sensitive to the people and the culture from whence they came. It does not have to be the entire, literal truth, however. Parents do withhold information that their children are not mature enough to understand or that might hurt them needlessly. There comes a point, eventually, at which the children take over the storytelling. If they imbue it with fictional elements, it is probably because it makes little sense or offers insufficient comfort otherwise. The adage "truth is stranger than fiction" is certainly borne out by international adoption. Fantasy can make the strange and unfamiliar parts less remote.

Parents can even help in that process by using their own imaginations to apply the special knowledge they have. After reading *Yogong: Factory Girl,* Robert Spencer's anthropological study of young women working in South Korean industry, I asked the girls to come and listen to a story. As we lay on my bed, I constructed a scenario in which we were a family in rural Korea: I, a widowed mother and they, two sisters approaching adulthood. I made up a brother to whose education the sisters would be expected to contribute. I described our house and our daily routine and then sent the older sister, shortly followed by the younger sister, off to the city to look for work and housing. Eventually, the story brought one of them into a relationship with a young man whom she cared for but whose parents had persuaded him to agree to a marriage arrangement with another woman. A baby was born and the question then was how best to provide for it. The answer the girls gave was to have the baby adopted, which they undoubtedly figured was the "right" answer. Grace took part but shortly returned to *Nancy Drew.* For a few days after, Maria asked for additional details: "Do we have a dog? What do we wear?" It was no longer a tale about the why of adoption but a fantasy trip to the country where she might have grown up otherwise.

Even before the children arrived, I expected to be supplanted in their affections at some time in their life by a fantasy birthmother much like the mother that Snow White lost. This struck me as natural but also troubling—who wants to be the wicked stepmother who usurps the place of the lost mother? Reba Perlitz had to choke back tears when she heard five-year-old Leah tell her grandmother that she had a mother in Colombia whom she loved more than her mom. Geographical distance and racial similarity might even endow the fantasy mother with special romantic appeal. Both my experience with my children and the interviews I did have taught me something I would not have expected—birthparent fantasies are not necessarily secret or guarded as private property. Amy Andrews publishes stories about her fantasy Korean family in her school magazine. Often, imagining what the birthparents are like is a joint endeavor of child and parent, as Mary MacNamara tells:

Katie will say to me, 'What do you think my Korean mom"—that's what she calls her unless she's mad at me—"is like?" "Well, I think that she was probably very pretty, and I really think that she was very strong-minded." And I really do, because for an unmarried woman to live with her boyfriend in Korean society—that takes a real independent woman. Now that's not something I want Katie to do, but I think that she must have been real strong-willed, like Katie is. The challenge for me is to try to channel that will in appropriate directions.

Mary's answer to Katie's question offers her a mother who is the source of personality traits that Mary wants to affirm and nurture—a birthmother who is like her. Yet she also makes clear that the birthmother is living in a different cultural context.

In aiding our children's fantasies, we can derive images both from what we observe in the birthparents' offspring and what we know about their life circumstances, including knowledge of their culture. But we can still leave room for pure make-believe. In answer to my question about how she imagines her birthmother, eight-year-old Margaret Chatten told me that she "maybe has curly hair." I bit my tongue when I heard myself say that she must have a permanent then. I didn't really need to check Margaret's knowledge of Korean physical features. A curly-haired birthmother is a fine fantasy, and anyway, permanents are in fashion in Korea. Children's fantasies about their birthparents can, of course, run counter to the information we have so carefully provided. I got an unexpected reminder of that when Maria came home from first grade with a drawing she had made for me. It showed a round-bodied woman with a tiny stick figure in a circle in the middle of her body. As you unfolded the piece of paper, it became a series of such pictures, and on each one, the stick figure, its arms and legs jutting out, became a little larger. "Can you tell me about this picture?" I asked, holding my breath a little. "That's me when I was a wee little fellow in your tummy," she said. At six and a half, the best birthparents the imagination can yield may well be the parents you know best.

Meeting Ruth Kim Schmidt and hearing her perspective as an adult looking back on childhood and adolescence helped me avoid being alarmed at Maria's "mistake." Ruth describes her own story as a "life journey":

> It's amazing, but adoption and being adopted is not something that you sit down and figure all out, and then you leave it and go on. It's a constant process of finding out who you are and what it means and how important that is. And it changes. At one time, all I could

think of was adoption issues, and then you kind of put it in perspective, and then something else happens that brings it all back out again. It's an ongoing process, and it's just amazing to me that you think you're at a certain point in your life where you really know yourself and you know why you do things and why you react, and then . . . A good part of your life is lived in your subconscious. I'm just sure of that.

If that is the case, then parents have little chance of transmitting the story whole, though we can do a great deal to help make it coherent. Whether it is drawn from the child's memory, from the referral papers, from books about their birth countries, from imagination or all of the above, it is a never-ending story. As long as it continues to unfold, it is full of promise.

7

What Are You?

A few years ago, public television broadcast a documentary series on the civil rights movement in the United States called "Eyes on the Prize." It came on right at the girls' bedtime, but I was intent on watching it. Although they were too young to follow the narrative and make sense of all the events depicted, I decided to keep them up for it, thinking it might be as good a way as any to introduce them to this critical phase of American history. Maria, only three years old, was mesmerized by the flickering images, but had little to say. Seeing the violence inflicted upon black people, Grace, then six, said with proper indignation, "They'd better not do that to my friend Charisse." Her promptness in putting a real human face on history was exactly the response I hoped for. Yet I never expected her to take this new knowledge about racism as personally as she did. As we watched the segment on the Montgomery bus boycott, she turned to me and asked, "Where would I sit on the bus? Am I black or white? What would I be if I lived in those days?"

I was stumped. Were the few Asian people in the segregated South "colored" or white? I didn't know, nor had I ever wondered about it. I didn't have to. I had lived this history as a Northern white student sympathetic to the Afro-American struggle for social equality, an easy and unambiguous role to assume. Attending meetings and turning up for demonstrations had not made me feel the impact of race as heavily as I did when my own daughter asked, "What would I be?" And how could I begin to explain that "those days" are not over, that race is still the most polarizing factor in American life.

Ruth Kim Schmidt, Asian in appearance but biracial in origin, recalls her confusion about where she fit in the racial scheme:

> I went to an all-white elementary school and an all-white church,
> so I was the only person of color. It was, My God, isn't anybody

else Korean in the whole world? By contrast, I went to a junior high and high school that were predominantly black. That was the only other identified minority group that I was familiar with, other than American Indian. I felt that I was unfortunate that I wasn't black, which I know is a real reverse for a lot of people. That really takes them aback. But to me, if I could have made my life better, I would have been black, because that was the time when they were coming into their own and my best friend was black. I spent a lot of time with her family and always felt kind of second class, because I wasn't black and couldn't be involved in certain activities, wasn't invited to be part of the clubs that the black girls were involved in. And I think I was kind of a mystery to them. It was like, "What are you? You're in a white family, but you're not white and you're not black and you're not Indian. Korea? Where is that? Is that sort of like being Japanese or Chinese?" Naive as I was, I would say, "Yeah, sort of."

What are you? is a profoundly American question. I know of at least one young woman, born to a Korean mother and an African-American father, who coyly answers "Presbyterian." She knows full well what kind of information is being sought. Silvia Kowalski, aware of differences in skin tone, first encountered the concept of race when she came to the United States at 12:

I really did not know black and white when I lived in Colombia. I learned black and white here. Here when you go to school or you apply for a job, you have to write your race. In Colombia, under no circumstances, anywhere or for anything, did I have to write my race. Here I have to specify. Why is that? The first time I had to do that, I was very confused. What am I? Am I medium? Am I brown? Am I black? Am I Hispanic? When I had to specify myself as being other, or being dark, or Hispanic, that really affected me a lot.

In a nation populated by waves of immigrants arriving in succession—some as captives, some as refugees, some of their own free will—race and ethnicity are both divisive and unifying. Knowing someone's ethnicity can give clues to other divisions, such as religion, social class, and political affiliation. At the same time, race and ethnicity serve as rare sources of community in this very diverse society. Being among others who are what you are can offer a sense of belonging that is otherwise hard to come by in this huge country.

Another question central to American life is, Who are you?, which we hear more often internalized as, Who am I? It refers not to membership in a group, but to an autonomous "true self," which we think of as inherent in the human psyche. The authors of *Habits of the Heart*, a provocative book about American culture, see this notion of the self as a cultural product, arising out of our "habit" of individualism. In other cultures, including some of those in which our children were born, the answers to these questions are simply given and immutable, so that they need not even be asked. Once in the United States, however, our children quickly become subject to what the book describes as "the quintessential American task of 'finding oneself.'" Growing up in America means wanting to be distinctive as an individual yet still be part of the group.

Both the professional literature and the public discussion about international and transracial adoption entwine these two matters—ethnicity and self-concept—into one phenomenon called "identity." People opposed to the adoption of black children by white parents, for example, warn that the children will be confused about their identity and perhaps become dysfunctional adults. Having a family that is not "what" they are will leave them troubled about "who" they are. Advocates of transracial and international adoption acknowledge a risk of identity confusion, but see it as avoidable if parents take care to provide the child with a sense of heritage derived from knowledge about the culture of the child's birth. This continuing debate has a great impact on how conscientious adoptive parents approach the task of child-raising. Mary MacNamara is a case in point:

Before the children came, I sort of had it in mind that we would do Korean-like things—have a Korean vase in the house or whatever. I don't think I really understood how involved it would end up being. You really have to work on teaching them about their heritage, and sometimes it's a lot easier not to, to just sit back and be a regular family, but you can't. If you do, your kids are the ones who pay for it. When they get to be about thirteen years old and have the normal teenage crisis anyhow, and on top of that "I'm adopted," and an interracial adoption on top of that—boy, that's a heavy load for little kids. So I think it's real important that they always know who they are. When they go off to college, people are going to expect them to know all sorts of things about Korea, and I think it would be embarrassing for them, if nothing else, not to know, so I want them to know. And I want them to have a high regard for Korea, Korean people, Korean customs, because in a way that's self-love. The more they appreciate their heritage, the more they care for themselves. That's the best way to deal with teenagers. Can you tell I'm not looking forward to teenagers?

If the truth be told, many of us parents do live in fear and dread of our children's adolescence, expecting an identity crisis of greater magnitude than that faced by children who were born into their families. Expert advice and frequent newspaper articles about adopted teenagers acting out "identity issues" feed this fear. We hear less often about children like Ruth Kim Schmidt, who says, "I didn't have a lot of information, and to be honest, I didn't want a lot of information. I spent a lot of my early adolescence just trying really hard to fit in." Curiosity about her cultural heritage came with leaving home and going to college and, while her efforts to recover a Korean identity caused some emotional distress, her psychological core remained intact. Nor do we hear much about children like Debbie Balcom, who has had a stable adolescence, is comfortable in her family, and describes herself as "practically 100 percent American."

> I never really wanted that much to get into being Korean. I know I'm Korean and it's always been a mystery to me—where I was from and what we did do. I always wondered about it and I probably always will, but it wasn't enough to make me go looking. Eventually, when I've got time, I would like to find out something.

In a fifteen-year study reported in the book *Transracial Adoptees and Their Families*, Rita J. Simon and Howard Altstein found that the adolescents' self-esteem was not necessarily associated with racial identity but depended most heavily on having a "strong sense of belonging" in their families. Ruth and Debbie are both good illustrations of that. Simon and Altstein's findings are helpful to parents because they disentangle What am I? from Who am I? and allow us to work at answering the one with less anxiety about how our children themselves will answer the other. The book *Adoption and Race* by Owen Gill and Barbara Jackson offers the same sort of relief. They regard "identity conflict" not as "pejorative" and "pathological" but as "possibly offering the scope for creative development." Nancy Bledsoe, a Korean-American college student quoted in the newsletter *Adopted Child*, seems to have taken it that way:

> I do think if you're a minority with white parents it makes you a more interesting person. It gives you a lot of depth. You've thought about some serious things and may be more reflective, and that's an attractive quality. (March 1989, p. 4)

There are some parents who set aside issues of race and ethnicity altogether. A few of them have no interest in such things and no perception that they matter. Armando Jordan feels that his parents are indifferent to his Hispanic background and that disappoints him. He has had to seek out support for his ethnic identity on his own. Other parents believe that the best way to ensure the health of their children's psyches is to raise them exactly as if they had been born into the family. They practice a deliberate colorblindness, which they regard as a virtue. Their children, however, are not colorblind, nor are the people around them.

There is no doubt that children experience some degree of psychological complexity in growing up adopted in interracial families, but that does not make them decidedly more volatile than their peers. For children with private sorrows of any kind, growing up in the United States today is a risky proposition. A child's acquisition of a sense of self is subject to so many influences beyond parental control that it becomes both mind- and heart-boggling. For the sake of clarity, this chapter will focus not on internationally adopted children's deep psychological yearnings to know *who* they are but on society's expectation that they know *what* they are.

Disentangled from Who am I? What are you? remains a critical question for anyone living in a multiracial and multicultural society. If our children do not look like the majority of the population—and not even like their parents—they will need clear and knowledgeable answers for their encounters with this question. Psychological health and self-esteem do not negate the significance of What are you? The reality of difference asserts itself the first time a stranger asks, "Is that your baby? Where is he from?" Even the "practically 100 percent American" Debbie Balcom has to identify herself in new situations.

One of the most recent happenings that I ran into was finding out who my college roommate was and telling her that I was Korean. I couldn't even tell her over the phone. I wrote her a letter and the first thing I said was, "There's one thing that you've got to know about me. I am Korean. This may come as a shock to you, but . . ." With people I don't know and won't see right away and have to communicate with, that's important, but I find it hard to tell them. What worries me is that not everybody is accepting.

To avoid these awkward moments, Ruth Hofbauer changed her name upon marriage, not to the expected Ruth Schmidt, but to Ruth Kim Schmidt, inserting her birth name to signal her ethnic identity and prevent double-takes.

With some exceptions—Jewish or Hispanic parents, for example—most internationally adoptive parents have little personal insight into what it is like not to be white and of European, Christian heritage in a society dominated by people of that type. We are, of course, minority families, and as such, we are singled out for scrutiny by the curious. Separate from our children, however, we pass as ordinary, majority Americans. Separate from us, they are still visibly out of the mainstream. Ruth Kim Schmidt is passionate about getting parents to realize that:

Parents need to consider, when they are adopting, how to provide their children with opportunities to be around other people of the same culture, or at least be in an integrated area. Whether they recognize it or not, the children are looking. Even when I was little, if I'd go into a room, I'd check out how many other people there were nonwhite. It's so unconscious, but you do it, and it's part of being a minority. I was having lunch with a black friend this week, and we were talking about relationships with nonminority people, and that there are some things that they will never understand and that you can't explain to them. It's something intangible, something you can't teach in college classes, starting with simple things, like how you choose a restaurant based on whether people are going to give you weird looks when you go in. Little things like that seem really insignificant, but they are second nature to someone who is a minority. That's the life you live. Your whole life is built upon those experiences—how you view the world and everything. It happens at a very early age, much earlier than I think most people imagine.

For Joy Egholm, being the only nonwhite child in her elementary school led at a very early age to a form of racial self-hatred:

I'd really get teased. They didn't call me Korean, they would call me Indian or something. My sister would always beat them up for me. I thought the reason they were teasing me about it was that they hated me, that they wanted me to leave their school. When I was little, I did not like being Korean. I thought that God had cursed me for some reason. Either I was bad or my mom and dad were bad, but He cursed me. I didn't want to tell my parents about it because I didn't want them to think that they chose something bad. I used to pray every night when I went to bed that God would make my eyes round.

Even if we can't experience it directly, many parents are concerned that our children's minority status will have such consequences, and we take that into account in deciding where to live, what schools the children will attend, where to seek out friends. When their family outgrew their house, Betty Ringstad and her husband decided to build on so they could stay in their integrated inner-city neighborhood.

This was a very definite choice for us. We saw our friends moving into neighborhoods where everyone was the same. We said, "Oh, how boring." Everyone was the same age, the same color, the same amount of money. The houses were the same, the yards were the same, the kids were the same. We said we'd rather stay here.

The MacNamara family lives in a fairly new suburb, and their children are the only minority children in the neighborhood and on the school bus. Mary had believed that raising the children in a stable environment, where others would get to know them as "just Billy and Katie down the street" would make their racial difference irrelevant. A timely trip to Korea made her think otherwise.

It was shortly after Billy had experienced his first bout of racism. For a while after that, he was real self-conscious about being different, and afraid to go where there were new people. He would say, "What if they don't like me? What if they don't like my color?" I'd say, "Billy, what's not to like? You're a great kid. Your color's beautiful. I don't understand." But I did understand. That was on my mind when I was in Korea. I saw all these kids walking to school. In Korea, elementary school boys put their arms around each other. Girls do, too. There's lots of physical contact among kids of the same sex. Even young women hold hands. I'd see these hoodlum looking boys walking down the street, bumping into each other and just acting like normal little school boys, having big fun. And I would picture my son in there with them—not being shy, not being worried about What if someone doesn't like me? Just happy and comfortable. I felt really bad. It was the first time I ever realized that adoption wasn't just a 100 percent wonderful experience for my kids, which is what it was for me. They would have to deal with being a minority.

This experience has made the MacNamaras firmly committed to learning, as a family, about Korean culture and getting to know other people, children and adults, from Korea.

By breaking their isolation from others of their ethnic background and giving them information about the culture they were born in, parents can at least help their children equip themselves to respond to the racism they are likely to encounter at some time in their lives. Margaret Chatten is only eight years old, but already she has been called "the Chinese idiot" and "pancake face" and was harassed on her first day at a new school by a classroom bully who made slant-eyes at her. Nevertheless, Margaret takes great pride in her heritage and can even conclude that "it's special being different." Her parents' interest in Korea and attendance at a weekly Korean school have bolstered her pride.

Some parents who adopt from Latin America expect that their children will be less subject to racism than black or Asian children. The incidents may be fewer or more subtle, but Hispanic children are not spared vituperative comments. While riding in a car packed with teenagers, Armando Jordan heard an unfamiliar boy in the backseat complaining about Latin Americans who come to live in the United States and "want us to feel sorry for them." Armando identified himself as Colombian, but the boy persisted, "I can't stand them. They should all be shot." The only Spanish-speaking people that residents of the Kowalskis' hometown had come in contact with were migrant workers from Mexico, some of them illiterate. "I always found myself trying to prove to that little town that Hispanic does not equal stupid," Silvia recalls. "If you criticize a Mexican in front of a Colombian, it's still the Hispanic culture. However, at the same time, don't mix me with a Mexican, because I am from a different culture. It's a very delicate balance." Mix-ups certainly do occur. Cesar Connor and the Frazee children have been called "nigger" by children confused about their ethnicity. That occasionally happens to children from India as well. This confusion brought the Frazee children face-to-face with their own racist attitudes. They were more upset about being mistaken for African-American than about the prejudice itself. Their mother had to explain that no, they were not black, but if they were, it would be just fine.

Racism can take seemingly benign forms, as well. Those of us who have very bright Asian children are easily seduced by the stereotype of Asians as intellectually superior. It is nice to think of your child as gifted and to be assured, as Nancy Bledsoe put it in Adopted Child, "People don't associate 'airhead' with Orientals very often." This stereotype causes extra difficulties, however, for children who were placed for "special needs" adoption because they have developmental delays or learning disabilities. It is also hard on children of average intelligence whose teachers have inordinately high expectations of them. It is important to know the reality that underlies the stereotype: In East Asian cultures, education and mastery of skills, such as musical performance, carry far greater prestige than they do in the United States. Parents who want the best for their children see to it that they study rigorously and practice a skill with strict discipline. Immigrant parents who want their children to succeed in the United States hold fast to this aspect of their culture. As a result, many Asian-American children perform exceptionally well in school and appear to have prodigious musical talents.

My daughters are both very pretty, but when people enthuse over their beauty, it makes them uncomfortable and me wary. The "exotic flower of the Orient" is another seemingly positive stereotype that can have negative consequences. The image of Latin women as flirtatious and hypersensual "Carmen" types falls in the same category. Ruth Kim Schmidt explains:

> There's a mystique around Asian women. Men sort of think, Oh, geisha girl. There's a very strong stereotype that is still pervasive: meek, submissive, slavish to men's desires. There are all these television commercials with the comb floating down the long hair, bathing in a spring pool with lotus flowers all around. They're like love objects. That's their sole purpose—to bring pleasure to men. I surprised a few men myself—"Oh, you're not at all what I thought you were going to be like."

This stereotype, too, has its origins in a very specific reality. Historically, American men have encountered Asian women for the first time while in the military in Korea, Vietnam, the Philippines. For all too many women, the only way to survive the hardship of war has been prostitution or an informal "marriage" to an American soldier, both of which depend on heightened sexual attraction and submissive behavior.

Parents who have not had personal experience with racism are hard put to know how to respond when it afflicts their children. We feel angry, frightened, protective, eager to soothe. A common response is to tell the child that everybody gets picked on for something or other, and to cite "fatso" and "four-eyes" as examples. In our eagerness to empathize and heal the wounds, we may pull up some memory of a time when we were singled out for ridicule. That often works for the moment, as Mary MacNamara discovered.

> When I was a kid, I had lots of freckles. Kids on the bus called me "Frecklebutt," and it used to mortify me. First of all, I was so embarrassed that they talked about a butt at all. And I didn't have freckles on my butt, and I wanted to say so, but I was too embarrassed to say that word. Well, my kids love that story. They think that's hysterical.

Mary knows that this response alone would not be enough. If we try too hard to find common ground with our children, we end up trivializing the minority experience. Racism is different in kind and degree from ordinary childhood nastiness. Overweight people have not been sold into slavery, and people with glasses would surely sacrifice clear vision to avoid genocide.

Hundreds of families in the Upper Midwest learned first-hand how terrifying racism is when they were targeted for hate mail from an anonymous opponent of international adoption. The diatribe typically included a photocopy of a newspaper article or photograph featuring their family or one of their children, accompanied by a typewritten text that said the following, or a variation of it:

> Will these adopted Korean children marry of their own race or will they marry our white sons and daughters? Was God wrong in creating different races and therefore the church and its people must now destroy God's human races, called racial genocide, today's holocaust. God created racial purity, man destroyed racial purity. Why? . . . What ever happened to sex-responsibility? Why should other people take care of other people's children? . . . God does not want his

people to lay and have fun with each other's body and then if a child is born, let their neighbor care for that child. . . . Married couples, who sit and wait for someone to commit adultery, so that they can have a child to adopt, are selfish and sinful . . .

It was not just Korean children who were targeted. The Kowalskis collected a stack of letters in the first couple of years after adopting Silvia and her sister. The perpetrator was caught after years of daily mailings that went, as well, to African-Americans with white spouses, Jews teaching in church-sponsored colleges, and Catholics who married Protestants. He turned out not to be an isolated, dysfunctional sociopath but a successful businessman, who had just made a generous endowment to a college. He left his victims wondering how many other placid exteriors conceal such hatred.

Because we love our children, we want so much to ease their discomfort with minority status and protect them from the further harm of racism. That is not entirely in our power, however. Debbie Balcom describes her parents' anxious efforts to keep tabs on her well-being:

My parents were always worried about if I was getting accepted. They were always worried about, Are you having problems? Are people giving you trouble at school? Do you get along with people? Are things OK? Do you feel like you blend in? My mom always says, "If you have a big problem, come and talk to us before you run away or do something foolish."

Trying too hard can backfire, as Ruth Kim Schmidt explains:

I can remember maybe twice in my whole life telling my mother that someone had said something racially inappropriate to me. I was very hesitant to tell her, because she was so-o-o sympathetic. It almost made it worse, because she was so hurt by it, and thought it was so awful, and made such an ordeal out of it. If she were to say, "Gol, that was really crappy of those kids to say that. I sure hope that didn't upset you," and then just leave it . . . But instead it was, "Oh, you poor thing." I think it's real hard for nonminority parents to teach children how to respond to racism in an appropriate way for a minority to react. White people react very differently than a minority person reacts, and that's due just to learning survival. That's what we're talking about—teaching minority children the survival skills of living in a society that is very racist, institutionally racist.

With or without parental help, children find their own ways to survive. Margaret Chatten advises, "Just ignore it." Daniel Molinari's mother calls him "unforgiving." "You do that to him and you're off his list." Michelle Gaartner has a book on self-esteem handed out at Sunday School that talks about the Great Me and the little me. When someone makes a racist comment to her, she explains to her parents that they have their "little me" out and aren't feeling good about themselves. Her mother says,

> Her approach mostly is to do something internal with herself about it and then leave the person alone. Just walking away from the person seems to give her a sense of empowerment. Jack and I would, of course, go beat up the kid and then find the parents that are responsible and beat them up too. The last thing I want to do, though, is single her out more by doing these big battles for her and also taking away her opportunity to learn how to cope with that better for herself.

To do "something internal" that wards off racism's potential damage to the psyche, you need to have a strong, realistic, and affirmative sense not only of who you are but of what you are. It is the "what" that provokes bigotry.

There is a very appropriate way for parents to handle this issue—by opposing racism itself, in all its varieties. Aware that her sons' skin color limits where they are welcome to go and what they might be encouraged to do, Elsbeth Saunders believes that she must be "an active participant in the minority struggle rather than just an observer." Many parents declare themselves ready to speak out if they hear racist comments, but the situations are often more awkward than we might imagine. They may, for example, expose prejudice in people we hold dear, as Chuck Stensrud remembers,

> We were having a Sunday family gathering with my sisters and brothers, and they were telling racist jokes. First, I just didn't laugh. I thought, They'll see me not laughing and that will be enough. Well, then they told a second one, and it was clear that they didn't get the idea. And I said, "I have to say, you guys, that this is really uncomfortable. I don't like you telling racist jokes. You've got to be aware of the fact that I have two children of another race here and they encounter racism. It's damn hard for me to hear you laughing about that kind of stuff when I know about the pain of racism."

They were really surprised. They hadn't considered that it was offensive, and they were really chagrined and apologetic, and they've never done it since. I kind of chalk it up to the fact that they've sort of become colorblind. They see Susan and Tony as part of the family, and so they forgot that they were of another race.

Chuck's comment did change his family's behavior, and he was glad that he had done more than just not laugh. The effort to change old habits can at times seem futile, but there is good reason to persist. When Jessica Martinson objected to a relative's use of a racist epithet, others in the family warned that she would never change. "That was not my point in saying it," Jessica explained. "Much more important to me is what the kids hear and what Anita hears about how I feel about prejudice toward all peoples."

Avoiding the issue of race within the family can, indeed, perpetuate racism. There is a loud message in what is not talked about. Even some very young children who know nothing of racism are aware of their difference from the majority and may ask, What am I? of their own accord. Grace began noticing racial distinctions much earlier than I expected she would. Just before her second birthday, we enrolled in a parent and toddler swimming class, along with a friend and her Korean-born daughter. There was another adoptive family in the class, with twin girls from Korea, and a Japanese mother and daughter. Our first time there, Grace toddled around the locker room pointing at each of the other children in turn. She identified all the white children as "Baby," but each of the Asian children was "Dace," her name for herself.

Children newly aware of skin color may seem preoccupied with it for a while. Bob Garman says of Benjy, his seven-year-old Colombian-born son, "He talks a lot about being brown. His skin color is this beautiful golden brown, and he's always asking me, is this guy brown or is that guy brown, about athletes and people like that." Of course, such fervent curiosity about skin color can mean that the child is already aware of its social value. Benjy asked his mother if he will still be brown in heaven, because he would rather be white. She answered the question directly, without showing alarm, yet built in the message she wanted to convey: "I really don't know, but whatever God decides it's going to be, it will be the best way, because He wants the best for us. Maybe we'll all be purple. I have no idea."

Many parents try to ease the pressure of What are you? by applying it to themselves and explaining that everyone in the family has a distinct ethnic origin. Chuck Stensrud and Margo Speiser take that approach.

> In our house, we have a lot of cultural conversations and talk about Margo's Germanness and Swedishness and my Norwegianness and what all. And we also talk about being Korean. That's a deliberate way of saying that we all come from different places and there are some things about us that are very different because of our heritage and culture, and then some other things that are the same because we are all in the same family. We can bring all these things in and they're neat things to have and they're all different.

As these "cultural conversations" proceed, the children do their own sorting into categories, filling them out with whatever information they have at hand. Because they themselves are of different religious backgrounds, Ron Josephson and Gwen Ryan especially want their children to appreciate ethnic diversity. One day Seth Josephson called down the stairs to his dad, "Am I Korean and you're Jewish, or am I Jewish and you're Korean? Who gets Hanukkah presents?" Obviously, the ethnic labels make no sense on their own but need some real-life referent. Americans do habitually say, I'm half-Irish and half-French, as though nationality is genetically transmitted. Though that is the common practice, people who look "foreign" in the eyes of the majority are pressed to supply more information about what their identity means. Irish we know—the Kennedys are Irish—but Paraguayan?

Children adopted as infants arrive in the United States as cultural tabulae rasae, with no memory of life in their birth countries. Whether they will have a sense of cultural heritage to go with their ethnic identity depends upon whether their parents choose to provide it. Even older children with memories to draw on may be unaware of having a heritage as such. Beverly Biehr, the mother of two Chilean boys adopted at six and seven, writes in OURS magazine:

> Our children know they are Chilean and are fiercely proud of it.
> But they didn't know they lived in Santiago—their knowledge does not extend beyond the places we visited while we were there. They knew the big river meandering through the city is named the Rio Mapocho, because someone repeatedly threatened to drown them in it when they misbehaved. Their overall lack of knowledge about Chile is significant: It means that the boys will form not only their American but also their Chilean cultural identities based on the

information that we, their parents, provide them. (September/October 1989, pp. 22–23)

Providing our children with a cultural heritage is a daunting task. How do we give them something we do not possess ourselves? How do we transmit to our children practices and habits and values that are not part of our daily life? How do we know for sure what Chilean or Filipino or Thai culture is? How many of us could even give a comprehensive description of American culture to a curious outsider? As much talking as adoptive parents do about the importance of a cultural heritage, we seldom consider what that includes. What aspects of the culture do we inform our children about? On what basis do we pick and choose?

The easiest way to define ethnic heritage in the United States is to look at what remains of the various immigrant cultures after a period of assimilation. The features most evident are distinctive foods, holiday rituals, music and dance, and assorted artifacts, especially folk arts and costumes. "Swedish" in Minnesota, for example, means potato sausage and painted wooden horses, rather than conflict avoidance and emotional restraint, even though the latter have had greater impact on Minnesota culture. These more obvious elements of cultural heritage are, indeed, the ones most accessible to adoptive families. My children know that if we go to an event planned for families with Korean children they can expect to wear a *han bok*, if they choose, eat *man du* and *bulgogi*, sing "San to ggi," and beg for the fans and drums and dolls and masks and hanging ornaments offered for sale.

These features, which Roy Brower calls "the trappings of a culture," make for great fun, and they give the children something concrete to identify as their own and to display to their classmates at school. Beth Larsen tells what interests her most about Korean culture:

I'm really interested in their colors. They have lots and lots of bright colors, they have really elaborate dances, and they say that most of the finest pottery is made there, or in Oriental places, especially Korea, because there are a lot of people that do pottery. I'm interested in their dances, especially the fan dance, because I think that's really a colorful and delightful dance. I go to a camp called Korean culture camp, and if my friend came, and she wasn't adopted or she didn't know anything about Korea, she'd be really, really pleased.

A sense of culture derived from "trappings" alone does, however, give an anachronistic picture of the birth country. Nowadays, you see more

Reeboks than *han boks* on the streets of Seoul, and the traditional crafts that survive the advance of technology do so in part because the government gives stipends to craftspeople who have been designated as "national treasures." Moreover, it leaves an impression of cultural uniformity that obscures internal ethnic, regional, or class divisions that have profound significance to people living in the birth country. Older children adopted from India feel uncomfortable participating in holiday rituals associated with a religion or a caste other than their own. A teacher eager to make instructive use of Anita Martinson's Guatemalan origins asked her to talk about holiday customs, a subject she had learned nothing about. Her mother explains,

> Anita doesn't remember anyone ever celebrating her birthday. One day was the same as the next for her. There were no Christmas celebrations. She didn't go to school. She didn't go to church. So all those things that break up our daily life, that give it a special timing, did not exist in her life until she came into the orphanage.

"*That's* the story that should have been shared in school," Roy Brower responded when I told him about Anita's experience.

> It's *that* part of their heritage and culture that should be valued and understood and appreciated, not that we eat Colombian rice on this holiday. I'm not putting that down, but if that's the extent of the cultural awareness, then I think it's a mistake. It's giving the kids a false sense of their own culture. There's not much about the present situation, the political situation, or the real poverty that exists in many of these countries and out of which many of these kids came.

When Armando Jordan arrived from Colombia at nine, he walked into his new bedroom and found a big box full of separately wrapped gifts. They were not unexpected. "I think every orphanage tells its kids, 'They're going to have presents for you. You're going to have everything you want.'" For months afterwards, he rummaged through drawers looking for more. I think of Armando now when I buy new things for my children, and of what culture shock he and other children must have endured in going from few or no possessions to "everything you want." As eagerly as I buy almost any Korean artifact my children show interest in, I find it ironic that this is probably teaching them less about Korean culture than about American consumerism and the importance it places on owning material things.

The cultures the children were born in may place far greater value
.on human relationships and membership in a community than on possessions. Children's play may thus rely more on group games than on
toys. North Americans, on the other hand, see each of the things we
own as having some inherent value—apart from its economic worth—
that will enhance our well-being in some way. There is a Barbie doll,
for example, with generically Asian features (except for her unhumanly
long legs and awesome figure) who comes in Japanese or Korean dress.
Along with the Peruvian and Mexican Barbies, these are popular items
for adoptive parents to buy as a way of bolstering the children's self-
esteem. I am glad to see alternatives to the basic blond Barbie that my
daughters adore, but I can't help but wonder where ethnic Barbie fits
in the larger context of international adoption. Mattel has located its
main Barbie manufacturing plant in Kuala Lumpur, Malaysia, to increase
profits by paying lower wages and fewer benefits. Who molds Korean
Barbie? How much is she paid for this work? Is it enough to raise a
child on?

As long as we are intent on "giving" our children a cultural heritage,
we will probably tend to think of it in very concrete terms. Instead,
we might look at their heritage as a gift that our children bring to the
family—a precious opportunity to expand our vision of what is valuable
in human life and to free ourselves from the constraints of our own
culture. It cannot be stressed often enough that in adopting children
internationally we become multicultural families. The daily presence
of this child born elsewhere gives us an intimate link to that other
place and those other people. When one of "them" becomes one of
"us," we have a chance to make the foreign familiar. This is a distinct
privilege that benefits the whole family. As thanks for this gift, we
owe "our family's other country"—to quote Pat Cantor Petrucelly in
Latin American Adoptive Families Quarterly (Spring 1989, p. 21)—our
genuine interest and respect, and a commitment to inspire the same
in our children.

Many parents first notice their vision expanding in a changed perception of the physical appearance of people of their children's origins.
Peggy Gaartner describes this:

When I visualize my daughter, what I see is her black hair and her
eyes, and that's with a lot of fondness. I love those qualities about
her. I love when she smiles and her eyes disappear. That's just *her.*

I like the appearance of Asian children and feel an automatic affection. I just love to look at all the faces in the Korean choir that she sings in. Now, from what I've been raised to think about what's pretty, a lot of Korean girls don't have the kind of features that I think of as pretty in a technical way. They have big faces or wide noses. So there's something that goes beyond head learning that has really gotten my heart.

Besides being attracted to faces that resemble our children's, we find ourselves more able to distinguish the features that make each of these faces individual. We soon realize the absurdity of the claim that Oriental people or Indians or Mexicans or whoever all look alike. At nine, Beth Larsen has already noticed how easily white Americans lump people of other colors together:

My friends can be kind of irritating sometimes, because they come up to me and they say, "If you're not really sisters, you sure do look alike." There are a lot of Korean people here, but it's not natural to have like five Korean kids in your class. So people think that everyone looks different in Korea, because in America, people could have blond, black, brown hair. In Korea, everybody has black hair, unless you're real strange. If I took two people who looked exactly, totally different, and they were both from Korea, people would think they were sisters or something.

Learning to see the individual differences in apparent sameness is an important beginning step in bringing the birth culture into sharper focus and recognizing a common humanity with the people who live there.

We should not be content, however, with distant admiration. The best method for learning about a culture, and for seeing it as dynamic and changing rather than as fixed forever in folk artifacts, is by meeting people who actually live it. Most of the countries that send children for adoption are also experiencing emigration, in some cases for the same economic reasons that make adoption necessary. Adoptive families living in certain urban areas have newly arrived immigrants close at hand for whom Filipino or Salvadoran culture, for example, still determines daily habits and outlook on life. They can shop at immigrant markets or attend ethnic festivals and cultural programs that are open to the public in a relatively effortless way to bring their children into contact with people of the same origins.

Turning to individual people as cultural resources is not as easy, however. I find myself smiling at anyone I pass on the street who looks at all Korean, but I am not ready to stop them and ask, Will you come over to our house and teach my children about your culture? For me, the hesitation is partly natural reticence, partly a concern about exploiting people's good will, and partly worry that they might not approve of our family make-up. I know that in the Korean immigrant community, there are some people who oppose international adoption on principle and some who are embarrassed by the numbers and visibility of children born out of wedlock in their home country. Polly Sonifer, the former president of Adoptive Families of America, told an audience at the AFA annual meeting that she too held back because she was afraid that immigrants from India would think that she had stolen one of their children. She then introduced to us an Indian man who happened to move in next door to her family. He advised her, and us, not to be apologetic but to celebrate the opportunity to be a cross-cultural family.

Bill MacNamara's initial hesitation to make the contact was also based on the possibility of disapproval: "In the back of my mind, I thought, I don't think they're too happy with me because I have Korean children." Since becoming involved with a Korean institute that runs a Saturday school for children from both immigrant and adoptive families, he has learned that a large segment of the community welcomes the children and is heartened to know of their parents' interest in their heritage. Bill and Mary are as involved as any parents are likely to be with a community of immigrants from their children's birth country. Because they also commit a good deal of time and effort to raising funds for the Korean social service agency that cared for their children, they also have frequent visitors from Korea in their home. They have learned that Korean people who work in adoption are very touched by evidence that an appreciation of the children's cultural origins is being fostered. Bill describes an event at their house:

We had some people from Korea who only speak a few words of English over for dinner. Besides the guests, we had thirteen kids and fourteen adults. We packed them in. We had an authentic, American-cooked Korean dinner, and they just loved it. Everything went fine. But the thing that stopped them was, we had the kids stand up in front of the family room and sing the Korean national anthem. They all knew it because that's the way they start the day

at Korean school. They didn't need any books or music. The Korean
people wept. They wept because they realized that even though the
kids are over here, they're being taught their heritage. They thought
that it was just wonderful. That's a good feeling, to have them go
back and say, You should see what's happening over there. That
really makes me feel good.

There are, however, cultural barriers that prevent adoptive families
from feeling truly comfortable in immigrant communities. Language is
an obvious one. "You smile and you nod a lot," Bill explains. Meeting
people from our children's birth countries shows us our common humanity
but also heightens our differences. We may even feel a little jolted to
find that the people who resemble our children physically do not seem
so familiar after all. Their bearing is different, their gestures and their
voice inflections are different. As a result of our parenting, our children
have become Americans in behavior and attitude. Living intimately
with them does not make us honorary members of their birth culture
nor initiate us into its most deeply rooted beliefs and values. Children
who have been told over and over again that they are Korean or Colombian or Indian must feel this jolt when they meet people who "really"
are. It took some time for Billy and Katie MacNamara to feel comfortable
mixing with the immigrant children at Korean school. "And I think
the kids from Korean families had to get used to the kids from adoptive
families," their mother says, "because their backgrounds are really different and they have whole different lifestyles."
Encountering these differences is both frustrating and enlightening,
in that it challenges us to examine our own cultural habits and our
illusions about what is universal. Parents of Latin American children
express amazement at how slowly and seemingly inefficiently the adoption
process works in their children's birth countries. As Jessica Martinson
attests, "Everything happens mañana." This is highly stressful for North
Americans accustomed to fast-paced productivity, especially ones who
have been expecting a baby for more than the natural nine months.
Nancy Cameron, the U.S. representative of the LIMIAR agency in
Brazil, says, "If there is one notable characteristic of us Americans as
seen by other countries, then surely it must be our lack of patience"
(OURS, November/December 1986, p. 6). These same parents are, on
the other hand, impressed by the spontaneous gestures of friendliness
that only a slower pace of life allows. A cultural disparity in operation

at Korean school has stretched the MacNamaras' thinking, as Mary explains:

> As the kids get older, the teachers are starting to talk more about a sense of duty and responsibility. Sometimes they say things that are not necessarily acceptable in our society but are perfectly normal in theirs. For instance, they will say that if you act up in class or you do this or you do that, you will shame your parents. We never would say a thing like that to a kid.

Bill describes how the MacNamaras approach the issue of responsibility: "We say, 'Eh, if you want to do it, you can do it.' They're not kids long enough. They grow up so fast, I never put pressure on them. If they can't do it, don't worry about it." Yet, they see a virtue in the Korean emphasis on duty, and they are glad to have their children exposed to it at Korean school, by Korean adults. Mary says,

> There's been a loss that I guess anyone who emigrates has to cope with, except that my kids didn't have a chance to learn about it at all. Because I have such respect for their culture and their value system and their sense of honor, that's why I feel the loss. Their work ethic alone! Holy smokes! If I could get the kids to work like that it would be wonderful. I'd like them to have that back, which certainly is not totally possible.

What the MacNamaras illustrate is an ability to respect, and regret the loss of, a cultural trait that they cannot and would not try to replicate in an American setting. Passing on such values as part of our children's heritage is far more difficult than buying them a folk costume, as immigrant parents also know well.

Nevertheless, we ought to make a reasonable effort to help our children learn what is fundamental to their birth culture—how the people view the world and what they believe to be true and good. This means being prepared to find factual answers to the questions they ask—by reading books, talking with people who know the culture, maybe even learning enough of the language to find clues to how its speakers organize their knowledge of the world. In presenting this information to our children, we should be careful not to fall into the Western habit of seeing things dualistically and making either/or choices. Jim Willwerth, the father of two Thai children who was interviewed for the newsletter *Adopted Child* (February, 1990, p. 1) advises parents not to say, "this is positive about Thailand and this is negative," but "this is Thailand." The Latin orientation toward time, the North American emphasis on productivity, Korean duty and filial devotion, American freedom and permissiveness each contain their own benefits and dangers.

Religious beliefs and practices are especially subject to misinterpretation and negative judgment. It is often hard to find commonality with people whose spiritual faith seems alien to your own. Sally Anderson mentions a difficulty she has encountered:

> Religion is such a part of Indian life, and we are nowhere near being Hindu or Moslem in this house. A lot of the traditions and even the stories in children's books are just steeped in the religion and have a lot of their gods and goddesses involved. They go around chopping each other's heads off. Not that our tradition is all nonviolent or anything. I want them to believe like we believe but still feel part of India, and it's hard to draw the lines there.

Sally would feel more confident about reading these stories and preserving some rituals if she knew what meaning this violent imagery actually has for Hindus. The image of an emaciated man hanging on a cross with his wounds oozing blood would be nothing but gory if deprived of its message about suffering and redemption. In explaining, for example, that the goddess Kali embodies both creation and destruction because life and death cannot exist without each other, Sally would be telling her children *about* Hinduism, not giving them instructions in the faith. She wants her children to believe as she believes, as do most actively religious adoptive parents, whether Catholic, Jewish, or Protestant. My children are being raised Presbyterian, which happens to be the largest Protestant denomination in South Korea. If they were to grow up Presbyterian in Korea, however, their faith would have an underlay of Confucian morality, they would show reverence to their ancestors on holidays, and they might even consult a shaman or an astrologer at critical times in their lives. I would like them at least to know about these things.

What, then, if there are aspects of the birth culture that are simply incompatible with our most closely held values? Confucianism, for example, prescribes a hierarchical relationship between men and women that I cannot present to my daughters without editorial comment. I have an overriding conviction that the subordination of any one biological group to another is a violation against the human spirit. Moreover, my children's separation from their birthmothers and from Korea itself can be attributed to the male dominance in Korean society. Margo

Speiser tells of trying to explain this to her daughter "at an age where fairness is a big issue." It made Susan angry, and Margo says, "I was afraid she would feel negative about Korea, but I've learned to switch that into more of a male-female theme in general and say that some things in Korea haven't changed as much as they have here, but they are still present here." But even that approach can leave Korea in a bad light as a less progressive country, rather than one with its very own cultural agenda. Another answer occurred to me when I heard a little girl tell her friend, "My mom says that they don't treat girls very well in Korea." What popped into my head was, Do we treat girls well here? Then why can't they go out alone after dark? Confucius aside, there is plenty of justification for patriarchy—even for violence against women—in Christian Scripture and American popular culture.

All parents have an obligation to prepare children for making ethical decisions about the problems that life poses for them. To do that, we cannot avoid being selective about what we value. While it is important to guard against ethnocentrism, we must not be so leery of making judgments that we end up romanticizing their heritage. Jack Gaartner warns of the risks involved in that:

> I think it's important for kids not to get too much of either "It's an awful place" or "It's the most wonderful place in the world to live," but a much more balanced, realistic sense of what the culture is like. If you create this massive myth, especially with kids, it can be real distracting to them when they bump up against the things in life that we all bump up against no matter what color we are. Then they have this notion that there's this paradise where people just dress up in costumes and everything's wonderful. I don't think it's helpful to the kid. Illusions rarely are.

Above all, we do not want our children to have an ethnic identity that is embarrassing or shameful, so that answering the question What are you? subjects them to ridicule. If the public image of the birth culture is negative, our children need both knowledge and a strategy to counter that. This has been difficult for children from Colombia, which has been portrayed in the American media as a country overrun and corrupted by the cocaine trade. Cesar Connor feels the hurt that such an image inflicts.

> Here in America, it's hard to be an immigrant. I like my country. I think it's a very good country, but here you get the opposite. I went

to the library yesterday and looked up under Colombia. The things they had were hunger, drug dealing, tourists. It's weird how America sees other countries of the world, because besides those things, Colombia is a beautiful place.

I was talking to a lady in the park one day and she asked me, "Where are you from?" And she goes, "Oh, I think Colombia is a sad place," and I said, "Why's that?" She said, "Because there's so much drug dealing." I said, "Don't be sad for all that. There's also natural beauty. Be sad about some of the things that are here." Then she kind of backed off. Sometimes I just have to bring something up to keep people from thinking about Colombia as just a bad place.

"Be sad about some of the things that are here" is appropriate advice in this case. One thing to be sad about is the shadow that drug abuse has cast on life in the United States. Coca plants, used to make a tea-like stimulant and for pain medication in the Andes, have been grown in large quantity and converted to cocaine powder to supply the American demand for "recreational" drugs. This is one case in which knowledge of the present reality is vital to the child's sense of heritage. Silvia Kowalski explains, when the subject comes up, that most Colombian people are very distressed by the cocaine trade and the violence it has provoked, while only a tiny group of people has gotten rich. The farmers in the Andes grow it because it is their best insurance against poverty, "the only crop that brings them any cash flow." Like Cesar, Silvia makes a point of finding good things to say about Colombia, to offset the negative impression. Every country, even the most impoverished and the most oppressed, has people of vision and courage whose stories we can tell.

Cesar and Silvia are lucky to have their own store of memories from which to derive positive images of their birth culture. The most instructive way to learn about a culture is, of course, to experience it first-hand. My perceptions of Korea were very much altered by a short visit to Seoul, and I hope I can afford to go back with my daughters in a few years. Many of the parents I talked with would like very much to visit their children's birth country as a family. The major uncertainty, besides the cost, is at what age the trip would be most fruitful. The parents' estimates vary from "at least ten" to "when they're teenagers" to "after high school graduation." The question really is, at what age can the children comprehend what they see enough to bear the inevitable culture shock? A Guatemalan social worker who assisted in Anita Martinson's adoption was adamant in warning Jessica about the harmful effects of an untimely visit:

> "Do me a favor," he said. "Don't bring her back until she's old enough to understand her country." I had mentioned to him, "Gee, Latin American people seem like they love their children so much," because I saw enormous displays of nurturing going on that was really nice. And he said, "It's in a very different way. Life for children here can be very harsh. You don't get to be a child very long in this country—not like in the United States. So don't bring her back until she can understand that. If you bring her back too early after being in the United States, she will feel like you've taken her out of hell. That's the one thing I would not want her to believe about her country."

The desire for a regular, consistent means of teaching children about their cultural heritage, short of the immersion that travel allows, is one factor leading to the creation of culture camps in various parts of the country. Generally, they are week-long day camps administered by parents where elementary-age children learn elements of art, history, music, and folklore, plus a little vocabulary. They provide an introduction to the birth culture accessible to isolated families who have the time and means to travel to them. For example, parents from as far away as Pennsylvania and Florida spend a week's vacation in Minneapolis chopping onions, scrubbing rice cookers, or pushing the playground swings while their children learn Korean songs and the martial art *tae kwon do.*

Ideally, the instruction is done by people from the birth countries—immigrants or temporary residents—who have special knowledge of the subjects they teach. Transmitting this knowledge in a form that the campers will absorb and retain is a recurring challenge. While volunteering as a classroom aide at Korean camp, I left the room on an errand as the history teacher was lecturing to twenty-four squirming third graders about Yi Sun Shin, the national hero who built the first armored ship in the world. When I came back he was drawing a picture of an Oriental toilet on the blackboard. He had gotten the message that comes through clearly each year at culture camp: The children's knowledge of their birth country is rudimentary and their primary interest is in the very mundane—Do you eat candy? Do you have Hallowe'en? Obviously, these are not little Koreans living in the United States but little Americans born in Korea.

These American children, then, are learning only bits of the whole, with no context ready in which to fit it. Even simple information about present reality is hard to comprehend in a vacuum. When I asked what she knew about Korea, Margaret Chatten recited, "The villages are shrinking and the cities are growing larger," but she wasn't sure why. Beth Larsen has acquired some inklings about the Korean economy:

> Most Korean people are sort of medium or poor average. Not many of them are like real rich. In America it sort of goes rich-rich-rich-medium-poor-poor. In Korea it probably goes medium-medium-medium-poor-poor. I don't always hear about people making millions of dollars in Korea. There are lots of people who have just enough money to get along, but they can't just buy everything they want.

Yet, for all that they don't quite grasp, Margaret and Beth are far better informed than Brad Crosby, who had to depend solely on the television show "M*A*S*H." "I always pictured Seoul as a little, run-down, slummy city," Brad recalls. "Just before the Olympics, I saw a picture of Seoul, and I thought, That is a major metropolis."

The oldest of the culture camps are into their second decade and a few have spawned separate overnight camps for teenagers. The parents who administer them have had enough experience to know what works and what doesn't and what limitations the camps operate under. La Semana, the Minnesota camp for children from all Latin American countries, relies on experiential education, such as a simulation of daily life in a rural Guatemalan home. Barb Strandemo and Mary Ness of the planning committee explain the rationale behind this:

> We are keenly aware that our children are in our families as a result of the poverty and economic conditions that are so pervasive in Latin America. And so we struggled with how to give them an accurate picture of everyday life in a Latin American country without offering them only poverty and despair with which to identify. . . .
>
> Our specific goals at La Semana were to give our children: an understanding of the needs basic to children everywhere; hands-on methods for discovering ways to meet those basic needs; and an appreciation for the resourcefulness and work that it takes to feed, clothe, and house a Latin American family of limited means without the conveniences we take for granted. (*OURS*, March/April 1990, p. 18)

Children who have access to special supplementary schools and the time to attend them regularly have the advantage of a consistent education in their heritage, in which new knowledge is continually reinforced. Learning a language, especially, requires regular, ongoing instruction. Roy Brower's children are enrolled in a public school that offers a bilingual education, with some instruction in English and some in Spanish. Some of the other children at the school are from Spanish-speaking families. Roy and his wife have chosen this program because it "provides another link to their own heritage." What Margaret Chatten likes best about Korean school, besides the opportunity to own a *tae kwon do* outfit, is learning the Korean language. She envisions going to Korea and staying there so that she can speak it.

Betty Ringstad, whose children attended both Korean school and culture camp all through childhood, has concluded that the curricular content is not of primary importance for most of the children. "The first priority," she says, "is for the children to have Korean adult role models," to meet adults of their own ethnic background whom they can both like and admire. This is probably best achieved by having young adults available who have immigrated with their families or who have come to the United States to go to college or graduate school. Their own lives bridge the two cultures in a way that allows the children easier passage. One of the most moving sights at culture camp is a group of kids clinging to a favorite teacher in the lunch line.

The greatest benefit that most parents see in the culture camps became evident to me in the first few minutes of our very first day there. I was towing four-year-old Maria by the hand through hallways crowded with more than 400 children looking for their assigned classrooms. She looked up at me and sang, in a taunting little voice, "You-ou don't have black hai-air." It was the only time since her arrival that she had been one of the majority, and she clearly felt emboldened. Donna Frazee's children did not want to go to La Semana at first and wanted nothing to do with being brown-skinned or of Hispanic heritage. But they did go and they let her know that, regardless of what they learned, it felt good to be with children who were the same color. Because they are organized by adoptive families, the culture camps also make international adoption the norm for that precious week. The children meet others who are not only of the same national origin but have similar personal histories.

Like school itself, culture camp is a mixed blessing. Making new friends and learning new information take hard work. Tina Molinari's children—both the Asian and the Caucasian ones—"throw themselves on the floor and bang around" at the mention of Korean culture camp.

They are not alone in this. Betty Ringstad made the whole family go to camp every summer. One year her birthdaughter asked, "Do I have to go to camp? Everybody there is Korean. I'm the only blond." Betty answered, "Yes, it's really important. Just think of how many places we go where the only people who are Korean—or different—are Todd and Kathy. Just think of how you sometimes feel."

How much authority should parents exert in providing their children with a cultural heritage, especially if the children resist it? Parental opinions differ on this matter. The Gaartners follow a policy of self-determination:

> We've let Michelle take the lead in terms of the identity issues, so if she wants to do more Korean stuff, we'll do more Korean stuff. If she wants to do less of that, we'll do less of that. If something came up and we said, "Here's a deal that you might be interested in," and she said, "Absolutely not," we would then drop it.

So far, Michelle has shown a good deal of interest in her heritage, unlike Melissa Woodrow, whose family has dropped their involvement in programs for Indian children at her request. Debbie Balcom, whose parents also practiced laissez-faire, was not interested and thus knows very little. Bill MacNamara is much more forceful in getting his children to Korean school:

> We fight them every Saturday morning. "Do I have to go there?" "Yes, you do." I think in the long run it will pay off, but right now Billy would rather be out playing hockey or baseball. It's tough. It's five days of school and then the sixth day you go right back to school. They don't see it being beneficial to them right now. But I think as they grow older they will.

Parents do make decisions on behalf of their children all the time. We make them eat vegetables, take music lessons, learn the multiplication tables, all with vague promises of future rewards. What parents offer children, at best, is consistency to counter the children's fickleness. Their habits change, and likes and dislikes come and go as they grow and mature. Interest in their cultural heritage fluctuates, too, and not always on a predictable schedule. After two years of pretending away her ethnic origins so she would fit in with her friends, Anita Martinson is studying Spanish and has joined a Latin American dance group. From her vantage point in adulthood, Ruth Kim Schmidt urges parents to be sensitive to their children's developmental stage in determining how hard to promote cultural identity. There were times in her adolescence when she "could have crawled under the desk" at the mention of Korea in school. She would even cross the street to avoid other Asians. It is encouraging to know that she outgrew this self-denial and has ended up with a firm Korean-American identity, which she hopes to pass on to her children.

The consistency we offer should come from a genuine, informed interest in our children's birth culture. My trip to Korea piqued my daughters' curiosity because the snapshots I brought back and eagerly passed around are concrete evidence that this place called Korea really exists. They will sit inside for Korean camp in the hottest week of August as long as I am willing to do that, too, as a classroom volunteer. Our show of interest must not seem phony, however, nor give the impression that we are misappropriating a heritage that is rightfully their own. I draw the line at wearing a *han bok* or trading in my silverware for chopsticks, but I do sing them the Korean national anthem every night as the one constant in my repertoire of lullabies. I only hope that if they hear it in the future at some ceremonial occasion, they won't fall asleep. Betty Ringstad's children are now grown, and she has reason to call her approach successful:

> We never hit them over the head with their differences. But at the same time—by the things we were interested in, by the things we did, by the fact that we lived in an integrated neighborhood, by our reactions to people—we were showing our children that we respect differences. By the fact that we committed ourselves to going to OURS, going to Korean culture camp. By the fact that we had Korean magazines in the house. By the fact that I would buy books and books and books, and I would read them, and I would read to them. But if they weren't interested in reading those and wanted other books, I never stuffed it at them. But they saw. We cook Korean food. We cook lots of Oriental food. We go to the Korean restaurant often. We have dolls hanging from the chandeliers. Our house is filled with Korean things. And I loved it. They knew I loved it, and that conveys a message without any words.

The most convincing rationale for encouraging children to learn about the culture of their birth comes from young adults who regret not having that knowledge. Many times, I have heard older adolescents say, "I wish my parents had been more interested. I wish they had pushed me harder." A statement from a Korean-born college student quoted in OURS magazine says it well:

> As a child, being adopted was like being left- or right-handed, it was just something about me. As I grew older, I wanted to find out more about my background and Korea. I started classes in college and made Korean friends. Then I discovered a barrier to my desire to "become Korean." I lacked the cultural identity background. Although I felt a pull toward my Asian friends, I was unable to understand and identify with them. The Asians expected me to have an Asian consciousness because I looked Asian. I realized I'd never become "Korean," but will always be a Korean-American. Now I am back to being "just myself."
>
> As a child, my family did not make an effort to share my Korean heritage with me. Now, they send me every article they find about Korea. I feel an earlier exposure to my culture would have helped me, giving me information on a gradual basis. It can't be pushed like I feel my parents are doing now, but just making it part of my life would have helped. (November/December 1983, p. 4)

There is something else intriguing about this young woman's longing to become Korean. It is so very American to seek a sense of belonging in your ethnic origins—to trace your genealogy, to revive old holiday customs, to give your children old country names, or to make a pilgrimage to your ancestral home. My curiosity about my heritage led to a Ph.D. in Scandinavian languages and literatures, but that has not made me a true Scandinavian. My experience is not identical to this young woman's, however. I am three generations removed from Denmark, born to an American mother embarrassed about her foreign-sounding middle name. My roots were stretched, not severed. No one ever stops me on the street to ask, in slow and precise English, where I am from. Internationally adopted children with a longing for ethnic roots have reason to feel it much more intensely.

"I will always be a Korean-American" is a crucial revelation for this young woman to have. Even if her parents had taken her to Korean school and culture camp and on a trip to Korea, they could not have replicated the "Asian consciousness" that her friends acquired growing up in Korea or in immigrant families. "Do not pretend that you are raising a little Indian," Polly Sonifer warned the audience at a workshop on adoption from India. Internationally adopted children have a dual heritage. As Michelle Gaartner sees it at age eight, "I'm special because I have two countries." The most accurate answer our children can give to the question What are you? has a hyphen in the middle. To keep from slipping into the void between the two cultures and feeling at home nowhere, they need to be firmly rooted in both. Children adopted at an older age have remedial work to do in becoming American. Jessica Martinson still reads 13-year-old Anita nursery rhymes and classic children's books so she will share in the common fund of symbols and idioms that her friends take for granted.

No matter how much emphasis we put on the heritage of our children's birth, we ought to be at least equally affirmative of their American identity. A teenage girl who reported on her trip to Korea to an audience of parents said she felt awkward because people assumed that she spoke Korean, and she could only shake her head in response. Here, on the other hand, people assume that she is a foreign tourist, "because I don't look American." She had a permanent that made her hair a long tangle of little ringlets moussed into place. Her speech was peppered with expressions such as "And I'm like, Wow!" What does an American look like, anyway? When my children use "American" to mean white, I am quick to correct them. Our families need frequent reminders, and we need to remind others, that the United States is made up of all different sorts of people with origins all around the world.

"American" is thus subject to many interpretations. Learning our children's cultural heritage should make us more aware of the precise nature of our own. Ultimately, we do offer a more particular identity to our children in the loyalties that we live by. This is already evident to parents who see themselves as different from the majority. Asked what identity he would prefer his children to have, Michael Perlitz says, "I'd like to have them think of themselves as Jews first, culturally, and as Americans, and basically I'd like to have them think of themselves as my kids. I'd like to have them know that they are Colombian and Honduran." Rita Garman's preferred identity is Christian, of a type that stresses "a personal relationship with Jesus Christ." She says,

We are real country conscious, but not for nationalistic reasons—just seeing it as, God did a beautiful job when He created Colombia. Look at all those beautiful mountains. They are aware of their countries, but still, someday they're going to leave all of that behind, and it's not something that's going to make any difference. We try to give them eternal values. That's their real grounding. It goes beyond nationalism.

All of us, in overt or subconscious ways, are acculturating our children to feel the allegiances that we ourselves feel. The forms that this can take challenge the imagination. One of my favorite stories in OURS magazine is about a Korean-American girl who won a trip to Dublin in a national Irish step-dancing competition.

There is yet another culture in which our children partake, this one determined not by geography but by historical moment. They are part of a worldwide diaspora of otherwise homeless children, unprecedented in size and scope. It pleases me, and I think Maria, that her first grade class includes six children who know the meaning of "when I came on the airplane." Imagine, then, if Maria, away at college, meets a handsome, dark-haired, high-cheekboned young man named Krister Johansson who speaks with unvoiced s's and elegantly pure vowels. "What are you?" she asks, though I hope more politely than that. "I was born in El Salvador and adopted in Sweden when I was three years old," he answers. Immediately, there is an affinity, despite their ethnic differences. They have a shared history of abandonment, displacement, and minority consciousness, enriched by curiosity about their genetic and cultural origins and a sense of multiple loyalties. The comfort and security that people derive from a common ethnicity might come to them through the common experience of international adoption. The best and most affirmative answer that both children and parents can make to What are you? is We are an internationally adoptive family. This is the heritage that we truly have "given" our children. Filling it out and giving it meaning is a shared family endeavor, which we must undertake with deliberate care and sensitivity.

8

Back to Beginnings

Amy Andrews' bedroom is a typical American teenager's refuge. Her bed is a mattress on the floor with a curtain drawn in front of it. The walls are covered with shelves of personal treasures and posters of handsome young men. Her desk is heaped with books and papers and tape cassettes. Amy's room has its own distinctive character, however. The curtain that hides the bed is a Korean flag pinned over a length of clothesline. The collected treasures on her shelves are mostly Korean dolls and ornaments. The handsome young men on the walls are Asian pop stars and athletes, and the pile on her desk contains study materials for teaching herself the Korean language. At 14, Amy readily admits that she is "really into being Korean." In her first month of high school, she has made many new friends, but talks with most excitement about her Asian friends, some born to immigrant parents and some immigrants themselves. They have sought her out, she says, and seem to accept her as she is, with no probing questions about her background.

Unlike the college student in the previous chapter who felt bereft at discovering that she had no "Asian consciousness," Amy does have something to go on. Her parents have always encouraged her to keep her heritage alive by sending her to Korean culture camp and taking interest in Korean matters themselves. She appreciates their efforts, though she sometimes used to resist them, and she advises other parents to follow their policy: "Influence your kids on their heritage. Keep hounding on them. Keep giving it to them." The most important contribution Amy's parents have made to her sense of heritage, and the cause, clearly, of her current enthusiasm, is a family trip to Korea, taken just four months prior to our interview.

The trip had long been planned for when Amy got to be a teenager. As the timing worked out, it marked the end of the rage that had made her lash out at her parents, withdraw from her friends, and feel miserable herself. Whether or not her abandonment was the cause of the rage, the trip has made a difference, even though she was wary of making it:

> At the beginning I was really nervous and I didn't want to go, because I didn't know what was going to be there. Just to know I was going to be in the country I was born in was kind of weird. But when we got there, everything seemed just fine. That first night, my Mom said that I woke her up screaming, "I don't want to go back to Korea!" I have no idea what I dreamed, because I woke up that morning feeling good that I was in Korea. I think some feelings deep down inside me told me, What am I doing here? I loved it, though. I just had a really good time.

Included in the three weeks of sightseeing was a site not frequented by other American tourists: a neighborhood police station near the U.S. Army base in Seoul where Amy was left a few days after her birth. That was as close as she could come to her roots. It was presumed from her lighter complexion and high-bridged nose that her birthfather was American. She has no easy way of tracing her birthmother, nor would she do so.

> You know how you hear about a lot of adopted kids wanting to find their birthparents? Me, I feel so different, because I don't think that I should do it. Even if I did have the right information, I wouldn't want to bring the pain into the family, because that mother gave me up. She's no longer my mother. She must have had a reason, so I should respect that reason.

As impressed as Amy was with the Korean landscape, the culture, the friendly people she met there, she knows that her adoption was not a fall from paradise.

> I have a feeling that if I'd stayed in Korea, I probably wouldn't be alive today, because I'm Amerasian and they have a big prejudice against Amerasians. My foster mother did not take care of me. I came here malnourished. They did not pick me up or give me attention. That's what we know.

Some of the people she met in Korea confirmed that her life would have been very difficult. Despite having been told before the trip that Korean people do not like to talk about adoption, she found them bringing up the subject again and again. People would smile at her and say, "Very lucky girl. Very nice parents." "They said how wonderful it was that I was in America. They said I looked so happy and healthy."

In spite of the prejudice she might yet encounter, Amy now envisions returning to Korea as an adult and living there. At this point, however, her future seems built more on a newly roused enthusiasm than on concrete plans. "I plan to move back to Korea when I'm older and be an English teacher. In a way I want to raise my family there, but I'm not sure. If I don't make it to Korea, I'll probably teach at a college with Asian-American students." She imagines either getting married in Korea or marrying a Korean-American and returning together. But, "if I fell in love with a white guy, this is the man I'd marry—no hesitation." The drawback to that, she says, is that her children would be only one-quarter Korean, unless she adopted a Korean child.

Amy's identity is still as mutable as any 14-year-old's. She perceives herself, with her dual heritage, as caught in a tug-of-war:

> There are two sides that want you, and you don't know which one to go on. You can't stay in the middle, going back and forth, because you feel like you're about to be ripped apart. But if you go on one side, you'll feel guilty for not going on the other side.

The struggle ends, not when one side wins, but when it feels comfortable to declare, like that college student, "I will always be a Korean-American."

Sitting in Amy's bedroom, surrounded by her Korean artifacts, I felt that I was in a major way station on a life journey that is not really so unfamiliar. Most of us who grow up in this amalgam of peoples called the United States do undertake that "quintessential American task" of shaping a persona that we can comfortably wear. Part of the task is to claim our right to the identity we forge for ourselves and to begin to live by it in the present, with an eye to the future. But unless we are imposters, we never fully re-create ourselves. We also have to reclaim the elements of the past on which our identity depends, including genetic heritage, family patterns, place of origin, and significant life experiences that demand interpretation: Why did this happen to me? What does it mean for my life?

We all engage, at varying degrees of consciousness, in a continual revision of who we are, where we belong, and what we ought to do with our lives. At critical moments, when the life journey has led us astray or we have come to a standstill, our imaginations take us back to where we began, to get a fresh look at where we are headed. For people who have been adopted, the task is, of course, more complicated because the beginnings are obscured and the patterns have been rearranged. Among significant life experiences, adoption itself looms large and may dominate the reclamation process, barring the way back. Sometimes it can feel as if there were no past at all, as Brad Crosby describes it: "I have no pictures of myself before a year and a half. I didn't exist before that. I wasn't born to anybody. I just existed all of a sudden. Everything starts from there on."

Central to the reclamation for some—but certainly not all—adopted people is a compelling desire to find their birthparents. People who cannot empathize with this desire often misperceive it as a sign of discontent with present reality or with the fact of being adopted. There are, however, many positive, healthy reasons for tracing these very personal beginnings. Brad Crosby has been engaged in a search for his birthparents for two years. Finding his "real parents" as he calls them, with no animosity toward his "mom and dad," is something he always counted on doing "someday." Although he knew he was Amerasian, he imagined his parents married and living together in Korea and he was simply curious to see them. In adolescence, about the time he realized that he was probably born out of wedlock, the curiosity took on a different quality:

> One thing every child has to do as a history project is a family tree. So I had to pretend doing a family tree of my adoptive family. I'd turn it in and get good grades on it, but in reality, that family tree starts with me. I am the root of that tree, not that big branch out on top. I want to fill it in. I want to become that branch up there and see what the roots are.

This longing for roots took on practical urgency when his wife became pregnant with their first child and he could not fill out the medical questionnaire at the doctor's office. "I don't know what I have to expect," Brad explains. "I don't know what my children have to expect." That was the motive he needed to make "someday" happen.

To initiate the search, Brad had to get access to his case history file, which had been closed at the time of his adoption, the common practice then. What he found there gave him another motive, besides self-interest, for finding his birthmother.

I had seen a movie about a girl who was 15 and had a child, so she had to quit school and she took care of this child for nine months. Her mother kept trying to talk her into giving it up for adoption. At the end of the movie she does. I couldn't imagine anyone keeping a child for nine months. How, after nine months, could you give up a child? Six months later I got the case study: My mother had me for fourteen months! That tells me that it's not that she didn't want me. She had to love me extremely to fight to keep me for over a year. The easy way out for her would have been giving me up at birth.

He also read about her trip to the orphanage, which told him how difficult their short life together must have been. The day that she had arranged to bring him in, she called the orphanage director and asked if he could send a cab to pick her up. She was only a mile away, and the director asked why she didn't just walk. She had tried to do that, she said, but her son had blond hair, and people swore and spit on them and threw stones. What Brad found most troubling in the case history was a brief account of his birthmother's departure from the orphanage. A social worker had coaxed the little boy to her side with some food. He sat there calmly and didn't cry or get upset when his mother left.

Just the way it's written, it seems like I didn't show any particular emotion while she was leaving. She was my mother, and I'd lived with her for over a year, and all of a sudden she leaves and it seemed like I didn't care. That's one of the reasons I want to find her. I want to tell her, I understand why you gave me up for adoption. Not showing any emotion then makes me feel emotional about it now.

After two years, Brad does not feel much closer to finding his parents and realizes he will have to go to Korea himself to continue the search. He is a young father with two jobs and two children, so time and travel money are short, yet he is optimistic about getting there, whether the trip takes him to his birthmother or not. In the meantime, the search has satisfied the longing for roots somewhat by showing him that he did not just materialize at an airport one evening at almost two years of age.

At the time I opened my case study records, my son was almost the exact age that I was when I was put up for adoption. It gives a little description of your characteristics and traits and the way you acted when you came to the orphanage. I was reading this, and my son was sitting and playing in the living room, and I was constantly looking over at him and going, He's exactly like I was. That means he seems to take after me somehow—all these little things that I would do, little quirks and things that little children do. It gave me a little sense about me. By watching him, I started thinking, That's how I was as a child.

There was also an early photograph of himself that Brad had never seen before.

I have that picture hanging above my desk at work. A lot of times I'll sit and stare at the picture, and I'll try to put myself into the picture, looking out at whoever was taking the picture, just to try to remember something out of my past. I try to imagine what things were like when the picture was taken.

Brad has found a partner in the searching process in Joy Egholm, who, quite coincidentally, lived at the same orphanage and came on the same flight that he did. A little less certain about finding her birth-mother, she, too, derives some satisfaction simply from knowing more about her origins:

With the case history file opened, she's a person now, and my father has features now—brown hair and blue eyes. Before they were almost like things that brought me into the world. But now they have an age and a description of what they looked like. I think that might be enough, because now I have something to fill the gap. I think I'd be satisfied. I'd feel a little disappointed maybe if I never saw a picture, but I feel better just having my case history file opened.

Whether or not she expects it to come true, Joy does replay the potential meeting with her birthmother in her imagination. "I've thought about this so many times, I cannot tell you. I lie in bed at night thinking, Now what would I say? The answer both she and Brad have hit upon is, Thank you.

Not every adopted child dreams of a reunion with birthparents. For every Brad Crosby anticipating "someday" there is more than one Beth Larsen who says, "I don't have this destiny to meet my birthmother, because I'm happy where I am and it's not any different than if I was living with my birthmother. It would be nice to meet her someday, but I don't have to. I wouldn't look. Maybe she'd come to me." Beth is only nine, and her sense of "destiny" may change as she grows up. Debbie Balcom, once immersed in the present like Beth, has become more curious about the past as a young adult, though she has no immediate plans for a search. Maybe in ten years, she says, after she has finished her education and entered a career and started a family.

Interest in finding birthparents varies greatly by age and psychological development and, even more, by individual inclination. It is by no means correlated with how easy the process may be. Betty Ringstad's son Todd, who spent his first six months with his birthmother, arrived with a letter from her giving her name and address. Betty has sent pictures a few times, but Todd, now 16, has shown no interest in communicating with her on his own or in meeting her. Betty's 21-year-old daughter Kathy, who was abandoned and has no information to go on, is the one who wants a reunion. Nor does such a longing imply discomfort in the adoptive family. Kathy is as close to her parents as any of the four children. Her favorite show of affection is a hug and her pet line, "You're my fambly."

Very many internationally adopted children have no names to trace or clues to follow. Unless Amy Andrews advertises for the person who left a baby at that police station on a particular day, the search does end there. This fact alone may be used to curtail interest in finding genetic roots. Melissa Woodrow wonders whether her parents are still alive, but she has no expectation of finding them and does not plan to search on the trip to India that she looks forward to taking when she finishes high school. Children adopted from countries where life expectancy is short and early mortality is high among the poor have real reason to doubt whether their birthparents are living. Ruth Kim Schmidt suggests that there are psychological motives for this, as well.

I don't think putting a lot of time and energy into a search right now would be that beneficial to me. I don't think it would make that big a difference, and it would be virtually impossible. I guess part of me feels fairly confident that she's probably dead. I don't

know why. I just have always had a sense that she would probably
not still be alive. Maybe because of the impossibility of searching
for her. Maybe that was a real easy way for me to accept it.

Children who have memories of their birthparents, as well as names
and other data, clearly have a head start on the search process. Whether
they proceed with it or not has more to do with the nature of their
separation than with how much knowledge they have to go on. For
them, it is not so much a search for roots, as Brad and Joy describe it,
but an attempt to heal wounds sharply felt. Armando Jordan lost his
mother in a very tragic way. Even if she is alive, she will probably not
recognize him or understand why he is there, yet he wants to look for
her as soon as he can afford the trip.

What I plan on doing is to go down there and ask for the hospitals.
I don't remember the hospital where she was, but just all the hospitals
possible, and I will go to all of them. And I hope I can find her
alive. I don't think she will know me, because when she became
terribly ill, she didn't know who I was. But I just want to touch
her. That's the main thing that I dream of.

Armando's genetic heritage is not the issue, because he knows a significant
part of it. She had a beautiful singing voice and she taught him songs
that he still remembers. He has inherited that gift and he uses it. If
he can manage, singing will be his profession, as well as a way of continuing his Colombian heritage and introducing others to it. Even if he
never sees his mother again, he still lives with her legacy.

Whenever I sing, I'm not doing it for anyone else. I'm doing it for
my mother. I hope people enjoy it, but mostly I do it because I was
given that. And that's the only thing I have to remember her. I
have no photos of her, I have nothing of hers. I can't even remember
what she looks like anymore.

Soon Hee Truman's link with her birth family was not immediately
broken by adoption. Her older sister wrote letters for the first couple
of years, but gradually she and her parents stopped answering them.
"There were so many things going on in my life, and I was so angry
about what they did, and they weren't telling me anything." Her sister
has made contact again, but Soon Hee has not written. "There are
times when I'm actually about ready to sit down and write but something

in me stops. Maybe it's because I have to write it in English. Somebody has to read it to make her understand." She has her birthmother's address and has considered going back to visit, but her anger about the separation gets in the way:

> I could if I really wanted to, but I'm just not motivated to do it. Maybe later on I'm going to regret it, because she's not getting any younger. Maybe one day I'll get my courage up and be able to do that. I think the feelings are always going to be with me, until I confront them with it one day. I think maybe then it wouldn't be so bad or so hurtful. But maybe you're going to get hurt even more if you do see them. What if it was worse than I imagined? Then I would always remember that, too. This way I can feel safe, not knowing exactly.

In some cases, there may indeed be more comfort in ignorance than in having all the blanks filled in. At an unhappy time in early adolescence, John Frazee began talking about finding his birthmother and learning if his father was still alive. After his parents sent in a request for information, his interest dwindled. "It was almost like he wasn't so sure that he wanted to know," his mother recalls. "Is he afraid of what he might find out?" Silvia Kowalski thought she should try to solve the mystery of her father's violent death and her mother's disappearance and began to contact people who could help. However, when one of them actually offered her some information, she declined to hear it.

> I was too afraid to find out what it was. I thought about it a lot and decided I'm not ready at this point. Is it going to give me peace of mind? Is it going to bring me despair? When I can say I really want to do this and not feel as apprehensive about it as I feel right now, I'll be ready. I'm OK the way it is.

For children born in one country and adopted in another, there are barriers to reunion that a child who was simply transferred to the other end of the home state does not encounter. There is a special poignancy in imagining a meeting of parent and child who have no common language, or who behave in ways that seem strange or inappropriate in each other's cultural settings. Brad and Joy assume that their mothers do speak English, because of their relationships with American soldiers, and they wonder whether they might even have immigrated to the United States, as many Korean people have. But for most children, the birthparents, no matter how close in fantasy, are distant in reality. In countries where out-of-wedlock birth is taboo, the sudden appearance of a child whose existence was kept secret can damage the mother's life. Half of the women surveyed at the Ae Ran Won home in Seoul in the mid-1980s want information about what becomes of their children, but most of these still want to remain anonymous and not be exposed. Joy is aware of this risk: "What if she's married now and has a family of her own and nobody knows? What if her parents didn't even know she was pregnant? Do I want to go into her life and just disrupt everything?"

If the birthmother is willing to meet the child, there is still no promise of a significant ongoing relationship. Even people adopted at older ages have acquired new loyalties in the meantime, to a job or a spouse or to goals more easily met in the United States. A young woman who speaks on occasion at programs on Korean adoption told of visiting her widowed birthmother ten years after her adoption at age 12. Her mother's relatives and friends were very dismayed to hear that she was not planning to stay and support her mother in old age, as Korean children are expected to do. She felt guilty leaving and does feel obligated in some way, but she was also homesick for family and friends in the United States.

Hearing how much Brad Crosby and Joy Egholm have benefited from the very process of searching, and how emotionally delicate the prospect of a reunion is for Armando and Soon Hee has impressed upon me that whether or not to search is a question my children should be allowed to answer for themselves. It is their right and I should neither push nor hinder. Nevertheless, like several of the parents I interviewed, I have my own longing to bring the story back to its beginning.

In contrast to the popular image of how search and reunion affects the adoptive family, most parents do not feel threatened or insulted by the prospect that our children will want to meet their biological parents. "I would really love for them to find their birthmother," Donna Frazee says of John and his sister and brother. "I wouldn't mind going back to Colombia with them and helping." "I certainly want my children to know their ancestry," says Tina Molinari. "I'm glad to be the front line of mother, but I think that to finish the story you have to go back and find that." Laurie Means believes that she has two responsibilities to fulfill to the birthparents. One is to convey to her daughter that they were wonderful people who "did the very best that they could."

The other is to try to find them, "to reassure them on a personal level that their child has been well taken care of." Laurie wants to take the initiative on this because she has a good friend who relinquished a child years ago and is hesitant to inquire for fear the child has not had a good life. I, too, want my daughters' birthmothers to know how they are doing, and so I send letters and pictures to be filed away at Eastern Child Welfare just in case they come looking. But I have yet another motive for wanting a reunion: to see for myself the women who gave birth, beauty, and personality to my children, and to say, "Thank you," or better yet, *"Komapseumnida."*

Geographical distance from the birthparents spares internationally adoptive families from the compulsion to be always on the lookout. Amerasian children, however, may have a sixth sense in operation: "I could be working for my father and I wouldn't even know it," Joy Egholm says. Since it occurred to her that her birthmother could have immigrated, she is more keenly alert. "Sometimes when Oriental women come in where I work, I think, This could be my birthmother and I would never know." When Mary MacNamara went to Korea, she was "strongly tempted" to initiate searches for her children's birthmothers.

> My son is from Seoul, and I was going through the city thinking,
> She's around here someplace, someplace in this city. Once I saw a
> woman on crutches, and I nearly jumped out of the cab. I wanted
> to run over and talk to her. Well, I'm sure she didn't speak English,
> and crutches are not the only requirement it takes to be Billy's mother.
> But I'd sure like them to know that the kids are OK and that they're
> happy and that they haven't forgotten about Korea, nor about them.

I had Mary's experience in mind when I went to Korea, and I found myself doing the same thing. I looked into the faces of as many women in the crowd as I could see, waiting for a resemblance. It surprised me that I saw no one with my children's distinctive features. I came away marveling at the array of faces in a country where coloring is not what distinguishes people. I also realized how difficult it might be, in such a populous country, to find my kids' birthmothers, even though I do have their names—names undoubtedly borne by many different women.

It was with the encouragement and support of her adoptive family that Colleen Griffith found her birth family in Korea. "I feel so much closer to my parents because of that," she says. Colleen was adopted at seven, after a year in an orphanage. Prior to that, she had lived with her mother some, but mostly with her grandparents. The families exchanged letters for a time, but lost touch when the grandparents moved. When she was fourteen, Colleen went on a tour of Asian countries with her parents and her brother, who was adopted from Vietnam. The adoption agency had arranged for her to be interviewed by a Korean newspaper for a feature story about the returning child. The paper published her picture and her history and an address to which anyone knowing her origins could send information. "We got just tons of letters," Colleen remembers, "not necessarily from people saying they were my mother, but just people wishing us good luck. It was so neat that that many people really cared." There were fifteen letters from women wondering if she might be their daughter, but the sixteenth came with photographs that were obviously of Colleen as a small child. A correspondence began.

Three years later, Colleen went to Korea on a youth exchange program, and the family she stayed with arranged a meeting with her birth family.

> It was a pretty tear-jerking experience. We embraced and we were crying and we were really happy. My grandmother was there, and I was closer to her, so I recognized her right away. She was at my side, hanging on to my arm. She wouldn't let go. She just kept thanking God for finally bringing us together. They couldn't speak any English at all, and I couldn't speak any Korean, so we had a translator. My mother wanted me to stay with her that night. I was kind of apprehensive. I was alone, and I was eighteen at the time. I wasn't necessarily worried about what would happen, but just that it was a new experience. Here's this lady saying that she's my mother, and I didn't recognize her. It was a strange feeling, but I did stay with her. She had the whole neighborhood come over and see me, and we just sat there and stared. We couldn't talk or anything.

She has gone back to visit three times since then, once with her adoptive mother. It was shortly before her marriage, and the two mothers helped her to pick out her wedding gown and bridesmaids' dresses. That trip also cleared up the remaining mysteries about Colleen's early life. "My Korean mother was finally able to explain to me why she put me up for adoption, and it made me feel better, because I always wondered why she didn't want me." Her mother was married to Colleen's father, an American serviceman who was killed accidentally not long after her birth. The mother then married a man who was alcoholic and prejudiced against Amerasians and mistreated Colleen. Housing her with her grandparents was a temporary solution. "She was nice enough to realize that I would have a better life in America," Colleen says. "I thank her for that. She did the right thing, and I'm glad she did because I came to a great family."

In the time since they were first reunited, there has been one major instance of cultural conflict. Colleen's "Korean mother," which is what she routinely calls her, needed an operation and asked Colleen to send her the money to pay for it. Her expectation was based in part on filial duty and in part on a common belief that all Americans are rich. Colleen had to write and say no, that she didn't have the money, and she didn't feel obligated in that way. "It was a hard thing to do," she recalls. "I think it hurt her to finally have it dawn on her that even though she is my mother from birth, she has no claims on me as a daughter." The relationship survived, and Colleen intends to continue to visit every few years. The real attraction, however, is Korea itself, not a deep attachment to her birthmother:

I feel like my Korean mother is like an aunt. I don't even consider her my mother anymore. I don't have any close bonds with her, like a mother and daughter bond. I kind of feel sorry for her because I know she would like to have a closer bond, but it's just not there. I'm glad she gave me a good start in life, because I know I was really loved over there. But for the rest of my life here, I was raised to be an American.

Even if the search for beginnings does not result in a continuing relationship between parent and child, it can enhance the child's sense of belonging to a loving family before adoption. Ruth Kim Schmidt's reunion with her foster family certainly gave her that. For many children, the only loving family to be reunited with is the adoption agency responsible for their early care, or the orphanage in which they lived. There is value in preserving that connection. Silvia Kowalski appreciates seeing a woman from Los Pisingos in Colombia who comes to the United States regularly to visit children she has placed here. On one of these visits, at a picnic reunion, Silvia met a little boy whom she had helped care for in a group home. "I was really attached to that baby," Silvia says. "It was so much fun seeing him running around." On my visit to Korea, I was astonished to see the shelves of file folders—not a computer in sight—that represent the thousands of children that Eastern Child

Welfare has placed. I was afraid my pictures and letters might just be
clutter. I learned, however, that the staff and the foster families truly
want to hear what has happened to *their* children, in whom they have
invested so much care and concern. Whenever children leave for the
airport, there is a brief, tearful going-away ceremony, at which Dr.
Kim, the founder of the agency, kisses each child good-bye and says a
prayer for its safety and welfare. It must be very rewarding to see some
of those children come back, safe and faring well. As the usual work
of placing children in other countries ceases, the intercountry adoption
department at Eastern Child Welfare expects to turn its attention to
follow-up, including assistance to families that want to come back to
the agency to visit, whether they search for birthparents or not.

Brad Crosby has had help in his search from both the American
agency and the Korean agency that worked together in his adoption.
He describes himself as "just a watcher" for the first year. When he
decided to get more actively involved, he went through the papers
and memorabilia that his mother had saved, looking for clues. In the
stack was a membership list from OURS, which was founded just after
Brad's arrival. Some of the names were highlighted, and he asked his
mother if she remembered why. Those, she said, were the families whose
children came on the same flight as Brad. By the time the twenty-
second anniversary of his arrival came around several months later,
Brad had organized a reunion of those seven families with help from
the agency. He sees fate at work in the fact that the arrival date fell
on the same day of the week as in 1967, and that the weather fit the
description in the newspapers his mother had saved.

Joy Egholm was one of the now-grown children who showed up for
the reunion. She and Brad, it turned out, were the only two members
of the group who were searching for birthparents, or who had any inclination to do so, which gave them a special affinity. They also learned
that they were brought to the orphanage within a day of each other.
Like some of the others, they both grew up in a setting where they
were "very, very minority," to quote Joy. This was relatively early in
the history of Korean adoptions, before culture camps, and before the
wave of Korean immigration. It was a rare treat for them to share childhood experiences with someone who understood, and that is mostly
what they talked about that evening. Accomplishing this reunion has
meant a great deal to Brad:

I started considering the seven of us as a family. We were together in the orphanage. It's ironic that Joy and I showed up on almost the same day, so we lived together for the six months before we were adopted. And so we were a family. Granted, I don't know if anyone ever felt that way. I didn't, until I started the search, and then I started thinking that way: Gee, we don't have a past. I'll create a new past. The seven of us are now a family in my mind. I'm going to consider Joy sort of a sister to me for the rest of my life.

Creating a family, but one with genetic ties that would continue into the future, was immensely important to Joy. She and her sister, who was adopted locally, used to worry, as teenagers, that they might be infertile.

We wanted something of our own, our own flesh and blood. I love my mother and dad dearly. I never wished that I lived with my biological parents. I just wanted my own child. I wanted something of my own that I could say was *my* child: He acts like me, he does this like me, he looks like me. I have no future. I have no past. There's just me. No ending. No beginning.

Joy has a son now, and she finds that the need for flesh and blood is satisfied. Next time, she may carry on her heritage in a different fashion:

I would like to adopt. I think it's neat what my parents did for me. I would like to help another child, the way my parents brought me into their home, loved me as their own, and gave me a wonderful life. I told my mom, "I have the best parents I ever could have even dreamed for. I would like to give all that love and everything that you gave me to another child." I would really like to adopt.

Choosing to adopt is a way of affirming one's own adoption and celebrating through imitation the adoptive parents' role in one's life. We parents do hope that in reassessing their beginnings, our children will assign us a place of importance, too. Marlene Duval's daughter Anne, who, for a time in adolescence, wanted to dissociate herself from her family, has named her children after Marlene's ancestors, a good sign of reconciliation.

I was interested to know whether passing on their ethnic identity to children was important to the adopted adults I interviewed, as it is, at the moment, to Amy Andrews. The five adults I talked with who are married and have children are all from Korea. The four Amerasians have white spouses. Soon Hee Truman's Hawaiian husband has Asian, Caucasian, and Polynesian ancestry, and they are raising their child in a racially integrated setting where his coloring and features will not set him apart. Colleen Griffith, pregnant with her first child, expects to make frequent trips to Korea, so the child will know her birth family and be familiar with the culture. Continuing the Korean heritage was not especially important to Brad Crosby, but Joy Egholm intends to pass her birth name on to a daughter, as a middle name. Ruth Kim Schmidt echoes Amy's concern about the Korean identity fading away: "I very much enjoy the cultural heritage, and my kids are very much aware of their one-quarter Korean. It's getting less and less. I'm hoping they both marry Asians and keep the flow in the family."

If returning to genetic roots to get one's bearings is not a possibility, visiting the place of origin may offer the comfort of having begun somewhere, of having a life prior to adoption. Cesar Connor, who has spent seven years each in Colombia and the United States, still thinks of Colombia as home and expects that going back to visit or to live will resolve some of his sorrow and regret and help him decide "where to go," as he puts it. Like Cesar, we all carry within us "places in the heart"—experiences of place that make up the interior landscape of our psyches. And like Cesar, we may not realize how embedded we are in a particular place until we are away from it. I didn't know, for instance, how much my imagination depended on lakes and cumulus clouds and the rich blue skies of a cold winter until I lived in another part of the country that lacked those things, though it was beautiful in its own right. But "place" is more than geography. One evening I got an unexpected phone call from a high-school classmate I have seen only once since graduation. Raised in a smalltown, working-class family, she has married into upward mobility and lives in a fairly wealthy suburb of Los Angeles. "I still feel like I belong in Minnesota," she told me, and she was not only talking about lakes and prairie. The place from which we originate is not just a spot on the map, but a collection of emotions, sensory impressions, images, mores, "scripts," as some psychologists call them. We do not always long to return to this place, but at critical moments, when we need a fresh start, we do at least think back to where we feel we belong to see what other direction we might take.

Children who have left their place of origin at an early age may have no conscious memory of it, though their first sensory impressions—the sound of Spanish, the heat of India, or the smell of *kim chi* and soy sauce that pervades Korean cities—must be recorded somewhere. The environment where the children actually grow up may determine the contours of the psyche, but the minority experience can inhibit feelings of belonging. The circumstances that led to her adoption and the teasing she endured left Joy Egholm longing for a place where she would fit unconditionally.

> Somewhere along the line it was explained to me that my mom
> gave me up because it was best, because I was half and half. I wouldn't
> have a good life in Korea because they wouldn't have accepted me.
> So I went through this big crisis, like an identity thing. I thought,
> OK, I'm not full Korean, so I don't belong in Korea, and I'm not
> full American, so I don't belong here. Is there some special island
> or something that I could go to? Where *do* I belong?

Soon Hee's husband might suggest Hawaii. "There are a lot of people that are mixed bloods," Soon Hee explains. "That's one thing that's neat about Hawaii. There are so many different kinds of people on the island, and everyone can get along." Curiously, Joy has married a man whose last name is the name of the island in Denmark where his ancestors lived. He can point to the map and show their son precisely where the family's roots are. Joy would like the security that gives, and she does plan to visit Korea, whether she can find her birthmother or not: "I think it would be enough to go back to Korea and see the last known address that she lived at, the house that she grew up in, and to see the agency offices and the orphanage, and to see where you lived for six months."

Brad echoes Joy's question, "Where are we supposed to be? That's where the fantasy world comes into play, because we are trying to make up our own identity." A natural course for anyone's fantasy to take is to ask What if?—to alter the place of birth or upbringing and imagine how differently life might have proceeded. What if I had stayed where I was born? is an obvious departure point for children who did not. This is a difficult scenario to play out, because it is not likely to be a happy one. Ruth Kim Schmidt has tried it, but can't make herself fit.

I think there was so much negative input when I was younger about "what your life would have been like if you had been left over there." When people would talk about biracial children in Korea, it was "these kids would have been either this or this." And then there's all the media stuff about the Amerasian children in Vietnam and how they are basically street kids. I heard that you would either work in a sweatshop or you'd be a prostitute. That kind of narrows the options. I think a part of you says, Isn't that awful? That's probably what I would have been like. The other part of you says, No, I wouldn't. That's not what I'm like. That's not who I am. I think there are some ingrained things in you. I'm not a victim person, and I don't think I would have let myself be victimized by the society that way.

It must be very sobering to think about how much impact poverty and ostracism might have had on your character had you never known anything else. It makes me sad to think of my children, even in the best of orphanages, getting little of the personal attention needed to encourage their distinct gifts, and having no opportunity for education beyond elementary school. It is not surprising that children like Melissa Woodrow, who assumes she would have died in India, do not engage in What if? fantasies. Ruth is fortunate enough to have an alternative scenario: Had her foster family been allowed to adopt her, she would have had their love and protection to bolster her. In fact, they gave her that in the time that she lived with them, and that may help to explain why she is "not a victim person."

In order to work effectively in the process of reclamation, the What if? fantasies might have to follow two courses—one based in reality, and an ideal version: What if I had grown up in the situation I was in before I was adopted? and What if I had grown up in my birth country, but in better circumstances? The thought of being dead may bolster Amy Andrews' sense of purpose, as it does for many survivors of hardship, but knowing that she would have been mistreated in the country of her birth is not what she needs to nourish a love of her Korean heritage. Yet, it is very important to her to affirm herself as Korean and to reconnect with her past. The trip and the kind welcome she got even from people on the street certainly helped with that. But she has also discovered on her own a way to fill out the picture and to satisfy the longing for that special place where she fully belongs: Imagining what it would be like to be born into a Korean family and immigrate with them to the United States. She would be Korean-American, which she already is, but with a firmer grounding in Korea.

Like the wish for a reunion with birthparents, thoughts of returning to the birthplace depend on individual inclinations and may come and go throughout a single lifetime. Beth Larsen is consistent in her indifference:

> It's kind of like meeting my birthmother. It's not one of my destinies. It's not like when I grow up, I have to go to Korea. It's not something I really have to do. But it seems interesting, and if I had a chance I would. I wouldn't say I'd put all my money into it and then come back just poor and not have any money.

She doesn't expect to feel at home, but wants to stay with someone and have them go along to interpret. "I wouldn't want to just go around and hear things and not know what they are and not know what they're saying." Eight-year-old Margaret Chatten, on the other hand, is very eager to go back. "To get to know a different language" is what appeals to her most and speaking Korean figures highly in her attempts to imagine what her life would be like there. She talks about going to Korea and staying there, though she would still go to her grandma's once in a while. She knows that Korea has mountains, and her grandma lives in the mountains, too. Margo Speiser describes nine-year-old Susan as very much attached to her birth country, despite having left it in early infancy.

> We were reading the newspaper, and Susan saw this picture of an anti-American demonstration in Seoul, so I explained it to her. She said, "I hope they don't hate *me*. I'm Korean. When I go there, I hope they don't hate me." I said, "Oh, when you go visit?" and she said, "No, I'm going to go back there." She's said that to me more than once. And so I was joking with Chuck, and I said, "Enough of this Korean culture camp!" But that would be like saying no to the boyfriend. Besides, I want her to be that proud. She's said that she's going back to find somebody in Korea to marry. She's quite confident of that. She has a real fixation on it. She gets a lot of strokes for being Korean. People reinforce it and are very positive with her about that. It might be something about wondering what it's like to join the others that are like her. I really don't know what it's all about.

These children, young as they are, may simply imagine themselves planted, as is, in native soil. They are not fully aware of the hardship they would have faced had they grown up as orphans, nor of how foreign they will likely seem to lifelong citizens of Korea. Colleen Griffith, a voice of experience after five enjoyable trips to Korea, says,

> I can't imagine wanting to live there. It's a great place to visit, and I love going over there, but this is where I live now. I would feel out of place in Korea. I'm so American. Some people might have dreams of going to Korea, but when it comes down to reality, you just don't fit in anymore.

Melissa Woodrow, who plans a return visit to India when she finishes high school, has no romantic illusions about what life would be like there. In fact, her image of Calcutta is quite gloomy, based on her own history of abandonment and malnutrition. She expects it to be "so dirty and everything, worse than it was before." Melissa is not currently interested in reading about India or watching television reports about life there, so there is nothing to challenge her negative image. A trip may well surprise her and revise the story of her origins.

Older children who miss "the place that is home," as Cesar Connor calls it, do have a natural tendency to idealize it. The clash of ideal and reality can leave them feeling "in a no man's land," as Silvia Kowalski describes her experience on a return visit to Colombia as a teenager.

> It was this dreamy sort of feeling. I was there and I wasn't. Within three short years I had lost something. I couldn't understand the language when I first got there, and when I spoke, they looked at me kind of odd because I sounded different already. It was really hard for me to accept that. This was *my* culture. This was *my* country of birth. For three years I had claimed I was going to go back. Suddenly I'm back in it and people look at me like I no longer belong there. Plus, things about the culture started to bother me. I was embarrassed to acknowledge that I was Colombian, but I didn't want to acknowledge the fact that I was American, either, to myself or to anyone else.

Silvia plans more trips in the future, but will carry with her a mature understanding of each culture's virtues and weaknesses and of her right to claim a place in both countries. She is no longer hesitant to call herself an American, by which she means born in South America, living in North America.

Many parents do intend for their children to visit their birthplaces and even look forward to a family trip as a rite of passage that will enable the children to claim, with pride, the dual heritage to which they are entitled. Many adoption agencies encourage such visits. Various Korean organizations are arranging low-cost "homeland" tours especially for adopted children. A family trip is expensive, of course, and not everyone can manage it, but it is a luxury worth scrounging for. I hope to save enough to take my daughters when they are teenagers, but I also hope they will find their way back on their own terms. While walking through the campus of Yonsei University in Seoul, I envisioned them there on a college year abroad, as Americans born in Korea, learning the language, making friends, and getting a Korean perspective on whatever subject they might be studying. And what if they fall in love—with the country or one of its citizens—and decide to settle there? That is a risk we take in adopting children from other parts of the world, but it is not such a dangerous one. So far in the history of international adoption it seldom happens, and if it does, the place of childhood memory, where the family lives, will probably become that place in the heart that exerts the attraction of home.

There are, in fact, "islands" in the United States where people of dual heritage can live out an identity that is not always bifurcated by intrusive questions and competing loyalties. It remains to be seen whether internationally adopted children, once grown, will seek out ethnic communities and be welcomed there. Soon Hee Truman has found a home in one of these, but her name, her husband, and her ability to understand spoken Korean give her a rare advantage. Her halting attempts to speak Korean do arouse curiosity, and when she explains that she was adopted, she senses that Korean immigrants feel sorry for her, though she doesn't want them to. Ruth Kim Schmidt sought out an Asian community when she left for college, but felt "almost shameful" because she spoke no Korean. She backed away for a time, but is now attending events and meeting people and looking on it "as an educational opportunity." Silvia Kowalski tried out a Hispanic group on her college campus but did not share their outlook or sympathize with their reason-for-being.

They isolated themselves. It took me so long to feel that I was accepted by the average American person and nothing different. I worked really hard at integrating, but they went out of their way to isolate themselves. I said, Well, I'm not going to put myself in a little clique simply because they're of the Hispanic persuasion.

Even if they don't entirely fit there, adopted children can "pass" as members of the ethnic community to some extent. At least it is a place to blend in and be anonymous, and it can function, even temporarily, as a place to define one's self, apart from the adoptive family. Barb Holtan, in an article in *FACE Facts* in 1985, described her encounter with a Vietnamese community as the moment when she realized that her twelve-year-old son would soon be heading out in his own direction:

> He's moving out into the world, his world, private and one which no parent can completely share—nor should we try. And for us Caucasian parents of non-Caucasian children, that world is rather more private, more unknown to us than usual. . . . We recently drove to Arlington, Virginia, to the "Little Saigon" area of town. We browsed in the shops and purchased some ethnic foods to sample. I watched how people were reacting to our family. I and my two Caucasian daughters were seen as "tourists" and accepted as such. . . . Tim? He blended right in, not even a curious glance coming his way. . . . We talked later, Tim and I, and the realization came to us both that he must make his way in that world. I cannot do it for him. (A hard lesson for us parents! It admits of powerlessness.)

Earlier in the article, Ms. Holtan described children in need of adoption as coming "with varying degrees of hurt or need or emptiness" and parents as wanting "so much to 'fill up' our kids, to make up for their early wounds . . ." She ends the article with a statement about her role in her son's personal development that reflects a very American sense of family relationships. The individuation that American culture regards as critical is offset, in Asian cultures, by a continuing obligation to parents.

> With Tim, we've had ten years to give to him, to "fill up" his empty basket, to reiterate our love and commitment—our family-ness. We will continue to do this in the years ahead but we have definitely passed a life-marker of sorts (as do all parents) and must now guard against that dangerous over involvement. We must now just hope fervently that the roots we created are strong enough and vital enough to withstand the wings he has sprouted and is anxious to try out.

The metaphor of "roots and wings" is a popular one among adoptive families. It is interpreted in various ways: that we give new roots to children who have been uprooted, or that their birthparents and birth culture give them roots and we give them wings. In either case, the necessity of both is affirmed. Adopted people who hope to draw strength from their roots do not curl into a figurative fetal position, seeking refuge in a primal past and mourning what might have been. The object is to begin afresh, with a richer appreciation of the past and its significance and a renewed impetus to ask, Why did this happen to me? What does it mean for my life? The answers can be very positive ones, which see dual heritage not as confusing, but as life-enhancing.

Among the older "children" I interviewed, there were two who were indeed ready to fly. Both Ruth Kim Schmidt and Silvia Kowalski have discovered that proceeding with their adult lives takes more than knowing their genetic and cultural heritage and having a place to belong. It also means coming to terms with the experience of separation and adoption itself. Ruth says,

> I know a lot of adopted people, and there are some fairly damaged folks. They have a lot of baggage that they carry around. I guess in some ways I understand it, but in other ways I'm like, Good grief, would you get on with your life? There are decision points in your life where you say, I am who I am, and I'm going to work on these things, but what happened happened, and I can't go back and reshape the past. I'm going to build myself a future based on who I am now and what I want for myself, and not have a future filled with, Gee, I was a victim. I was abused, or I grew up in an alcoholic family, or here I am abandoned, and have that be your life script. I don't think it has to be that way.

Silvia says she believes "very much that the negative can be turned into something positive." Looking back at the horrible trauma of her childhood and the turbulence of her teenage years, she watches herself developing a strength that she knows she can count on in her life to come.

> I went through a lot of emotional adjusting, which I did on my own. I have never in my life had counseling of any kind. My parents didn't think it was necessary. I guess I've been my own counselor. I never had anyone to confide in until later on in college. I feel I'm pretty strong because I managed to handle it myself. My thought was, I've always been strong, I can be strong this time too. That's how I've faced life.

In asking themselves, Why did this happen to me? What does it mean for my life? both Ruth, 30, and Silvia, 25, have settled on a "destiny," to borrow Beth Larsen's word, that is very specifically related to their life histories. Ruth is a social worker who works with children in foster care, and she also does public speaking on adoption from the child's point of view. "I don't know if being adopted has anything to do with wanting to be an advocate for the underdog or whatever," she says, "but I feel a real strong need to work out the injustices of our society or be the safety net for the people that don't fit in. I think that has a lot to do with who I am and the struggles I've had in my life." Silvia is in graduate school, preparing for a career in intercultural relations—not political diplomacy, but a kind of mediation that will help people of different cultures work cooperatively on global issues such as care of the environment. "I'm starting to feel I have a purpose," she says. She realizes that without adoption, she would not have the education she needs to do this, and without her move from one culture to another, she might not have the sensitivity and the skills.

I certainly wish my children a destiny like that—a deeply rooted and firmly winged sense of purpose that makes the best of their life histories. I fantasize a lot: Grace, a staff member of an international self-development organization, coming home energized from another part of the world where she has visited a support project for mothers who are at risk of having to abandon their children. Now she is going to apply what she learned to help young, single, American mothers become free of dependence on public welfare. Maria, known profession-ally as Sookie Park, back from a year in Korea, where she has made films and learned new dances and mask dramas to perform on her high quality, multicultural television show for children. These are my fantasies, not theirs, and the details change from time to time. I balk at inflicting my kids with survivor's guilt. They do not have to prove themselves worthy of selection, since every child is born with the same innate worth and the same right to a healthy life. Nor do I want them to feel that they owe me the fulfillment of my fantasies for raising them. They have already given me rewards enough for a lifetime. I simply want them to find destinies that, to paraphrase Ruth, have a lot to do with who they are. They will, if all goes well. Whatever Grace does, she will do it with fashion and flair. Whatever Maria does, she will find a way to make people laugh.

To be good American parents, we need to follow Barb Holtan's advice and "guard against that dangerous overinvolvement." As internationally adoptive parents, we have other tasks as well. We, like these children whom we claim so adamantly as our kids, have deeper roots than we knew, an enlarged sense of family, another place in the heart, and a rich and varied history of facing life issues we would never have encountered without them. We, too, can look back and ask, Why did this happen to me? What does it mean for my life?

9

The Global Family

Early one morning, the clock radio clicked on just at the start of an on-the-hour news report. I dozed in and out, missing key pieces of information, but one brief item was startling enough to take hold in my memory: A mudslide in São Paulo, Brazil, had buried a community of women and children living in fifty shacks on a hillside. Once awake, I looked over the newspaper headlines but found no reference to it. The day's demands quickly took over and I never got to check the inside pages, where short international news items frame the discount store ads. I still don't know the details. The mudslide took its place alongside so many other cataclysmic events barely comprehended:

- A news feature on National Public Radio estimates that 5,000,000 children will be orphaned in the 1990s by the AIDS epidemic in Sub-Saharan Africa.
- A letter to the editor in the *New York Times*, drawing on United Nations statistics, claims that 38,000 children die every day from starvation and illnesses resulting from malnutrition, the equivalent of 100 jumbojet plane crashes.

Numbers are mind-boggling and the memory easily drops and adds zeros, but graphic images remain—mud coursing down a hillside, taking bits of wood and cardboard and scrap metal. Why mothers and children? Where are the fathers? Why were they living on this muddy hillside? Where did they come from? How did they end up in this vulnerable state? To make sense of this, I thought through other associations with São Paulo:

- Carolina Maria de Jesus, scavenging for paper to sell and saving scraps on which to write her starkly powerful diary, *Child of the Dark.*

- The child welfare agency LIMIAR, whose U. S. representative, Nancy Cameron, writes articles in *OURS* magazine urging American parents to be more patient with foreign adoption agencies and to understand how burdened they are.
- Casa da Mamãe, a shelter that offers transitional support to destitute mothers who want to raise their children themselves—like the typical mother described in publicity about the shelter:

If and when a young Brazilian mother decides she has no choice but to abandon her child to the streets or to FEBEM (the state agency that has responsibility for abandoned children), she is almost invariably alone in the big city. Usually she is a migrant who has come to São Paulo from a rural area, accompanied by a husband or companion. After weeks of unemployment and despair, the man often becomes discouraged and disappears from the scene. With a young child or children in her care, the mother is unable to get any kind of job and has no one to whom she can turn for help. Nothing is left for her but to face starvation in the streets. To such desperate young women, Casa da Mamãe offers a temporary haven.

I think, too, of the children I saw on my visit to the local La Semana culture camp. Who among them spent their infancy in a shack on a muddy hillside?

As the parent of children adopted internationally, I hear the news about the mudslide, or the orphans or the starving children, with a refrain at the end: These could be my kids. I have made the joyous discovery that I can feel complete and natural parental love for a child who is related to me by neither blood, race, nor cultural origin. Perfect as the match seems, and as willing as I am to attribute it to fate, I know that I would feel the same attachment to virtually any child who might have been placed with me. That realization exposes joy's sorrowful underside: How can I not mourn the mudslide victims? And how can I not mourn the lost gifts of children whose spirits are suffocated by poverty, hunger, disease, violence, and sexual exploitation?

Sad news about children is hard to live with and tempting to put aside. The circulars with photographs of missing children that come in the mail are tossed after one glance in the wastebasket, where they cannot arouse fears for my children's safety. Here in the United States, it is easy for many of us to isolate ourselves from suffering children. The drive from a suburban school to gymnastics class or soccer practice goes past shopping malls, not shantytowns. As we watch our children thrive on the material comforts that middle-class American life offers, we are easily convinced that this is, after all, their destiny. The life they might have lived as orphaned or abandoned children was never really meant to be—not for *these* bright and healthy kids. That risk was long ago and far away. Here and now, we are a family just like any other.

In the ordinary course of daily life, we certainly are families just like any other, and we deserve to have our family bonds affirmed as normal and inviolable. To underscore this, we tell ourselves and anyone who asks for explanations that we adopted our children out of purely selfish motives: We simply wanted to be parents. For most of us, that is perfectly true, and there is, ironically, some virtue in owning up to selfishness. Yet, even if we never set out on a rescue mission, rescues have been accomplished. Michael Perlitz first understood this when an application form he was filling out asked him to name his most outstanding achievement. "I really believe that the most—if not the only—outstanding thing I've done is to adopt two Third World kids and to have saved two lives—I mean literally. I do feel that those two lives have been saved." International adoption has kept some children alive, saved certain children from ostracism and abuse, and spared others a life of unrelenting poverty. It has only shaken the world a little, not transformed it, but the difference it has meant for our children is profound.

Adoption can make a meaningful difference for us parents, as well, if we take time to ponder the questions Why did this happen to me? What does it mean for my life? The more our children's lives have been changed, the more potential they have for changing ours. Rather than let parental love settle into a proprietary fondness for our own children, we can let the wonder we feel at watching them grow nourish a broader, loving concern for children who are not our own, children who still face the risks from which our children have been spared. I believe very firmly that being entrusted with the love and care of children born to someone else in another part of the world carries an obligation of stewardship. In becoming an internationally adoptive family, we claim a place in the global family.

Membership in the global family, like membership in our immediate families, obligates us to share in family responsibilities. There are many ways to approach this new role, but I would like to suggest three that the experience of adopting and raising our children particularly suits us for. First, we can make our voices heard in the continuing public discussion of adoption, whether we share our views on the propriety of transracial and intercountry adoption, or respond to media coverage of adoption, which often stereotypes adoptive families as either heroic or troubled. Second, we can work to improve the welfare of children worldwide, with special attention to family security. Third, we can seek and promote greater awareness of the global socioeconomic causes for family dissolution and abandonment of children, and help find just and equitable solutions.

Adoption still needs some conscientious and persuasive advocates. Internationally adoptive families have a richness of experience to speak from in explaining how adoption "works" over the long run. A good many of us do offer encouragement, in both casual and organized ways, to others wondering whether they should adopt. Our delight in our own children and knowledge about others in need of families motivate us to do so. I've lost count of the times I've said, "You'll never regret it," as though I had the power to make that promise. What it really means is, "I certainly don't regret it."

Yet, if we are to advocate for international adoption, we need to be careful how we portray it. It is not an absolute good to be pursued for its own sake, nor is it a baby market. It is a temporary and very limited solution to two concurrent problems: homelessness among children and infertility. Of these two problems, the welfare of children takes precedence. Children are entitled, as a birthright, to a loving family, adequate food and shelter, sound health, a safe environment, and education and training to allow self-sufficiency in adulthood. If the lack of a loving family puts the other rights in jeopardy, then adoption into another family is a worthy solution. But if the child already has a loving family, then the best we can do is to help secure the other rights so the family can stay together.

By no means are we entitled to claim the children of those who, by our own cultural measures, seem less fortunate: Wealth does not entitle us to the children of the poor. Higher education does not entitle us to the children of the illiterate. Marriage does not entitle us to the children of the unwed. Technological advancement does not entitle us to the children of "underdeveloped" nations. Religious faith does not entitle us to the children of parents who believe differently than we do. International adoption is an undeserved benefit that has fallen to North Americans, Western Europeans, and Australians, largely because of the inequitable socioeconomic circumstances in which we live. In the long run, we ought to be changing those circumstances. Adoption is paradoxical through and through, a mix of grievous losses and joyous gains, tragic separation and firm belonging. We who live with the paradox day by day can manage yet another one: To be advocates for international adoption while simultaneously working to make it unnecessary.

We can begin by asking whether our eagerness to adopt children from countries with poorer economies enables improvement or perpetuates inequity. There would seem to be simpler methods, such as that suggested by a four-year-old Korean-born boy who asked his mother, "Why don't the American moms and dads just send money to the Korean moms and dads so they can keep their children?" Roy Brower says of adoption,

> It's one way Colombia deals with its social problems, and the tremendous problem it has with poverty and streetchildren: Let's get them out of here. They're going to lift the lid on the pressure cooker a little bit, so they don't have to face the real change that may have to happen in Colombia some day. Let's face it: It's the policies of countries like ours that keep these countries in poverty, that put them in a situation of adopting out their kids. By making this choice, you're really participating in that cycle. I'm not saying that there isn't something humanitarian in it. For these kids, there is. These kids probably wouldn't have survived otherwise. But I don't think we ought to have any illusions about somehow we're changing the world by doing this. In fact, we may be deferring change.

Lourdes G. Balanon, assistant director of the Bureau of Child and Youth Welfare in the Philippines, also suggests that having adoption as a safety valve may delay efforts to secure the welfare of all the country's children. This does not make her an opponent of adoption, however:

> Follow-up visits and feedback on Filipino adopted children have shown that the needs of a foreign child can be satisfactorily met in another country. It has given family life to children in their lifetime. Foreign adoption, however, should be only an *interim or temporary solution* while services to families and children are being developed and strengthened, and the socioeconomic development and political stability of the country are established. (*Child Welfare*, March-April 1989, p. 253)

South Korea is a case in point. For thirty-five years, while the country recovered from war and gradually developed into a self-sufficient industrial nation, there was no better solution for individual homeless children than sending them abroad to waiting families. Now, there is both the national wealth and the public consciousness necessary to make provision within the country for children in need. Rather than bemoan the "closing" of Korea, we who have adopted Korean children can take pride in watching our children's birth country find permanent remedies for the problems that adoption was meant to alleviate.

Finding personal solutions for individual children does not have to impede efforts at reform that would benefit all children. Certainly, refusing to adopt children from other countries would not in itself bring about changes for the better. We can perhaps foster the change by choosing to adopt only in socially responsible and ethically sound ways that underscore the need for other solutions. Ironically, the social problems that make international adoption necessary also threaten its ethical integrity. In countries afflicted by war or political oppression, children are frequently separated from their parents by force or chaos, and placing them for adoption without first trying to reunite them with family members compounds the loss. In countries where many people live in abject poverty, there is room for profiteering off the desperation of parents who can't afford to raise their children. In countries where unwed motherhood is stigmatizing, women can be coerced into relinquishing children they had hoped to raise themselves. From time to time, misdeeds come to light that taint international adoption as a whole, especially in the eyes of people who are concerned about the loss of their country's children. If we are to be responsible and culturally sensitive advocates, we need to make our opposition to kidnapping, baby-selling, coercion, profiteering, and fraud very clear and avoid taking advantage of practices that allow such things to happen.

Unfortunately, there are no universal regulations governing the process of adoption nor are there consistent lines of authority and accountability. The United Nations' "Declaration on Social and Legal Principles Relating to the Protection and Welfare of Children, with Special Reference to Foster Placement and Adoption" suggests standards, but they are not legally enforceable. The Child Welfare League of America (CWLA) includes a section on intercountry adoption in its *Standards for Adoption Service*. Agencies that belong to the CWLA presumably follow these. The Joint Council on International Children's Services from North

America, which includes both agencies and parent groups in its member-ship, has published a statement of principles called "The Practice of Intercountry Adoption." Catholic Charities has set up its own monitoring agency—the National Office for International Child Care and Placement, and a number of placement agencies and social workers have joined together in the International Alliance for Professional Accountability in Latin American Adoptions. The guidelines of these organizations are helpful and need to be more widely distributed, but the lack of uniform, enforceable international standards still leaves adoptive parents and potential parents with the responsibility of acting ethically on our own initiative. If we were to compile a list of rules to follow, derived from our experience and observations as parents who have adopted, I would suggest the following:

- Agree to adopt only through agencies or institutions, both here and in the birth country, that have a more general concern for child welfare, which they demonstrate by offering services to children who are not available for international adoption and to families struggling to stay intact.

- Avoid entrepreneurial arrangements with people who are taking personal advantage of foreign citizens' desire for children. Ask for an accounting of anticipated expenses before you proceed and check it against average fees and legally mandated expenditures.

- Do not agree to adopt a child until you have been told why the child is available for adoption. If the birthparent relinquished the child, make sure there is legal documentation of this. If the child was abandoned, make sure that reasonable efforts have been made to find relatives.

- Do not adopt from a country where there have recently been reports of adoption fraud until you are satisfied that the case is being prosecu-ted.

- Make sure the child meets the basic legal qualifications to emigrate and to be admitted into the United States before you proceed any further.

- If you are adopting an older child, make sure the child has no objection to moving to another country where life is very different, or at least understands that there truly is no better alternative in the home country. Ask to correspond with the child or someone responsible for the child, and respect this person's linguistic abilities and workload in doing so.

- Ask what expectations those involved in the care and placement of your child have for the future. Do they want to stay in touch? Are they concerned about the child's sense of identity and knowledge about the birth country? Do they expect a return visit? Do they rely on continuing support from client families to continue their work? Be sure you are willing to honor those wishes or, if they seem unreasonable, to do them the courtesy of explaining why not.

Our resolve to do things right can easily waver under stress. Especially after the referral stage when anticipation is greatest, we have a tremendous personal stake in trusting the word of those who assure us that everything is fine. Adopting a child is an emotion-wrenching experience. If it takes longer than expected and we encounter obstacles along the way, we become much more vulnerable to compromising our standards. Remembering what that was like, those of us who have already adopted could help those still in process by urging agencies and governments to be specific about their ethical guidelines as well as their legal policies.

We who have looked beyond our national borders for healthy babies eventually have to admit that we overlooked many children in need here in the United States. In a 1989 report entitled *The State of Adoption in America*, the Child Welfare League of America estimated that there were at least 34,000 children "without permanent families" who had been waiting an average of two years to be adopted. A high proportion were older, mentally or physically handicapped, or had a history of abuse that may have left them wary of loving and trusting other people. We have each had our own very practical and sensible reasons for not choosing children such as these, and we might make the same decision in the same circumstances again. Some of us, assessing the skills that parenthood has taught us, may regret that we didn't take greater risks. Some parents may yet choose to do so. But even if we still feel inadequate to serve as parents to children with special needs, our advocacy must extend to them as well. The global family, after all, includes American children. Dr. Margaret K. Hostetter, the codirector of the International Adoptions Clinic at the University of Minnesota, made an eloquent appeal on their behalf in *OURS* magazine:

Enlarge your activism. We in the International Adoption Clinic cannot fail to be impressed with the enthusiasm, energy, and insight adoptive parents bring to their new roles. Parent groups, cultural activities, and nationwide networks of resources are an exceptional testament to the commitment of adoptive parents. But within this country, there remain children born of poverty and despair, children who are unwitting victims of the consequences of adult behaviors such as AIDS, alcoholism, or abuse. These children, too, need our energies, compassion, and willingness to transcend social and political barriers in the quest for change. Only when we become advocates for all our children will the future of each child be justly assured. (March/ April 1989, p. 21)

Advocating for adoption, and especially the adoption of special needs children, may be more difficult as medical solutions to infertility become more effective, and as more people make surrogacy arrangements. These developments have certainly provoked controversy about the ethical issues involved, and adoptive parents have useful insights and opinions to offer. The parents I interviewed had mixed feelings about the more radical infertility measures such as in vitro fertilization and surgical implantation. Most saw both pros and cons in the new reproductive technology. Chuck Stensrud, for example, says,

The first time I heard of that stuff, I was just shocked that anybody would think about "ordering" a baby. It just went against everything I believed. And then I said, Well, there is sort of the exciting, curious, interesting, technology-making-life-better aspect of it. Maybe it's not so bad. Maybe I'm sort of an old-fashioned stick-in-the-mud and just need to loosen up.

Margo Speiser, Chuck's wife, has similar feelings.

I used to feel pretty definite about it: Why in the world are these people monkeying around? Why all this manipulation of their bodies when there are children who need homes? And I thought, Well, I'll back away from that. There seems to be something intrinsic in humans that they need to see themselves reproduced. Because I don't feel it strongly in myself, maybe I shouldn't hassle with that.

Elsbeth Saunders emphasizes the value of personal freedom: "It's such a private choice that, frankly, people ought to try anything they want to try and feel is OK to them to do." She extends that to surrogacy, too, but referring to the Baby M case, qualifies it with, "Obviously it's so easy to have that bomb." Patti Cronin, who went through years of infertility treatment herself, says she can imagine being a surrogate mother as a gift to another infertile woman. Others describe surrogacy in negative terms like "scary," "weird," "obsessive and self-centered," or "clearly about money and power."

There was strong agreement among these parents that no matter what remedies there are to choose from, adoption is certainly not to be regarded as a last resort. On the contrary, they cited the unique value of adoption—that it aids a child already born—as a compelling reason to choose it. Making that choice themselves and living with its consequences had shifted their rationale from self-interest to the welfare of children. To advocate for adoption in these new circumstances, we need to talk about that shift in values and bring the discussion back to the basics: What are the best solutions for children without parents? What are the best solutions for would-be parents without children? To what extent are their interests mutual?

There are, unfortunately, many adoptive parents who settle back into privacy after their own families are complete, without allowing the experience of adopting internationally to have much impact on their habits. Others, however, remain concerned about "the children left behind" and feel an ongoing commitment to the agencies or orphanages or birth countries from which their children came. Bill and Mary MacNamara lend a good deal of their time to the support of child welfare in Korea. It was Donna Frazee's interest in the work of the International Mission of Hope in Calcutta that inspired her to adopt one more child. The Garmans have taken in a foster child from an orphanage in Ecuador so that he can attend school in the United States, and the Trumans have sponsored Asian refugees through a program for unaccompanied minors.

Although many adoption agencies rely to a great extent on continuing support from the parents with whom they place children, rarely do they require follow-up action. Adoption Advocates International in Port Angeles, Washington, has an unusual and admirable policy of asking each of its clients to write a "letter of commitment" explaining what they will do to continue to serve the needs of children. Collecting supplies to be sent abroad is the most common response. Some parents promise to write articles or conduct programs on international adoption, sponsor children in other countries, or lobby for legislative changes that benefit children here in the United States. One of the letters summarizes the agency's philosophy: "Adoption is not something to do *once*. It is a lifestyle. To this lifestyle we are committed." Other agencies use regular persuasion to convince parents to stay involved. Families that have adopted through International Mission of Hope, for example, receive periodic letters that make the need for support very vivid, and judging from the steady improvement of the agency's medical facilities, the response has been great. Though it does not make direct appeals, Eastern Child Welfare Society in Korea does benefit from the fund-raising efforts of adoptive parents. A visit to the agency convinced me to stay committed. I was most impressed with the broad dimensions of their work on behalf of children. Eastern encourages Korean families to adopt, runs day care centers in "financially disadvantaged communities" and a rehabilitation center for handicapped children, pays high school tuition for selected orphanage children and promising students from poor families, and has a sponsorship program for families that might otherwise have to abandon their children. The agency also operates sex education programs and birth control clinics in the areas where young factory workers live, "as an effort to prevent further increase of unwanted pregnancies."

Adoptive parent organizations routinely include the improvement of child welfare among their objectives. Adoptive Families of America, for example, commits 15 percent of its membership dues to "children without permanency." The many journals and newsletters for adoptive families—OURS, Roots and Wings, Latin American Adoptive Families Quarterly, The Adoption Advocate, News from FAIR (Families Adopting in Response) to name just a few—give evidence that adoption can expand the family's interest in the general welfare of children. There are solicitations for funds and for donated clothing and medical supplies, appeals to join sponsorship programs that benefit particular children or orphanages, and news about voluntary organizations serving needs that adoption alone can't fill. Americans for International Aid, for example, has organized a network of airline employees who collect and deliver medical supplies around the world. PACT (Partners Aiding Children Today) provides treatment for handicapped children in Korea, India, and Colombia, whether orphaned or living with parents who can't afford the cost of medical care. FCVN (Friends of Children of Various Nations) was originally Friends of Children of Viet Nam, which operated orphanages and hospitals there until the end of the war. In 1988, they were invited back by the Vietnamese government to continue their work, which is sorely needed. The daily maintenance of these organizations depends on a relative few parents, some of whom were already involved in charity and social activism and some of whom acquired a new sense of purpose through the experience of adoption.

Supporting the continuing work of agencies through which we have adopted is a direct and practical way to aid children in need, but there are other opportunities, as well. The most pressing problems facing the world's children, ill health and hunger, are certainly not limited to children without families. The success of campaigns that pose these problems to an American audience seems to depend, in part, on how effectively they can personalize the need. "Poster children" bring in money for research into the causes and cures of disabling illnesses. Sponsorship programs publish entrancing pictures of needy children in magazines and promise contributors a chance to correspond with the child they support. Since we already have a representative of the world's children sitting at the dinner table, internationally adoptive families can be a receptive audience for more anonymous appeals.

In fact, the most persistent needs of children around the world are not easily dramatized. It is always sobering to read the requests for medical supplies in magazines for adoptive families. There are no CAT scan machines on the list, but rather intravenous tubing, syringes, suture material, tongue depressors, alcohol, antibiotics, vitamins. Accustomed as we are to eleventh hour appeals for donated organs and the thousands of dollars needed to transplant them, it is hard to grasp how mundane children's most pressing health problems are and what simple measures it would take to alleviate them. According to UNICEF, the five illnesses that account for most deaths among children worldwide are dehydration from diarrhea, pneumonia, measles, tetanus, and whooping cough— illnesses that are either extinct or easily curable in the United States. Immunization and oral rehydration therapy—a simple solution of water, sugar and salt—would make a vast difference. Immunization would also prevent polio and other crippling diseases and thus reduce the number of children who are in need of adoption because their parents do not have the resources to cope with their disabilities.

The problem of hunger is equally mundane. Again, American concern is roused by pictures of famine victims with bloated bellies and protruding rib cages. Outright starvation, however, is not nearly so widespread as chronic malnutrition, which is less visible. Many adults and children in Latin America, Southeast Asia, Africa, even here in the United States subsist on one scant meal a day that is never enough to stave off anemia, keep them mentally alert, or boost their immune systems. For all too many families, abandoning the youngest child or two is the only way to keep the older children nourished enough to stay healthy.

It feels good to respond to appeals on behalf of children's health and nutrition because the simple measures we take as individuals do make some real difference. This is a good way to initiate our children into habits of giving, too, because the problems are easy to understand and the benefits easy to illustrate. Thirty-nine cents worth of loose change dropped in a child's Hallowe'en UNICEF box will buy a dozen hypodermic needles for immunization. Ten dollars is all it takes to make one child immune to all the major childhood illnesses. If money is short, time is welcome. Dr. John and Anne Murray and their family, natives of New Zealand now living in Minneapolis, spend their summers conducting a mobile medical clinic among the Masai people in Kenya in cooperation with a Kenyan clergyman. The most prevalent problems they see in children are scabies, which makes them scratch their skin raw so it is easily infected, and respiratory illnesses such as pneumonia. The scabies can be treated very effectively with an ointment that is inexpensive in the United States. Keeping the children warm in the cold night air decreases the incidence and severity of respiratory illness. Every year, the Murrays take with them a supply of very simple homemade fleece shirts in traditional Masai red. My daughters and I can cut and sew five to ten shirts on a single Saturday. Just one day out of each year can keep five or ten children better protected against pneumonia. It doesn't transform the world. It only keeps a bunch of little kids warm and, maybe, alive. And it plants another part of the world in our consciousness so that we do not forget our relationship with the global family.

Nevertheless, a good case can be made for transforming the world, and that effort deserves our commitment alongside the immediate needs. Destitution and despair are not the whole story of life in economically disadvantaged countries. Using American comfort as a measure of happiness, we sometimes have trouble comprehending that people with less material wealth draw satisfaction from other sources, and that they see us as impoverished in our own way. In every country, there are local people working with great initiative and optimism to transform living conditions, often in astonishingly elemental ways: drilling wells to bring fresh water to communities where the women otherwise walk several miles each day to fetch enough for their families, introducing fuel-efficient cooking methods to reduce dependence on diminishing sources of firewood, teaching people to read, helping rural communities reestablish farming that will produce enough food for local needs, organizing craft and marketing cooperatives, and so on. We can help to sustain their progress by linking up with American and international organizations

that offer special skills and material support to self-development projects—organizations such as UNICEF, Oxfam America, Bread for the
World, Save the Children, and the outreach programs of some religious
denominations.

To be conscientious members of the global family, we must also try
to understand the current social, political, and economic context in
which international adoption takes place. Why, we must ask, were
mothers and children living in a squatter community on an eroding
hillside in São Paulo? What hope do these families have for a more
stable and prosperous life? The abandonment of children is not the act
of just a few dysfunctional or unlucky parents. It can be traced to problems
that afflict whole countries and to an economic balancing act that is
precariously off center. In statistical measures reported by Oxfam America
in 1989, the imbalance is this: The United States has six percent of
the world's population, but uses more than 25 percent of the world's
resources. For example, we import more than one billion dollars' worth
of agricultural products from Central America every year while two
out of three Central American children are undernourished. Just knowing
about the imbalance is very frustrating, because there is a reasoned
difference of opinion about cause and effect and thus no consensus
about solutions. It is also both guilt-inducing and threatening, because
we North Americans have benefited the most and risk losing those
benefits if the balance is restored. The implications can be especially
troubling for adoptive families, as Chuck Stensrud acknowledges:

> I don't feel like I exploited anyone, but the reality is—underlying
> all my personal responses—that this does happen because there is
> exploitation in the world. There's no getting around it. Whether
> we get our babies from Colombia or India or Korea, there's exploitation,
> and people are economically distressed, and we have a lot to do
> with that. No one has to divorce themselves from that. We wish
> we could. But we also know that the reality of life for these kids is
> that they would be seriously deprived and underprivileged people
> without opportunities. That's their reality.

Michael Perlitz agrees. "The parents were at a disadvantage and the
children were at a disadvantage. Rather than feel guilt about that, I
feel a sense of pain for the entire country in which this child was
born. What we have done has altered—corrected—one little piece of
it."

"Don't feel guilty, feel responsible," is the advice offered by Philip

Tacon, the adoptive father of six children and the founder of Child-hope, an organization that works with streetchildren around the world. (Childhope was featured in a column by Colman McCarthy of the Wash-ington *Post* in April 1988.) What does another person's poverty have to do with my life, we might ask, and how can I live in a way that will alleviate it? On a recent trip to the grocery store, I bought bananas, imported from Honduras, at a bargain price of thirty-seven cents a pound. In the account of his son's adoption, Michael Perlitz referred to Honduras as a "banana republic." Indeed, it is the prototype of a banana republic. It was governed by the Spanish for 300 years, and then after a brief period of independence, economically "colonized" in the last century by North American entrepreneurs with the aid of military intervention, in order to keep U. S. markets supplied with food that doesn't grow in our climate. Bananas and other export products, such as coffee and sugar, are grown on large plantations, leaving little land to grow food for local use. Agricultural labor is low-wage work, so the campesinos, or rural workers, who pick the crops have little money to buy food. The 1989 *Information Please Almanac* gives per capita income in Honduras as only $700 a year, compared to $15,340 in the United States. Elvia Alvarado, a campesina herself, describes a typical diet in the book, *Don't Be Afraid, Gringo: A Honduran Woman Speaks from the Heart:*

> The campesinos live on tortillas and beans—three times a day, every day. When we have money, we buy other things like rice, sugar, coffee, and cooking oil. Sometimes eggs. Those of us who live in the valleys can't raise our own chickens, because there's a disease that kills them all off. Only women that live higher up can raise chickens.
>
> We don't have money to buy milk or meat or anything expensive like that. We buy cheese sometimes, because you can buy it in small amounts—ten or twenty cents' worth. And once in a while we buy bread at two and a half cents a roll. (p. 21)

In recent years, Honduran agriculture has been turning from the low-price crops to the more lucrative market for beef. Cattle ranching requires much larger amounts of land and far less labor—about 3 percent as much as coffee, for example. Elvia Alvarado describes how these changes affect the landless rural population:

> Many campesinos are forced to migrate in search of work. When it's time to harvest coffee, they go to the mountains where the coffee

is. They stay for a few months. Sometimes they take their families along so everyone can help. Sometimes the men go alone. In the south there used to be temporary work in the cotton fields, but no one seems to grow cotton anymore.

There also used to be more work on the banana plantations, but they use so many machines nowadays that there's hardly any jobs for the campesinos any more. Now they have planes to spray the fields with pesticides. I think they even have machines to cut the bananas from the trees. So not only do the banana companies take land from the campesinos to grow the bananas, but with all their fancy equipment they don't even give us jobs. (p. 20)

The trend toward large-scale export farming is worldwide: The Japanese get their bananas from the Philippines. A 1989 pamphlet from Oxfam America tells of a Filipino farmer whose parents lived sufficiently off a plot of land that grew corn, yams, and mung beans. Now the land is part of a sugar plantation, and the farmer is paid a daily wage of thirty-five cents to cut cane. He grew up healthy, but his son is malnourished. When rural Hondurans or Filipinos cannot make ends meet on the wages they earn and have no land on which to grow food, they have great difficulty providing for their children. Some move to the cities in the hope of better opportunities that may not exist. Often the father leaves and the family never manages to be reunited. Relinquishing a child for adoption may be the only way to keep the child fed.

It is hard to respond to this situation alone. We might do better thinking the issues through as a community of internationally adoptive families. What does it mean to feel responsible for these conditions? If the world's wealth were distributed equitably, what would the common standard of living be? What would we Americans have to give up? Would it mean sacrifice or simply trimming the fat? If we were to live more simply now, keep our consumption within reasonable bounds, and share the excess with others, would it make a difference? Can we in our daily lives make principled choices that, in the long run, enable these Honduran and Filipino families to provide for their children? These circumstances require far-reaching political solutions as well as personal measures, and adoptive parent groups tend to be wary of involvement in international politics. Political developments are rarely mentioned in magazines for adoptive families, unless they ease or complicate adoption. Partisan divisions threaten the fellowship we feel when we see a family with a child obviously adopted from another country. Instead of fearing ideological disputes, we can try to join in a common concern for the welfare of children and conduct our discussion of appropriate solutions from that shared vantage point.

The division of the world into rich and poor nations dates, of course, from the age of exploration and colonization, when Europeans "discovered" the rest of the world and claimed its resources as their own. Economists and social reformers have long debated how best to rectify the imbalance that colonialism created. The solution generally agreed upon has been technological development and industrial manufacturing for export, which would presumably bring more income into the developing country. For a time, this seemed to work well. Brazil, for example, was touted as the "modern miracle." Brazilian cities were built up and beautified, and the new urban middle class enjoyed a standard of living on a par with ours. However, to finance development, Brazil and many other countries had to borrow large amounts of money from foreign lenders. By 1989, Brazil owed 84 billion dollars, but the income from export goods had not met expectations. Repaying the loans requires severe domestic austerity. Even with partial loan forgiveness, the result for the Brazilian economy has been catastrophic, with rising unemployment and constant inflation that has lowered nearly everyone's living standards. For the rural poor, already displaced by the loss of land and agricultural work, life in the once booming city means destitution. The mudslide in São Paulo is not only real. It is a telling metaphor for the effect of indebtedness on hopes of prosperity.

According to a 1989 UNICEF report called *The State of the World's Children*, the international debt is greatly to blame for a measurable decline in the welfare of children in the debtor nations. To repay the debt, governments have to cut expenditures for health care, education and welfare programs. In the meantime, child welfare agencies feel the strain of increased need for their services. LIMIAR's Nancy Cameron writes in *OURS*,

> In these days of crushing inflation (over one percent per day) Brazilian families are being torn asunder as never before.
>
> LIMIAR, the child service organization I work with, is witnessing more and more children brought to the courts by their biological or adoptive families to be interned in already overloaded orphanages because there simply is no money for food.
>
> The work load is enormous! (November/December 1989, p. 28)

This does not mean that Brazil will be "the new Korea" in adoption terms. Cameron goes on to explain:

> In an orphanage of 500 children, perhaps 50 children may be adoptable, and of the 50, five may be eligible for foreign adoption. These numbers are low because the majority of these children have relatives who maintain bonds that cannot and should not be broken.

We who are willing to adopt the five children might show the same concern for the remaining 495 and do what we can to enable their families to reclaim them.

In some countries, notably South Korea and Taiwan, development has, in fact, bolstered the national economy and raised the average standard of living. But it has also brought about a social upheaval similar to that experienced by Western countries during their own industrialization. The new prosperity has social costs in the rupture of old and trusted bonds of family and community. This, of course, is one of the factors used to explain the high incidence of unintended pregnancy and the abandonment of children born to unmarried women. The mothers of urban children placed for adoption are primarily factory workers, many of whom have exchanged life in a declining rural economy for a steady wage earned by doing assembly work in an electronics plant or clothing factory, for example.

Very many women of childbearing age are employed by foreign-owned companies in manufacturing plants that produce goods for export. For some, factory work brings benefits otherwise unavailable—housing in a dormitory and basic health care—and hope of earning enough to help support their parents and siblings or to buy themselves some of the new consumer items on the market. Others turn to factory work because their former way of life is no longer an option. Most of the clothes and toys and household appliances that we buy, even those with solidly American brand names, are actually made elsewhere. U. S. companies have moved their plants abroad because labor is cheaper, the workday is longer, there may be legal prohibitions against labor unions, and there are fewer environmental and safety regulations and fair employment practices to comply with. Even with the cost of transporting goods back to the United States, there are much higher profits to be made. The hourly wage paid to an American worker may be a *daily* wage for workers in plants located abroad.

The multinational companies justify this arrangement by saying that they provide jobs for people otherwise unemployed and offer better wages and working conditions than they have been accustomed to. This may be true, but the standards are still inequitable when measured against the life style we enjoy. Long workdays and a preference for young, unmarried female workers make it especially difficult for those who need to earn a living and raise a family at the same time. Also, the profits earned benefit the American economy far more than that of the host country. Most of the goods produced are intended to be sold at competitive prices to consumers in the wealthier nations. The people who make them often can't afford them or make use of them. I once heard a Maryknoll priest who spent many years living among factory workers in Taiwan speak on the topic "Why Is Your Pocket Calculator So Cheap?" He illustrated for us how the low-wage work of people in other countries keeps us supplied with inessential goods at inexpensive prices. An example that has stayed with me is that most of his neighbors spent 12-hour days turning out plastic lawn bags for export to the United States. Yet these people lived in such crowded conditions that they had no green space. They had difficulty imagining why anyone would need a lawn bag.

If we are merely perplexed by global economic issues, we may be tempted to isolate ourselves from the rest of the world and take comfort in ignorance. However, we who have adopted children from the countries that appear on the product labels don't have the luxury of ignorance. "Made in . . ." is a reminder of our children's heritage, of the women who gave them birth, of the life they might be leading if they had grown up in their birth countries. If, instead of feeling guilty, we feel responsible toward the people who make the items we buy, how do we then act responsibly? Becoming knowledgeable about them and the conditions of their lives, rather than generalizing from our own standards, is a beginning. The more we know, the less likely we are to see the workers either as "cheap labor" or as anonymous victims of uncontrollable economic forces. They acquire human dignity as people trying to improve their working conditions, to gain more comfort and security, and to provide a better life for their children. We are invited to make common cause with them in working toward greater equity.

Easing the lives of people currently living in poverty would go far toward preventing the family dissolution that has become commonplace in many countries of the Third World, as well as in the United States. Yet it would not provide love and security to all the children of the world. There are certainly other problems to contend with. Most of the children brought to the United States for adoption as infants have been born to unmarried mothers who find it impossible to raise them on their own. Some, but not most, are younger than the age at which their culture considers childbearing appropriate. The issues that out-of-wedlock birth raises, for the women and their society, are not entirely the same as those raised by teenage pregnancy in the United States. As a single mother myself, I know very well the practical disadvantages that one-parent families face that would be relieved by having a second committed parent on the premises. Yet I also know how I would feel if I were to lose my children on that account. A loving mother who has reached the age of majority can certainly raise a family if she has housing, a job, and child care. Projects like Casa da Mamãe in São Paulo and the Ae Ran Won home in Seoul, which offer transitional help with the goal of independence, could save many mothers from having to relinquish their children. They receive little government support, however, and must rely heavily on church sponsorship and private donations.

To do justice to the issue of unwanted pregnancy, we need to look at two fundamental, worldwide problems: Women's lack of the knowledge and means to control reproduction, and men's lack of responsibility for the children they engender. Encouraging the prevention of unintended pregnancy seems like a reasonable solution, but one that often gives way to religious and cultural prohibitions against contraception. Even where birth control is available, it may be beyond the means of many of the women who need it. American efforts to encourage "population control" in other countries understandably raise suspicions of imperialist intent. Perhaps the soundest way we can help to reduce the number of unintended pregnancies, both here and abroad, is by supporting programs that empower women to feel as though they have the right and the resources to make decisions about their reproductive lives. In much of the world, this would include literacy campaigns and efforts to counter sexual exploitation and economic discrimination, as well as education about sex and reproduction.

In the public discussion of unintended pregnancy and birth control, a key ingredient is usually missing: men's responsibility for their sexual behavior and its consequences. To "father" a child is currently a very different matter than "mothering" one. As disparate as the cultures of the world are, this double standard is a seldom questioned universal that seems impervious to change. We who have adopted children from abroad, in the conviction that every child is entitled to a loving family, could easily extend our logic to claim that every child has the right to both a mother and a father. This does not mean that the parents have to get married or live together or even that they have to share equally in the custody of the children. What it means, at a minimum, is that every child, in every culture, should have a right to paternity: to an acknowledged father, an ancestral lineage, rights of inheritance, access to medical history, the same civil rights that children born in wedlock enjoy, and the right to financial support in keeping with the father's ability to pay. In the United States, the Children's Defense Fund has turned to paternity adjudication as a strategy for improving the economic well-being of children born to single mothers, now 20 percent of all births nationwide. On a global scale, the United Nations Convention on the Rights of the Child asks that governments "use their best efforts to ensure recognition of the principle that both parents have common responsibilities for the upbringing and development of the child."

There is one special case in which U.S. citizens have both the opportunity and the obligation to pursue a right of paternity: on behalf of the children fathered by American servicemen stationed abroad, children who, because of their mixed heritage, may face discrimination in their birth countries. There has been some improvement in this area. Since 1982, the Immigration and Naturalization Service has been required by law to give preference to Amerasians seeking to immigrate from Korea. The law was passed in response to lobbying by adoptive parent groups, and the immigrants need ongoing advocacy in finding sponsors to house them and provide initial support. The Amerasian Homecoming Act extended refugee status to Vietnamese children of American servicemen, about 30,000 of whom were awaiting resettlement at the end of 1988.

Much more needs to be done to make young American men more concerned with the consequences of the sexual license that military occupation appears to offer them. Ruth Kim Schmidt speaks to this problem with a passion befitting the daughter of an anonymous American soldier:

Where do you even begin to address something that is such an ingrained part of our culture—"Well, boys will be boys," "Men have to sow their wild oats"? When you think about the impact of servicemen in foreign countries producing children, and those children being discriminated against in their own countries because they are biracial, then being abandoned by the mother so they have to be put up for adoption, so they are transplanted into a foreign culture . . . When you think of the chain of events from one very simple thing, and the lives that are impacted as a result of that, it's just incredible that there hasn't been more work done as far as recognizing the problem and taking some steps to deal with it. It's incredible to me that it's allowed to go on.

Describing the global context within which adoption takes place may seem to complicate the task of promoting awareness and change, rather than encourage participation in it. To be realistic and avoid disillusion, we do have to acknowledge that we are not likely to attain the ideal of a world where no children are left homeless, where every child is raised in a loving family with sufficient resources to provide food, shelter, education, and health care. In the United States alone, our vision of the ideal is limited by a numbingly high incidence of chemical dependency, child abuse, and family violence. There will still be parents who cannot raise children. There will still be parents who *should* not raise children. In the tension between ideal and reality in a changing world that can never quite keep pace with itself, adoption will still be the best solution for many children.

Yet, if we can imagine our own children among those who are hungry or sick or homeless, and if we can imagine their birthparents—or ourselves—struggling to keep families together, we will feel a compelling need to do something for the well-being of the global family. What that might be depends on our individual talents and resources. Marlene Duval, whose family doubled in size when she learned about Amerasian children waiting for homes, puts it very simply: "You offer what you have." What we offer should, however, be given generously and sensitively, with a right of refusal, avoiding the condescension and control caricatured in the image of Lady Bountiful.

In offering what we have—whether compassion, intelligence, hope, time, advocacy, knowledge, money, moral support, strategy, special skills—to the welfare of children and their families, we have a chance to "intervene in history," Brazilian educator Paolo Freire's term for acting in a socially responsible way. As grandiose as "intervening in history" might sound, adoptive families have already done it, by taking a branch from one family tree and grafting it onto another. What usually stops us from intervening more deliberately is the sense that poverty and injustice are inevitable forces of nature that defy human efforts to control them. Like the mothers and children in São Paulo who saw the river of mud cascading toward them, we feel overwhelmed and powerless. Yet, it was undoubtedly human action that deforested the hillside in São Paulo, leaving it vulnerable to erosion. It will take human action to repair the damage. If each of us were to develop a genuine, fond commitment to the people of another place, we might keep some other family's hopes and dreams from washing away.

Selected Reading List

Adoptalk. Newsletter. North American Council on Adoptable Children, 1821 University Avenue, Suite N-498, St. Paul, MN 55104. 612–644–3036.

Adopted Child. Monthly newsletter. P.O. Box 9362, Moscow, ID 83843. 208–882–1794.

Adoption Factbook: United States Data, Issues, Regulations and Resources. National Committee for Adoption, 1930 Seventeenth St. N.W., Washington, DC 20009.

Alvarado, Elvia. *Don't Be Afraid, Gringo: A Honduran Woman Speaks from the Heart*. San Francisco: The Institute for Food and Development Policy, 1987.

Ballero, Mireille. *My Village in India*. Needham, MA: Silver Burdett & Ginn, 1985. (Children's book.)

Bartholet, Betsy. "International Adoption." *Adoption Law and Practice*. New York: Matthew Bender, 1988.

Bellah, Robert et al. *Habits of the Heart: Individualism and Commitment in American Life*. New York: Harper & Row, 1985.

Bothun, Linda. *When Friends Ask About Adoption: Question and Answer Guide for Non-Adoptive Parents and Other Caring Adults*. Chevy Chase, MD: Swan Publications, 1987.

Burns, W. J., and Kim, David. *A Letter From a Korean Village*. Seoul: Korea Save the Children Federation and UNICEF/Korea, 1987. (Children's book.)

Casagrande, Louis B., and Johnson, Sylvia. *Focus on Mexico: Modern Life in an Ancient Land*. Minneapolis: Lerner Publications, 1986. (Children's book.)

Child Welfare. Journal of the Child Welfare League of America (see below).

Chowdhry, Dr. D. Paul. *Intercountry Adoption: Social and Legal Aspects*. New Delhi: Indian Council for Child Welfare, 1988.

Convention on the Rights of the Child. Up for ratification by the United Nations General Assembly in 1990. Available from UNICEF (see below).

Cousins: A Newsletter for Young Korean-Americans. Korean Identity Matters, P.O. Box 4460, Berkeley, CA 94704.

De Jesus, Carolina Maria. *Child of the Dark*. New York: E. P. Dutton, 1962.

Dunn, Linda, ed. *Adopting Children with Special Needs: A Sequel*. Washington, DC: North American Council on Adoptable Children, 1983.

Elsberry, Jan. *Let's Visit Korea*. Jan Elsberry's Designs, 8000 60th Ave. N., New Hope, MN 55428. 612–533–0458. (Children's book.)

A Family In _____. Minneapolis: Lerner Publications. (A series of 28 children's books, each featuring a single country, with color photographs and a text about the life of a typical family.)

Feigelman, William, and Silverman, Arnold. *Chosen Children: New Patterns of Adoptive Relationships*. New York: Praeger, 1983.

Gill, Owen, and Jackson, Barbara. *Adoption and Race: Black, Asian and Mixed Race Children in White Families*. Child Care Policy and Practice Series. London: St. Martin's Press, 1983.

Gilman, Lois. *Adoption Resource Book*. New York: Harper & Row, 1987.

Han, Hyun Sook, and Spencer, Marietta. *Understanding My Child's Korean Origins*. St. Paul: Children's Home Society of Minnesota, 1984.

Holmes, Pat. *Concepts in Adoption*. Wayne, PA: Our Child Press, 1984.

Indian Journal of Social Work. Frequent articles on child welfare and adoption in India.

Jenness, Aylette, and Kroeber, Lisa W. *A Life of Their Own: An Indian Family in Latin America*. New York: Harper & Row Junior Books, 1975. (Children's book.)

Jewett, Claudia. *Adopting the Older Child*. Harvard, MA: Harvard Common Press, 1978.

Jewett, Claudia. *Helping Children Cope With Separation and Loss*. Harvard, MA: Harvard Common Press, 1982.

Johnston, Patricia Irwin, ed. *Perspectives on a Grafted Tree*. Indianapolis: Perspectives Press, 1983.

Kirk, H. David. *Exploring Adoptive Family Life: The Collected Adoption Papers of H. David Kirk*, ed. by B. J. Tansey. Port Angeles, WA: Ben-Simon Publications, 1988.

Kozol, Jonathan. *Rachel and Her Children: Homeless Families in America*. New York: Crown, 1988.

Lapierre, Dominique. *The City of Joy*. New York: Warner Books, 1985. (About rural migrants living in Calcutta.)

Latin American Adoptive Families Quarterly. Newsletter. 40 Upland Road, Duxbury, MA 02332.

McRoy, Ruth, and Zurcher, Louis. *Transracial and Inracial Adoptees: The Adolescent Years*. Springfield, IL: Charles C. Thomas, 1983.

Melina, Lois Ruskai. *Raising Adopted Children: A Manual for Adoptive Parents*. New York: Harper & Row, 1986.

News from FAIR. Newsletter. Families Adopting in Response, P.O. Box 51436, Palo Alto, CA 94303. 415–856–3513. (Special attention to needs of children with disabilities.)

OURS: The Magazine of Adoptive Families. Adoptive Families of America (see below). (Each issue includes a list of parent support groups around the country and a list of books and resources for adults and children that can be ordered through AFA.)

Report on Foreign Adoption. Annual. International Concerns Committee for Children (see below).

Roots. Newsletter for families with children from India. International Adoptions, 282 Moody St., Waltham, MA 02154.

Roots and Wings. Quarterly magazine for adoptive families published by New Jersey Friends Through Adoption. Cynthia Peck, Editor, 161 Twin Brooks Trail, Chester, NJ 07930.

Rosenberg, Maxine B. *Being Adopted.* New York: Lathrop, Lee and Shepard, 1984. (First-person accounts from children adopted cross-culturally.)

Schaffer, Judith, and Lindstrom, Christina. *How to Raise an Adopted Child.* New York: Crown, 1989.

Simon, Rita, and Alstein, Howard. *Transracial Adoptees and Their Families: A Study of Identity and Commitment.* New York: Praeger, 1987.

Smith, Jerome, and Miroff, Franklin I. *You're Our Child: A Social/Psychological Approach to Adoption.* Washington, DC: University Press of America, 1981.

Sobol, Harriet Langsam. *We Don't Look Like Our Mom and Dad.* New York: Coward-McCann, 1984. (Photo essay on family with Korean children.)

Spencer, Robert. *Yogong: Factory Girl.* Seoul: Royal Asiatic Society Korea Branch, 1988.

Organizations Mentioned in the Book

Adoption Advocates International, 658 Black Diamond Road, Port Angeles, WA 98362. 206–452–4777.

Adoptive Families of America (AFA, formerly OURS), 3333 Highway 100 N., Minneapolis, MN 55422. 612–535–4829.

Ae Ran Won, 127-20 Daeshin-dong, Sodaemun-gu, Seoul, Republic of Korea 120. (A transitional home for pregnant women placing babies for adoption and for single mothers intending to raise their children themselves.)

Americans for International Aid, 1370 Murdock Road, Marietta, GA 30062. 404–973–5909.

Bread for the World, 802 Rhode Island Ave., N.E., Washington, DC 20018. (An alliance of churches and individuals that pursues U.S. government policies that will benefit hungry people worldwide.)

Casa da Mamãe, São Paulo, Brazil. For information: Today's Child Charitable Trust, P.O. Box 4786, Santa Barbara, CA 93140. 805–684–5284. (A shelter for destitute women and children that helps them find means to keep their families together.)

Child Welfare League of America, 440 First Street, N.W., Suite 310, Washington, DC 20001–2085. 202–638–2952.

Childhope, c/o UNICEF (see below). (An organization supported by the UN, the World Council of Churches, and other groups that works with streetchildren worldwide.)

Children's Defense Fund, 122 C Street, N.W., Washington, DC 20001. 202–628–8787. (A nationwide research, education, and advocacy organization working on behalf of children in the United States.)

Children's Home Society of Minnesota, 2230 Como Ave., St. Paul, MN 55108. 612–646–6393. (A social service agency that has had a leading role in promoting international adoption and providing post–legal adoption services to families.)

Crossroads, 4640 W. 77th St., Edina, MN 55435. 612–831–5707. (An adoption agency originally founded to work with parents disqualified by other agencies because of marital status or physical condition.)

Eastern Child Welfare Society, 493, Changchon-dong (or P.O. Box 241), Sodaemun-gu, Seoul, Republic of Korea.

Friends of Children of Various Nations (FCVN), 600 Gilpin St., Denver, CO 80218. 303–321–8251.

Fundación Los Pisingos, A.A. 50090, Bogotá, Colombia. (A foster care and placement agency.)

Holt International Children's Services, P.O. Box 2880, Eugene, OR 97402–9970. 503–687–2202. (A social service agency active in many countries that was first organized to care for children left homeless after the Korean War.)

Immigration and Naturalization Service (INS), United States Department of Justice, 425 I Street, N.W., Washington, DC 20536. (Also regional offices around the United States.)

Indian Council for Child Welfare, 4 Deen Dayal Upadhyaya, MRYG, New Delhi, India 110 002.

The Institute for Food and Development Policy (Food First), 145 Ninth St., San Francisco, CA 94130.

International Adoption Clinic, Box 211, University of Minnesota Hospital, Harvard Street at East River Road, Minneapolis, MN 55455. 612–626–2928.

International Alliance for Professional Accountability in Latin American Adoptions, P.O. Box 430, Shepherd, MI 48883.

International Concerns Committee for Children (ICCC), 911 Cypress Drive, Boulder, CO 80303. 303–494–8333.

International Mission of Hope (India) Society, 2, Nimak Mahal Road, Calcutta-700 043 India (or c/o FCVN, above).

Joint Council on International Children's Services from North America, Inc., c/o Adoptive Families of America (see above).

La Semana, Parents of Latin American Children, c/o Jan Redpath, 2424 Sheridan Hills Curve, Wayzata, MN 55391. (A summer culture camp.)

LIMIAR: USA, 46 Ravenna Road, Suite B-11, Hudson, OH 44236. 216-653-8129. (A Brazilian child welfare agency.)

Los Niños International, 1110 W. William Cannon, Suite 504, Austin, TX 78745-5460. 512-443-2833. (A placement agency that finds homes for children from Latin America.)

Maryknoll Fathers, Catholic Foreign Mission Society of America, Maryknoll, NY 10545.

National Association of Black Social Workers, 642 Beckwith St. S. W., Atlanta, GA 30314. 212-749-0470.

Oxfam America, 115 Broadway, Boston, MA 02116. 617-482-1211. (An agency that funds self-help development and disaster relief in poor countries and educates people in the United States about world hunger.)

PACT (Partners Aiding Children Together), P.O. Box 80-100, St. Paul, MN 55108. (An organization that provides medical assistance for handicapped children in other countries.)

Plan Loving Adoptions Now, P.O. Box 667, McMinnville, OR 97128. 503-472-8452.

Resolve, Inc., 5 Water St., Arlington, MA 02174. (A national education and advocacy network for people experiencing infertility.)

Save the Children, 54 Wilton Road, Westport, CT 06880. 203-226-7271. (A voluntary agency that helps families in the United States and other countries achieve stability by supporting family self-help and community development projects.)

UNICEF, 3 UN Plaza, New York, NY 10017. Also United States Committee for UNICEF, 331 E. 38th St., New York, NY 10016. 212-686-5522.

Index